HE-MOTIONS

T. D. JAKES

G. P. PUTNAM'S SONS

NEW YORK

HE-MOTIONS

Even Strong Men Struggle

Foreword by Max Lucado

G. P. Putnam's Sons
Publishers Since 1838
a member of
Penguin Group (USA) Inc.
375 Hudson Street
New York, NY 10014

Library of Congress Cataloging-in-Publication Data

Jakes, T. D.
He-motions: even strong men struggle /
T.D. Jakes.
p.   cm.
ISBN 0-399-15196-6
1. Christian men—Religious life.   I. Title.
BV4528.2.J34   2004   2004048374
248.8'42—dc22

Printed in the United States of America
13 15 17 19 20 18 16 14

This book is printed on acid-free paper. ∞

To all strong men who struggled their way through tough times. I know you are better because you did not give up. I understand the weight you carry and I salute you for the effort it takes to be the man you are. This is my tribute to you!

ACKNOWLEDGMENTS

For me, the most difficult part of a book to write is the acknowledgments. There are so many people who played a part in making this book a reality. I have been blessed with so many wonderful people who have made such an impact on my life that trying to name them all is a bit intimidating. I am extremely fortunate to have so many great friends, but I am worried that if I tried to list them all, I'd leave someone out. So instead, just let me thank God for those special people (you know who you are) who have in many ways enriched my life. Thanks for the thoughtfulness, the well wishes, and the prayers. I deeply appreciate you because you have often been the catalyst for needed change in my life and the impetus for introspection, and without you I would be hopelessly malnourished as a person and grossly underdeveloped in my masculine soul.

However, in an elite category that demands mention are the following persons: The honorable Dr. Sherman S. Watkins—you have been my spiritual mentor and a father figure that I sorely needed as I grew up. I am thankful for the friendship we have—a friendship filled with deep and transparent conversation. It has been therapy for my soul. Perhaps some would never understand the rich relationship we enjoy. I am not sure that even you fully know how much you have blessed my life and made times of bleakness bearable, with your relentless humor, tenacious optimism, and keen wisdom. Thank you for making me laugh, forcing me to think, and provoking me to prayer.

A special thanks to my siblings, Ernest and Jacqueline. Boy, our mother did a great job! I am so grateful that she taught us to stay together. The longer we share the air, the better I feel the breeze of love and family on my soul. Calling you, seeing you, and knowing you has been a tremendous advantage for me. If I could have chosen a brother and sister I would have chosen you!

To my sons, Jamar, Jermaine, and T. Dexter, Jr., whom I love each in unique and unexplainable ways. I have enjoyed serving you as a father and providing for you those necessary ingredients for life. I only hope that I live long enough to be there with you in the tough places that are an inevitable part of manhood. I realize that being a man is the toughest thing you will ever do. Feel the fear but do it anyway. None of us does it without error, but I hope to lessen your learning curve by the things I share in this book. Maybe it will assist you in the journey and comfort you through the failures. I have left clues, like breadcrumbs in a fairy tale, sprinkled lavishly throughout this book. I want them to help you find your way back home when home becomes difficult to find. I wanted you to know my perseverance, my passion, my power, and my pain. Each of the four reveals me in diverse but significant ways.

To my daughters, Cora and Sarah, whom I love in ways that only true fathers can ever understand. You are beautiful girls, becoming women before my eyes. May your princes never turn out to be frogs! You deserve the best life has to offer. Hold out for it, and you will always get it. I love you differently because you are unique, but never doubt that I love you equally. Both of you hold a special place of my heart. I give you my heart for now and for always. We have shared moments that will never be forgotten, and I love you unconditionally.

To my wife, Serita: We have weathered some fierce storms together, and I have come to realize that your soft demeanor hides a very strong center. You have often been my strength, and for that I am eternally grateful. I deeply admire how you sashay through tornados and bring warmth to snowstorms in my soul. We have endured much together, and I am amazed at how you survive. Sometimes I think you have nine lives and each one is better than the previous. Undoubtedly, you are an extremely distinctive woman!

Thank you to everyone at Putnam. You always treat me and my work with great dignity and integrity. To Denise Silvestro, who tirelessly labored to enhance this project with her insights and creativity. Her grace to race as we edited and developed this book was a significant component in reaching the deadline and getting this timely message out to the people who need it most. Thank you, Joel Fotinos, for your enthusiasm, encouragement, wisdom, and for believing in my message and my method. My gratitude also goes to Susan Petersen Kennedy, Marilyn Ducksworth, Dan Harvey, Timothy Meyer, Dick Heffernan, Katie Day, and everyone at JMS Marketing & Sales, Inc.

Special thanks to Mr. Dudley Delffs, whose prolific literary experience and ability enhanced my ideas and inspired me personally. Finally, thank you to Dr. Tim Clinton. Your insights and expertise added much to this project and will help men and women truly better understand themselves and their relationships with each other.

CONTENTS

FOREWORD

How would you complete this sentence?

Real men _____

Think about it. What words would you place in the blank? Or, better still, what words *do* you place in the blank? You do, you know. Somewhere, you learned the image of a real man. Someone may have told you that . . .

- Real men *pump iron.*
- Real men *run the show.*
- Real men *never cry.*
- Real men *swagger.*
- Real men *woo women.*

Such messages billboard our society. The stereotype of the tough stud with washboard abs permeates catalogs and cartoons. But are these the measure of a man? Is gender defined by dumbbell lifting and female conquering? If they are, most of us guys fail the male test. Truth is, not all of us lift weights or lead groups. Some of us shed tears, walk normally, and, gulp, get downright nervous talking to ladies. There must be more to being a man than what we learn in the locker room.

Indeed there is. God's dream for men includes words of eternal consequence. Words like: "prayer," "joy," "father," "friend," "loyal," "humble." God equipped you with an ability to forgive, a desire to be loved, dreams to fulfill, and, most of all, a Savior to follow.

In God's economy . . .

- Real men *pray.*
- Real men *open up to friends.*
- Real men *cherish their wives and love their children.*
- Real men *kneel at the cross.*

If such an image intrigues you, then you are holding the right book. It's a great privilege to recommend this work of T. D. Jakes to you. I have watched, in amazement, as men fill arenas to hear this brother teach. Not only do they come, they listen! And not only do they listen, they *do!* T. D. Jakes speaks to the hearts of men. And he, with God as his helper, would like to speak to yours.

Practical, encouraging counsel awaits you in these pages. Bishop Jakes will introduce you to men of the Bible, like Saul, Abraham, and Isaac. He'll share wonderful lessons from the life of David. You'll read down-to-earth advice regarding budgeting, fathering, and enjoying your work. You'll be moved by his personal admissions and changed by his pastoral admonitions. And, whatever you do, don't miss the chapter called "Finding Our Fathers." It, alone, is worth the price of the book. But most of all, you'll gain a clearer picture of a real man.

Interested? Then turn the page. After all, real men read *He-Motions.*

—MAX LUCADO

INTRODUCTION

MEN IN MOTION

You are who you are before God, nothing more and nothing less.
—UNKNOWN

Years ago at a Back to the Bible Conference in Cincinnati, Ohio, I invited Jim Bakker, former head of the *PTL Club* and a recently paroled inmate, to speak to the men in attendance. It was a controversial decision, and quite a few people were offended at my choice. They couldn't believe that I would invite a convicted criminal to speak about what it means to be a man of integrity, a man of God. However, I felt myself led to invite Mr. Bakker and therefore was very comfortable with my decision. You see, I know that half the Bible is filled with stories of inmates, and parts of it were even written by people such as Paul, who had been incarcerated. I know that when a man is locked up alone, he is forced to come to terms with himself, with his God, and with the reality of his life before him. There's no place to hide—no remote control to channel surf, no job to work overtime, no toys or diversions. Often, men who have endured external imprisonment finally face the internal imprisonment that most men face each and every day. I knew Jim Bakker would have something to share that would speak to this self-imposed prison where so many of us find ourselves these days.

And indeed, his message spoke directly to the hearts of the many men congregated that afternoon, including my own. Jim shared openly and honestly, with a level of candor and vulnerability that captured everyone's attention. One of his most cathartic and captivating stories was about a man who loved exotic fish. This man kept a large fifty-gallon aquarium in his apartment and enjoyed watching the myriad rainbow of fins flashing within his miniature ocean. Since the man often traveled for his job, he equipped the aquarium with state-of-the-art mechanisms, which would automatically clean the tank, release food, and keep the water temperature constant. Once, however, while he was out of town for several days, the man returned home only to discover that he had not adjusted the thermostat on the aquarium. The water had over-heated and killed his beloved collection of exotic fish. In his grief over this loss, the man imagined what the fish must have thought and felt as the temperature rose and the water became hotter and hotter. "Did they scream in silence?" he wondered. "Did they wonder where I was and why I didn't save them? Did they beg for someone, anyone, to turn down the temperature?" He felt silly for considering such a possibility, know-ing that he was personifying the little fish. But he cared so much about them that he couldn't help but wonder.

BOILING POINT

As Jim Bakker shared this story, he began to tear up, and it became in-creasingly clear why he felt so moved. He knows what it means to emit a silent soul scream that no one can hear as the water around you goes from tepid to warm to boiling-point hot. He knows about the silent screams within men that will cause them to boil to death in their own aloneness. He knows what it is like to cry out in an enclosed cage, long-ing for someone to release you, and to wait in vain as no one comes. With this fish story, Bakker articulated a powerful metaphor for men today as we grapple with the rising temperature in our own personal aquari-ums. We are being boiled alive by our own fears and insecurities, those thoughts that gnaw at us below the surface of our attempts to look like we have it all together.

As I listened to Jim Bakker speak, I realized that I, too, know about reaching the boiling point. I experienced a powerful depression a few years ago. I would come home after church and sit in the dark and weep. I wasn't even sure why I was crying. I had lost my joy. I realized that I didn't know who I was apart from the roles I fulfilled: husband, father, son, brother, pastor, bishop, businessman, employer, on and on. But *who* was I? Where was that vitally alive part of me that longed to engage and cherish each day? It felt buried under a mountain of quicksand, sucked up in the endless responsibilities and overwhelming duties of my life, consumed by the multiple roles that had replaced who I was at the core of my being. I felt like a mound of papier-mâché that I've seen my kids use with their artistic endeavors: Each role and responsibility became another glue-soaked sheet of paper caked on to the one before it until the original form had lost its shape. And I didn't know how to break out of this cocoon of imprisonment, didn't know how to ask for help. I only knew that the water was boiling and that my soul was seared with scorching pain and that my cries were inaudible to human ears.

As Jim Bakker related how he felt like one of the fish in the over-heated tank, I reflected on my own life and considered other seasons when I'd felt the water temperature rise. Like so many men, my father never taught me how to scream aloud, and so I wept in the dark, my soul crying out for relief, for comfort, for camaraderie. I realized then that my prison was every bit as tangible as the one in which Jim Bakker had been incarcerated.

As Bakker went on to point out, if we are to lower the temperature and restore our environment, we must begin communicating—initially with ourselves, gradually with God, and increasingly with others. We must enter the dialogue that is already fast-forwarding through our minds and hearts and souls: Who am I? Why in the world am I where I am today, this minute? How do I feel about my identity? What have I quit hoping for in this life? Do I have what it takes to keep going, to attain my dreams?

Heavy questions, I know. But these are at the heart of most every man I encounter. And let's be real. You don't need another book on all the "shoulds" in life, all the easy steps to fixing your life's problems, your relationships, and your spiritual walk. There are plenty of those out there if that's what you're looking for. But I'm not here to waste your time or my own precious moments by telling you that I have all the answers or know the secret to being a man. What I am here to do, however, is to offer you ways to turn down the temperature on the boiling points of your life and consider some issues that can help you discover what is in your heart.

You may be thinking, "Yeah, yeah, I've heard all those big heavyweight questions before, Bishop Jakes. I know I should be dealing with those issues. And I appreciate your good intentions. But I don't have time to be navel-gazing and daydreaming about some secret identity and the meaning of life. I've got to earn a living, serve at my church, coach the kids' soccer team, and repair the leaky faucet at home." I hear what you're saying, and if you know me at all, you know that I'm not writing this to offer easy answers or false hope. I simply ask you to continue reading and acknowledge that you, too, have experienced the silent scream of your own soul. Maybe you gagged it by overworking, or you muffled it with alcohol or drugs or sex, or you drowned it out with the applause of others. But it's time you got real with yourself if you want to live life as God intended for you to live it. It's what you were created for and who you long to be. It's what *He-Motions* is all about.

FORWARD PROGRESS

When I work out, especially in the cold and damp winter months, I'm usually forced to run in place on a treadmill. But like a lot of folks, I often get bored with the scenery and can't trick my mind into thinking that I'm really outside on some beautiful trail or expanse of track while I keep staring at the same wall, window, or TV screen. I believe the same dilemma is escalating for men today as they run and run faster and faster, taking on more roles and responsibilities, perhaps earning more money and acquiring more things but feeling in their hearts that they're stuck in place. They feel they're not making progress on their journeys, not pushing through the hurdles of their destiny. It seems to me that men today are able to sprint faster than ever before, but even as their legs keep moving and their exertion increases, their hearts and souls trail along behind them aimlessly.

Where are your motions taking you today? Do you try to move forward but feel stuck, as if the soles of your shoes have melted into the hot, tarry asphalt? Or are you running in place like a man desperate to reach the finish line but who never makes actual progress toward his goal? Perhaps you feel like a hamster in a cage, spinning and spinning on your wheel, running from home to work to church, and wondering why you feel so detached from life, so empty at the core of your being. Why is there so much movement but little forward progress?

Yes, men today are in constant motion. As technology increases, as work demands clamor more loudly than ever for attention, as family and relational obligations accelerate, most men find themselves forced to move. While much of this motion can be a good thing, propelling men toward great accomplishments, new discoveries and inventions, it can also result in feelings of frustration, confusion, anger, and detachment. Oftentimes, we're moving so quickly, as is everyone around us, that we become so overwhelmed by the traffic of life that we can't focus on our own journey. Have you ever seen drivers on the Autobahn, the German equivalent of our interstate system? There is no speed limit, and cars in the slow lane often cruise at ninety to one hundred miles per hour, while those in a hurry whiz by at speeds that look like the time trials for the Indy 500. This often feels like the speed of our lives and, consequently, men feel like they must run or be run over, they must soar or risk being grounded permanently. The pressure consumes them as they race on the surface of their lives without realizing that they're running out of fuel and that their engine is in need of repair.

But how can a man slow down and refuel? Won't he be run over or passed by—left behind in the dust of those who can move faster or more tirelessly? Won't he fail to cross the finish line and lose the race? The truth is, it doesn't matter how fast you're moving, or if you're moving at all, if you're not running the right way.

> Do you not know that those who run in a race all run, but one receives
> the prize? Run in such a way that you may obtain it.
> (1 CORINTHIANS 9:24)

What is the right way to run? How can a man discover which way he should be going? Sometimes he just has to slow down and find the pace at which God created him to run. He has to discover his natural rhythm so that he can move forward with grace and determination, knowing that he is running in such a way that he may obtain the prize.

Perhaps it's time to step off the treadmill, to exit off life's Autobahn, and discover who you are and what you are made for. You may discover that you're on the wrong road for your true destination.

Whether you're a young man just merging onto the highway that society deems as the road to adulthood, or whether you're weaving in and out of the traffic of life's freeway, or even if you're stalled along the shoulder and don't know how to start again, all of us long to drive toward our destination. Regardless of the season of our sojourn, we desire to live fully as men.

We must acknowledge that manhood is the call of a lifetime. But what does *that* mean? Herein lies the problem. What is a *man*? If I asked different groups of men, I would get different answers. And God help me, if I ask women, I would get answers as diverse as the shoes they have in their closets! So regardless of who I ask, the myriad of answers ranges across a broad spectrum of perceptions and beliefs about what it means to be a man. Some people would say that manhood is sexual development. Maybe some would reason it is the destination beyond puberty. Others would say that manhood is having a job and being responsible. Some would say that manhood is working out and developing one's body. Some others might say that manhood is the development of the intellectual properties in each of us. And some may contend that, from a spiritual perspective, manhood is reached when a man has achieved God's purpose for his life. All valid answers, but no one fully captures the essence of what it means to be a man.

This last statement may surprise you. What higher level of manhood is there than fulfilling the role God has created for him? But who among us can say they have mastered the Master's plan? Who has accomplished all he was meant to do and be? I have yet to meet this person of perfection. Remember: Although we were created in the likeness and the image of God, we are not like God yet. Most of us are not even close. But thank God we are in process. We are in motion. We are in motion beyond the rat race and treadmills of life that drain our energy. We are a work of masculine artistry in process. He-motions. Men in motion, trying to move toward what God wants us to be.

Instead of considering the linear motion we often associate with a runner or a fast sports car, consider another picture of motion. Have you ever been to the beach and watched the gentle waves crash and subside, dance and collapse into one another? It's a beautiful sight, especially as the sun goes down and explodes its orange and red glory across the blue horizon. The water looks so calm and peaceful. But below the surface, the water is in constant motion. Warm and cool currents collide and create crosscurrents and riptides. Tides ebb and flow, storms peak and regroup their energies. Indeed, no matter how calm or how turbulent the ocean may appear, there's so much more going on below the water's surface. This seems to me a much more apt metaphor for us as men in motion. Each man is his own ocean in motion, with his own agony and ecstasy along his life's journey every bit as tumultuous as the tossing, turbulent sea. We are just as given to waves and billows as we grow into the fullness of our manhood over a lifetime. "He-motions" describes this movement of the masculine soul. This is not the same as simply running in place on your life's treadmill, faithfully dogging what others claim you should be moving toward. Nor is it trying to keep up with others racing past you on a freeway of competition and comparison. No, I'm talking about that soul motion that begins when a man realizes who he is and that he has a purpose in his life that is uniquely his own.

ANCHOR MAN

Some men never realize this sense of their true selves, and that is why their manhood never quite seems to flow outward to those who desperately need them to grow up. They run in place but never arrive. Or they go through the motions but without the peace and joy that come from fulfilling their destiny, moving reactively like a marionette whose wires are pulled by the actions of others. No, if we are to freeze the frames of a true man in motion, we must consider one who lived in the fullness of his masculinity, who loved and failed and wandered and returned, who battled and risked and won and lost, who persevered and danced and sang.

Do you remember David? As the only man in Scripture identified as "a man after God's own heart," he is a fitting model for a man living in the fullness of his masculinity, moving along the rapid currents of his life's calling not with perfection but with a passion and perseverance that has much to teach us today. He is also one of the players in Scripture who had virtually his entire life, with its various seasons, recorded and noted. While we will look at many biblical examples, David provides a complete and complex portrait of a man in motion, in pursuit of his God-given destiny.

In addition to using David as our "anchor man," I also want to share, as vulnerably and honestly as I know how, about my own experiences as a man. Like a reporter conveying essential news from the scene of a breaking story, I want to impart all I've learned. As a teacher and preacher of God's Word, as a husband of more than twenty years, and as a father to my five children, I humbly offer whatever lessons and insight I've gained through my own masculine journey in process. Based on my observations and relationships with other men, as their pastor, counselor, mentor, friend, brother, uncle, son, cousin, and confidant, I want to share what I've learned. I want to cut through so much of the junk imposed on men today and talk heart to heart about what it means to be a man, not in some touchy-feely group hug kind of way but in an honest, soul-bearing way, which also respects men and honors the women who love them and whom they love.

While I'm writing primarily to men, my hope is that men and

INCREASING YOUR RANGE OF MOTION—FOR MEN

Have you ever felt overlooked or unappreciated? Even by those you love?

What pressures are tearing at your heart and life right now?

What are you like when you are discouraged, even depressed?

Who are you in the dark?

How do you handle pressure? Pain? Loss?

What have you filled your life with?

Do these things honor God? Or do they pull you away from God?

INCREASING YOUR RANGE OF MOTION—FOR WOMEN

What are his silent screams? Do they awaken him in the middle of the night?

Can you still see him for who he is—his potential before God?

In what ways can you come alongside to support, nurture, and comfort him?

What do you want to see God do in him?

---

women can read these pages together and dialogue about the unique challenges to men and the impact on their relationships. Women cannot empower and activate a man's mission of manhood, but they often possess wisdom and vision into a man's soul that he himself cannot see. They know when his soul is screaming out in silence, when he has lost his way, and when he has work to do that only he can do.

Ladies, as many of you know, you cannot change him by yourself. Whether he's your partner, your son, your husband, your father, or your brother, you can't change him on your own. If you haven't learned this hard, brick-wall lesson, then please talk to other ladies and those you trust. It's not that you aren't a powerful influence on him, but it's simply impossible for you to activate the masculine furnace burning within him. Whether his pilot light is about to die out or whether he blazes with an intensity that is out of control, you can only relate to him as he is, not how you wish he would be. "If that's the case," you might be asking yourself, "what's reading this book going to do for me?" A fair and honest question. My hope and prayer for the women reading this book is that you will gain a greater understanding of the inner workings of a man's soul and a clearer perspective on how to love him as he finds the right speed for his heart-motions.

More important, sisters, this book is for you if you long to see your man change in ways that can only come from God working inside him. If you sense a silence in him that you long to decode and you fear that something is absent from your relationship with him, then I urge you to read on and travel the he-motions journey with him. Offer him no pressure, no false encouragement, no selfish expectations of who you wish he would be. If you truly love him, and I know you do or you wouldn't be reading this, then I ask you to make room for the new forward motion in his life. Walk alongside him and encourage him to experience a movement within that will change both your lives and how you relate to each other. Be patient with him and support his courage as he looks for a new rhythm and speed on his journey.

Men, if you're longing for your life to matter, if you long to know who you really are inside with a confidence that transcends the title on your door, the physical condition of your body, the number on your bank statement, and the size of the house you live in, then prepare to change. Prepare to have your hope rekindled that you are so much more than who you feel like at present. Prepare to have your hope restored that you have a unique destiny waiting to be fulfilled. Linger through these pages and immerse yourself in the truth of God's Word, the experiences and wisdom I humbly offer based on my own life and the lives of other men, and the challenge of applications that will make your life's motion count for eternity.

My brothers, it will likely not be a smooth journey. You may be forced to get off your present life's treadmill and find a new route to your heart's destination. You may need to question the familiar, autopilot motions of your present journey and be willing to blaze a trail toward new and greater heights. But if you are willing to explore the inward wilderness of your masculine heart, then I believe you will unleash the powerful, fluid motion of your soul that God intends for you. It's time to move, men. It's time to swim with the current of your maleness and discover the secret of who you really are. It's time to catch the wave of being a unique man in motion!

Part One

A MAN'S RELATIONSHIP WITH HIMSELF

"Why are many Christian men so frustrated? It is exactly because God has set eternity in our hearts, and we have a built-in sense that life does have meaning, and our frustration is that we have not yet found it. We don't have enough religion to make us happy men as we look in the mirror, but we have enough to remind us how unhappy we have become."
—PATRICK MORLEY, *"The State of Men in America"*

"For many men, one striking and far-reaching consequence of the mal-socialization ordeal is an inability to differentiate and identify their emotions. The technical term for this condition, alexithymia, *comes from Greek roots that mean 'without,' 'words,' and 'emotions.' People with alexithymia cannot put their feelings into words, and are often not even aware of them."*
—RONALD LEVANT, *Men and Emotions*

"You are as sick as your secrets. In the classic metaphor, family secrets are like the elephant in the living room that no one ever talks about. Eventually the elephant grows and takes over the room, spraying its waste on everyone and making it impossible for anyone else to be in the room. Still, no one ever talks about the elephant."
—DAVID STOOP, *Competent Christian Counseling*

ONE

—◁◦◦◦▷—

SECRET IDENTITY—
DISCOVERING THE KING
INSIDE THE KID

Failure is the greatest opportunity to know who I really am.
—JOHN KILLINGER

I can still remember those navy-blue camper shorts with the key chain on the side. My brown legs, freshly oiled with a thin coat of Vaseline, protruded out from under the shorts like chocolate marble pillars, albeit those pillars were short and chunky, as I was about only six years old and wrapped in a layer of baby fat. But that extra padding didn't diminish my energy as I came running down the path that led to the bus stop, where the school bus would pick me up. I imagined that path to be a magic conveyor belt, but it was actually a small, narrow stretch of hard-pressed Appalachian soil running narrowly but steadily behind my house down to the street, where herds of screaming kids congregated each morning. It was my first year of school, and I was excited finally to be a "big kid," joining the neighborhood children in a rite of passage that marked the transition from baby to student.

Now I don't have to tell you that children can be mean. If you ever had a childhood, and I know you did, you realize that facing children may be harder than standing before the Supreme Court justices. One might find more mercy at a tribunal hearing or a lynching mob than a group of kids who mask their own insecurities by revealing yours.

Even as a boy, I think I was fairly adept at people skills—that wasn't the problem. No, I liked people, and most people eventually grew to like me. The real problem was finding a way to face my problems without my peers detecting that I was a flawed, less-than-perfect little boy, who felt safer with Momma, Daddy, and my siblings than I was around them. While I worked hard to hide my imperfections, one secret in particular weighed me down, and though I have had worse ones since then, at this time my burden blocked my path. Literally.

When I came to this one spot on the path between home and the bus stop, I found myself stopped cold in my tracks. A big rock loomed before me in the middle of the path, a huge obstacle between me and where I was trying to go. What made it worse was that the other boys seemed well equipped to climb over it. Maybe I was too afraid of hurting myself, too afraid of the bruises and lacerations that I saw in my mind when I imagined myself trying to scale the rock. Maybe it was the fear of tumbling down the rock into the briary patches of blackberry bushes that flanked it on both sides. Each time I walked down the path, those bushes seemed to wait hungrily for me to fall into them, eager to make a fat, juicy hamburger out of my backside if I tumbled into them.

Whatever it was, each day I would valiantly run down the path, confident that finally I would conquer my nemesis. However, time and again, I would stand frozen at the foot of that great rock, fighting back tears, while all the other children mocked me. I would stare at the boulder, humiliated and afraid, paralyzed and defeated. Eventually, my mother or father would hear me crying and come to my aid. I would get a kiss on the cheek and be lifted over the rock and deposited on the other side to continue on my way.

One day, after many days of humiliation, I couldn't believe my eyes. My two-hundred-sixty-pound father—who I thought was a combination of the Hulk and Hercules—took a mallet and pick and went down the path to where I was always getting stuck. All I saw was the mallet swinging and the chipped rock flying out of his way. He hacked that rock in good fashion, and before he left, it looked like an escalator in a major department store. He had cut steps into the rock so that I could get to the other side. My father was my superhero, coming to avenge my adversary and carve a path for me.

As I grew older, I realized that even superheroes have their kryptonite, and my father was no different from all other men. He had some rocks he could cut through and some he could not. But from the ripe age of six, I thought he looked like an invincible giant, and I wondered if I would ever be able to cut through someone's rocks like he did mine that day. And now, I realize how fortunate I was to have such a father, willing to chisel and carve steps into the massive boulder blocking his son's path.

Looking back on that incident, I don't know what I enjoyed most: the defeated, blank stare that the rock gave me when I returned, the blackberry bushes' timid grin as I walked by them every day with ease now, or the fact that I momentarily had my father's undivided attention, that I was important enough for him to stop working and see about me. Perhaps most important of all, this incident gave me a glimpse of who I wanted to be—an overcomer—and a hope that no matter how large the obstacle, it can be overcome.

Little did I know that I would spend the rest of my life with a mallet and pick in my hands trying to help people who were stuck at their own big rocks, helping them over their hurdles into the field of their dreams.

SHATTERING THE SILENCE

It has been forty years since I was that little boy crying at the base of a boulder, and I have come to realize that life is full of big rocks that confront us as men, and sadly there are not enough fathers who have the tools—emotionally, spiritually, and financially—to cut steps into all of the rocks we face while trying to get to the other side of manhood. I have also learned that you can swing a mallet and crush a rock, but that doesn't mean that you can hack through all the pitfalls of life, and if you do succeed on occasion, you should expect to suffer a few bruises and lacerations. I call them the battle scars of those who fought a good fight. A good fight doesn't mean that you won't incur a bad bruise; it just means you didn't let the bruises stop you from fighting onward anyway.

If I had only known that many of the things we face in childhood offer a preview of what we may encounter as we travel the path to becoming men. Too many blackberry briars, too few fathers, and not enough time make it a perilous journey for most men, and only a few who are brave and relentless, wise and well tested have the wherewithal to make it past the rock. Most of us are stuck at the bottom of some intimidating obstacle, bemoaning our fate while all the others pass us by and mock us rather than help us learn to get to the other side of the barriers that are inevitable in the pursuit of manhood. Like the fish in the aquarium screaming silently as the water around them boils, we must learn to break the silence, to overcome the rock blocking our path and verbalize who we are and what we need. It's one thing to wait for Daddy to come with his pickaxe and bust up the rocks in your life when you're a boy; it's another thing when you're still waiting on him when you're a grown man. It's time to move beyond the voiceless cries and rocky barriers of life.

The first step, if you are willing to try to move beyond your obstacles, is to honestly assess your current condition and get in touch with where you really are. A man can't always locate himself: the women in his life may think him lost; even God asks the man where he is, much like He called out to Adam in the Garden: "Where are you?" (Genesis 3:9). Like Adam, most men hide from those who love them, hiding not beneath fig leaves as he was, but beneath mounds of work, hobbies, accomplishments, and anything else that will keep the issues that remain unresolved buried deep within the Garden of Eden. What should have been the utopia we dreamed of in our youth is now overgrown with unexpressed, unconfessed mistakes and liabilities. You and I both know that coming out from your fig leaves may be liberating, but it is also intimidating as well. But, in order to move forward in life, you must acknowledge your pain and recognize your needs and tend to your suffering soul.

We find one of the most famous instances of a man coming to terms with his circumstances in the story of the Prodigal Son (Luke 15:11). Here is a man whose soul was crying out, yet he sought to drown out these cries with the many diversions in life that tempt us. He drank, he partied, he enjoyed the leech-like friends that big bucks attract. It was only when he crashed and found himself tempted to eat the pig slop in the troughs he now worked that he finally realized he could no longer ignore the silent screams within himself. In Luke's Gospel, we find that he "came to himself." Alone at the pig trough, with time for true introspection, he had an epiphany of life-changing proportion.

> But when he had spent all, there arose a severe famine in the land, and he began to be in want.
> Then he went and joined himself to a citizen of that country, and he sent him into his fields to feed swine.

And he would gladly have filled his stomach with the pods that the swine
ate, and no one gave him anything.

But when he came to himself, he said, "How many of my father's hired servants have bread enough and to spare, and I perish with hunger!

I will arise and go to my father, and will say to him, 'Father, I have sinned
against heaven and before you, and I am no longer worthy to be called
your son. Make me like one of your hired servants.' "

For many men, it's necessary to come to this place of abasement, to
wake up the morning after, to see the evidence of your indiscretion or
the consequences of your addiction, to see your reflection leaning over
the pig trough. While it can be a time as confusing as being lost after mid-
night on the foggy country road without your GPS, you must learn to
navigate, to ask for directions if necessary (something we men find impossible to do!), to make a U-turn and redirect your vehicle's destination.
You must be willing to get comfortable with the journey of your life and
quit waiting for life to begin when you reach a certain destination. Even
the failed choices and wrong turns in your life can be redeemed by God
if you're willing to let Him.

The Apostle Paul knew about this process of going through the fog;
he wrote:

When I was a child, I spoke as a child, I understood as a child, I thought as
a child; but when I became a man, I put away childish things.

For now we see in a mirror, dimly, but then face to face. Now I know in
part, but then I shall know just as I also am known.

(1 CORINTHIANS 13:11–12)

Paul's phrase "when I became a man" indicates someone who endured
a process and became comfortable in his own skin, who was in touch
with himself, his personality, his needs and desires, his strengths and

flaws, his sexuality, his fears, a man who knows that accepting himself is just as important as improving himself. So often men improve themselves for other people—to fit in, to look good in a way others will notice, to change and adapt to a new environment. Some men learn what wine to order at the restaurant to impress their woman, they get the right suit for the job interview, they work out so that others will be impressed with our fine physique. But what do we do to get to know ourselves at an intimate level that isn't for external approval or perceptions of others? To become a man, as Paul indicates here, we men must be willing to stop thinking as a child, to wrestle with our thoughts, acknowledge them, and learn to accept who we are. "As a man thinks in his heart, so is he" (Proverbs 23:7).

As we explore who we are, we have conversations with ourselves, and there are constantly thoughts that we don't share with anyone: thoughts about money, about sex, about God. Many of us aren't courageous enough even to have these inner dialogues about these very important topics with ourselves, let alone with others. It's as if we're afraid to plumb the depths of our beliefs, our hopes, our fears. Generally speaking, men are much more prone to action without introspection, a natural reflex, perhaps, but one that will eventually get you in trouble. Come on, let's be honest. Have you ever acted first and then wondered, "What in the world was I thinking?" I know I have, but I'm learning that God has gifted us with intellects, with sound minds that can reason, remember, and reflect upon the data that each day brings into our lives. The great philosopher Socrates said that the unexamined life is not worth living; I say that the unexamined life falls short of who we could be and what God has empowered us to do, and makes it a tragedy, a life wasted.

> *Take responsibility for the direction your life has taken; only you have the power to change it.*

Please realize that this isn't a self-absorbed all-about-me exercise. As Paul explains, knowing yourself is a vital means to fulfilling the purpose for which you were created:

> Therefore, I urge you, brothers, in view of God's mercy, to offer your bodies as living sacrifices, holy and pleasing to God—this is your spiritual act of worship.
> Do not conform any longer to the pattern of this world, but be transformed by the renewing of your mind. Then you will be able to test and approve what God's will is—his good, pleasing and perfect will.
> (ROMANS 12:1–2)

How can we commit ourselves as living sacrifices, as we're instructed here by Paul, if we don't know what's inside ourselves? We're also told to be transformed by the renewing of our minds, but how can we transform what we haven't informed? Like the Prodigal squandering his future inheritance, we're in denial about ourselves, about who we really are and what we really want.

As a man who struggles on his journey, one who's come to his senses many times, one who limps like Jacob after spending all night wrestling the angel for his identity, I know what it means to struggle with the complexity of finding out who I am. The vast majority of the men I've known struggle at some level with what it means to be a man. The stakes are high and the consequences can be lethal if the conclusion is not correct. Armed with no manuals, few tutors, and a bus load of critics, we embark upon a journey to be correct and complete, but often we reach midlife defeated by the harsh reality that the conquest is far more challenging than we thought. This is true for men in the Bible and for all the many men I've known: sons, uncles, friends, some now dead, many still living, some Jewish, some Christian, some who don't believe at all, rich men and homeless men, men as diverse as any tossed salad. I've seen men at a bar mitzvah and soul food restaurants, men driving sports cars and go-carts, men who are professional athletes and those who are armchair quarterbacks. We're all on this journey together, and it's time we came to our senses and started making our way back home.

NET WORTH

How can we facilitate the process of coming to ourselves, of redirecting our course toward home? How can we know what we have in ourselves so that we might submit it to God as a sacrificial vessel for His purposes? We must be willing to know ourselves, to know ourselves intimately, and ultimately to become comfortable with who we really are. This must precede discovering and exploring our purpose, which we will discuss in the next chapter. For now, though, the starting point must be an honest, stare-yourself-down-in-the-mirror eyeballing of your soul.

QUESTIONS FOR RELATIONSHIP WITH SELF

1. How do you behave when you're alone?
2. Often, what you spend your money on is a direct reflection of where your values are placed. What do your spending habits say about your values?
3. How much do you enjoy your own company? What do you enjoy most about being alone with yourself?
4. What's the hardest part of being alone with yourself? How have you handled being alone in the past?
5. Can you write a letter or have a conversation and tell who you are without telling what you do?
6. Do you have a fair and objective sense of the intimacies of your character?

To answer this last question and to get to know yourself better requires a personal audit, a comparison of your assets and liabilities to determine your net character worth. So many men struggle to do this objectively enough to get a true glimpse of who they are. Their insecurities, failures, and fears either keep them from seeing their true strengths or cause them to ignore their liabilities. But to grow in maturity, to birth the greatness within, you must be willing to see yourself through new eyes. Can you compare your personal assets and liabilities and honestly assess your character? This means listing, without arrogance, the assets you bring to any endeavor, any company you work for, any woman or child to whom you relate. Stripped of your title, your toys, your bank account, your sports trophies, and résumé accomplishments, what positive traits remain fundamental to your being? What is in your character that makes you an asset to know? Are you loyal? Honest? Creative? A good listener? Generous? Tenacious? Relentless? Do you possess a gift for timing? A sense of humor? Don't pretend you're a Boy Scout if you're not, but on the other hand, don't be embarrassed to list as many legitimate strengths as you can think of.

In the same manner, you must be willing to be honest about your liabilities. Are you a procrastinator? Are you caught up in a secret lust or perversion? Do you struggle to follow through on commitments? Are you unorganized? Unfocused? Do you allow your desire for immediate gratification to make decisions for you? While you might not want anyone else to see this list, keep it real with yourself. Try not to be too hard on yourself for these shortcomings, to feel ashamed or guilty. Remember that every person has liabilities and that who we are is much more complicated than just a "good" and "bad" list of traits. There's an interplay between *all* our traits that can transform our weaknesses into strengths, depending on the context of our circumstances. Pretend that you are simply emptying your pockets of all your character traits and the negative ones must be examined and set alongside the positive ones. You must look at both or else you get a false worth, an inaccurate reading that's skewed by faulty information or inclusion of disparate data.

Now, you may be inclined to include on your list of assets the corner office in your firm's skyscraper, the size of your church, the net income on last year's tax return, the kind of car you're driving, and the number of women you've slept with, but you must focus instead on what truly are examples of good character. It doesn't matter if you wear FUBU or Gucci, drive a Porsche or own a sailboat. You must be willing and able to move beyond men's tendency to define themselves by things. Sure, it's tempting. We've all

> *You can often determine who you are by how you behave when visiting a place where no one knows you.*

seen the bumper sticker that says: "He who has the most toys when he dies, wins!" Yes, our consumer society certainly reinforces such a possession-based identity at every turn. But if you're honest and willing to look in your heart, you know that you cannot define yourself by what you own. The true net worth of a man can't be repossessed. Real soul-searching requires this intense scrutiny of the positives and negatives, your strengths and your flaws, your accomplishments and failures that reveal your character.

I recall my brother in the Lord, Jim Bakker, whom I mentioned earlier, as a prime example of a man who was forced to redefine his net worth. From his status as a founder of PTL and Heritage USA, and all his many possessions, homes, cars, and toys, he found himself a bankrupt inmate with nothing but time and his own character before him. He had to finally face who he was behind all the possessions, titles, wealth, and masks that all men are tempted to put on.

Whether we feel like successful men or failures at this point in our life, we must be willing to know where we are if we are to birth greatness and run into our future to embrace the imperishable prize.

EXPANSION JOINTS

So many men are afraid to do this internal audit on themselves for fear of what they'll find or not find. However, their standards and expectations are often out of whack with reality. They overlook or underestimate the need to forgive themselves, to embrace God's grace, and to get on with their lives as wiser and more experienced men.

Have you ever noticed how sidewalks are constructed? In between each concrete panel, there's an expansion joint, a divider of rubber or pliable mortar that allows the concrete to "breathe," expanding with the heat of summer and contracting in the frigid winter. Without these expansion joints, the concrete would crumble and crack and soon be useless for its intended purpose, reduced to a path of dry powder ground underfoot. These expansion dividers permit movement, ebbing and flowing, as temperatures and external conditions change. They keep the sidewalk intact and suitable for its intended purpose.

Most men have no expansion joint. They feel so locked into being "good" and "right" and "together" that they don't give themselves room to take risks and to fail, and then when they do inevitably fail—as we all do—they're crippled by their failures. But the human factor is unavoidable—all the more reason why we must know and take ownership of our weaknesses. If we are to remain whole and grow purposefully, then we should assume that there will be times when we fall, fail, and flounder on our journey. So many men feel pressured to have all the answers, to be competent in all areas—especially those arenas perceived as indicators of masculinity, such as sports, mechanical and technical ability, and lovemaking. But if men only allow their manhood to be measured by such external yardsticks, then they will consistently come up short, not because they're inadequate but because all of us struggle some, if not most, of the time. Let's face it, my friend, most of these attributes decline with time, and if essence is only configured from youth, then age will leave us feeling bankrupt and bewildered. Soon you find yourself not even trying, hiding instead by playing it safe, sticking with those areas that you have mastered or that come more naturally for your strengths.

Let's work for a moment on flexing our personal expansion joints. I want you to recall for a moment your top-ten-worst failures—mistakes you made, decisions that turned on you, temptations you indulged, risks that came back and bit you on the backside. For most of us, making such a list is a painful, shameful endeavor. But don't be afraid. This is for your eyes only. "What was I thinking?" you ask yourself, knowing you weren't thinking at all, at least not with your head. "How could I have been so blind?" you wonder. "Why did I ever think that I have what it takes to win that _____ (fill in the blank: woman, job, game, account, client, etc.)?" While you can't control your emotional response to this list, try not to get sucked into a vortex of self-contempt. Focus on being objective, knowing you're looking for something in this list that goes beyond the individual experience itself.

And what you're looking for is room to grow, the expansion joint in each of those items on your list. How did you pick yourself back up? What did you learn from the experience? How could you use this mistake to contribute to your character in a productive way? If you struggle to answer those questions and find your own expansion joint, then I encourage you to "retro-fit" an expansion into yourself and those times. Take some time now and consider how you can forgive yourself, and others if necessary, regarding these failures. If you are to know your identity, then you must be a student of yourself and know how to build in and exercise your own expansion joints.

Men must allow themselves permission to be in process and not completion. "Metamorphosis" is the word that comes to mind, from the Greek for "transformation." It's a process, something in flux, something moving and growing, not something static, that's arrived, that's finished and completed. We're not finished! Only Christ is complete and perfect in His being. And yet His entire reason for coming to this earth was to extend God's grace to us—not for us to compare ourselves to Him and feel inadequate and inferior. Men must allow themselves the grace to be traveling and not arriving, to know that they have weaknesses and flaws, and to allow for those times when they fall down. We must stop feeling guilty for simply being human!

Allow me to illustrate it this way: I have worked hard my entire life, from the time I was eight years old. I've always been industrious and set goals for myself. Cutting grass and doing odd jobs for neighbors provided my first income, and I was thrilled as a boy when I was able to buy my mother a suede coat. I saved up fifty dollars and thought it was the most beautiful thing I'd ever seen, something my momma wouldn't likely splurge on to buy for herself. I'll never forget the tag attached to the gorgeous suede garment: "Imperfections in this natural leather add to the beauty of the garment." This is so true of life! Our imperfections add to our own beauty, wisdom, and ability to birth the greatness of our true purpose. If we don't risk and fail, don't fall and get up, don't hurt and holler, then we are pretending that we were created perfect to start with—as if we've known all along who we are, what to do, and how to do it. And that's simply not true. It's not true because we are human beings, not perfect beings. Yes, we are created in God's image, and yes, we are being conformed to the perfect image of Christ Jesus. But because of our fallen nature, inherited from our ancestors at the top of the family tree, Adam and Eve, we are fallible, mortal, and flawed. To pretend that there are no imperfections in the garments of our identities is to imply that we are synthetic, for this is the only "perfect" material. Something man-made, unnatural, and unreal. Phony. I think men long to be genuine and to know that the imperfections they experience only add luster and contribute to wisdom in their character.

TLC (TOUGH LOVING CARE)

Another way to improve your expansion joints and to be more accepting of your own imperfections is to work on taking good care of yourself. We men must be willing to take care of ourselves and not feel guilty or less masculine or weak because of our needs. Lately, I've noticed more and more magazine and media coverage on the so-called metrosexual men, guys who are indulging themselves more and learning what many women have known for sometime: how to take care of themselves. I am seeing a trend, even among executives and businessmen, who are learning the value of pouring into themselves, detoxing from stressful days, and downshifting from the pressures of the world they live in. It is not uncommon to see men reclining in saunas and enjoying a moment of repose. Many men are opening up to the possibilities that once carried an effeminate or homosexual stigma: salon treatment, day spas, being fashion savvy, having decorating preferences, and appreciating art, music, and theater. Personally, I've always been an advocate of men being comfortable enough with themselves not to be threatened by self-care, to learn about healthy sensual pleasures (such as a pedicure, a relaxing massage, or a gourmet meal), and to know what genuinely restores their bodies and spirits. This not only helps dilute the toxins of stress, but such self-caring exploration can be like a journey deeper into who you are and what you need.

And this isn't just my personal preference, a cultural trend, or license for self-absorbed hedonism. Even in the midst of his life of sacrificial ministry and suffering, Jesus took care to ensure that he had time alone to pray, to reflect, and to imagine. He also knew when to indulge himself. Consider the time when Jesus was visiting and was gifted with something that his own disciples thought could have been put to better use.

And when Jesus was in Bethany at the house of Simon the leper, a woman
came to Him having an alabaster flask of very costly fragrant oil, and
she poured it on His head as He sat at the table.

But when His disciples saw it, they were indignant, saying, "Why this waste?
For this fragrant oil might have been sold for much and given to the
poor."

But when Jesus was aware of it, He said to them, "Why do you trouble the
woman? For she has done a good work for Me.

For you have the poor with you always, but Me you do not have always."
(MATTHEW 26:6–11)

We must learn from Jesus' example and be willing to let the oil be
used on ourselves. This is not a license for self-indulgence but rather a
call to do what needs to be done to restore your depleted energy and exhausted spirit. As we will see in the next chapter, you will not be able to
find your purpose and birth your true greatness if you don't know how
to recharge yourself. If you continually treat yourself as a kid instead of
the king who is inside you slowly coming out, then others will only see
you as the kid. People treat you like you treat yourself. Spoil yourself in
the appropriate ways so that you know you are a king, and others will too.

Have you ever met a man who was always so helpful, always willing
to do what needed to be done? Always willing to be someone's go-for-it
guy, dependable, trustworthy, solid? I'm sure you have. You may be one
yourself. Yeah, they seem like nice guys. Everyone seems to like them,
but soon everyone dumps their grunt work on these men: "Let's get Jim
to do it." "I know we can count on Jim." "Jim will get the auditorium
set up for the meeting—he always does." It's well and good to serve
others, so don't get me wrong. But too many men are hiding behind
serving others to avoid having to serve themselves. And truly, how can
they really love others if they don't know what it means to love themselves? I have counseled many men who were secretly resentful of the
endless chores, responsibilities and needs that were dumped on them

while seemingly no one took time to provide them reciprocal care. Ultimately, you have to make a deposit where the world you live in seems to make endless withdrawals or else face insufficient funds. Pretty soon checks are bouncing everywhere: morally, emotionally, sexually, and spiritually. Who will give back to you if not you? Men must be willing to pour oil onto themselves.

Too often men expect their women to do it for them. In reality, it is virtually impossible for a wife, no matter how much she loves you, to be 100 percent accurate in understanding and anticipating your needs. She often doesn't even realize that you are secretly burned out and drained. Many men get fulfillment from being needed, but eventually they grow weary of being counted on and start to feel taken for granted. You see, most men are ashamed to admit to anyone that they need anything at all. Consequently, his

Although you may have many responsibilities, you cannot take care of others if you don't take care of yourself.

signals for need are non-verbal in nature and often go unrecognized by those who have grown accustomed to calling him for help. This is tragic, because if you don't seek answers in appropriate places, you will inevitably seek help from some dangerous source. For example, you need oil and you look for it at Delilah's house. You're tempted to have an affair, because when you're with her you feel appreciated and valued, poured into. That's why Samson found himself with Delilah—not because she was such an incredibly sexy seductress, but because she knew his real needs for rest and she was attentive. He had no place to rest, no place for comfort, no escape from his life and his reputation. Delilah gave him that place to let his hair down, and then, of course, as we know, she exploited this need for his destruction. When we look to others to pour oil on us rather than pouring it ourselves, we often give footholds to the enemy to impede our journey toward greatness.

Men are told that they should love their wives as their own bodies, as Christ loves the Church. If we go back to Adam and Eve, we see him treating her like he treated his own body. And even today, show me men who are taking care of themselves and chances are great they also know how to take care of their wives, how to encourage and facilitate her own ability to receive oil from the alabaster jar. I've certainly seen the inverse when dealing with women who are victims of domestic violence. The abuser generally doesn't feel good about himself. His self-image is distorted by disappointment that, left unchecked, turns to rage. And they act out their anger, contempt, and shame on those around them, projecting outward as a means of trying to fight, literally, their own feelings of incompetence and inadequacy. They're often ignorant about themselves, about what's in their hearts. They only know how awful they feel and how desperately they want to feel better. I'm not making excuses for their choices to harm others; this is always wrong. But understanding does help to change their behavior and helps them understand why their choices feel so automatic. A man must value himself, or his emotional deficiencies will manifest themselves in his behavior and in his relationships with others. He will be looking to others to meet needs that only he can meet or that he can only experience in his relationship with God.

KING WITHIN THE KID

Just as many men look to others to take care of them, many also wait for others to tell them who they are. While we long for our true identities to be recognized and affirmed by those around us, our sense of self and our true value must start from the inside out. Consider David for a moment. It's tempting to think that because God chose him, and had Samuel anoint him as king, David had his identity handed to him on a silver platter. He was selected and told who he would be. But this is not quite what it appears to be, for what God does is *recognize* the man inside the quiet shepherd boy, the king inside the kid. Indeed, when Samuel is initially looking for Saul's replacement, he focuses on what you or I might look for: someone wise and regal in their bearing, someone experienced and knowledgeable of royal ways at court, someone who looks like a king should look. But God quickly sets Samuel straight: "Do not look at his appearance or at his physical stature, because I have refused him. For the Lord does not see as man sees; for man looks at the outward appearance, but the Lord looks at the heart" (1 Samuel 16:7).

It's interesting to note that not even David's own father recognized the greatness in his youngest son. Let's consider the scene of Samuel's visit to the house of Jesse:

> Thus Jesse made seven of his sons pass before Samuel. And Samuel said to Jesse, "The LORD has not chosen these."
> And Samuel said to Jesse, "Are all the young men here?" Then he said, "There remains yet the youngest, and there he is, keeping the sheep."
> And Samuel said to Jesse, "Send and bring him. For we will not sit down till he comes here."
> So he sent and brought him in. Now he was ruddy, with bright eyes, and good-looking. And the LORD said, "Arise, anoint him; for this is the one!"
> Then Samuel took the horn of oil and anointed him in the midst of his brothers; and the Spirit of the LORD came upon David from that day forward. So Samuel arose and went to Ramah.
>
> (1 SAMUEL 16:10–13)

In many ways, David's destiny was blocked by the way others perceived him just as much as my path was blocked by that giant boulder I described at the beginning of this chapter. And instead of having his father hew into the rock and make a path for him to discover his secret identity, his father's resistance is the rock itself! Examine this huge obstacle with me for a moment: David was the eighth son of Jesse, his father. The youngest child. He tended sheep while his other brothers had seemingly more exciting occupations: they were fighters, but he was only a baby-sitter for a group of musky, dank sheep. He doesn't seem to be a favorite child of his father, and most of his brothers see him more as an errand boy than a contributing sibling. His father doesn't consider him when Samuel comes looking in Jesse's house for a king. His dad brought everybody before the prophet in hopes that one of them might meet with the Lord's approval and end up as king over all of Israel. You know that would have made Jesse famous—the father of the king! That would be a real status builder. Perhaps he himself wasn't sure of his own identity and needed an external boost to elevate himself. Jesse had to put his best foot forward. So he garnered the support of his sons and brought all of them before the prophet—all but one. This one son was not mentioned.

It would have been better for David to have been brought before Samuel and had the prophet refuse him than to have his father ignore him and not allow him a chance to compete with the rest of his brothers. It's like Cinderella's wicked stepmother not allowing the young girl to try on the glass slipper when it was clearly made for her. Can you believe it? Everyone was there except David, who was either ignored or forgotten. I imagine that either ignored or forgotten would present a rock that was hard for him to climb over. And tell me this one: How does a boy cry for his father to cut holes in the rock when the old man's opinion of him is the very rock that the boy is trying to climb over? Haunted by the question of "Why didn't he choose me?" David is left throwing rocks at lions and killing bears, protecting his sheep even as he wondered who would protect him. "Who will cut steps through my rock?" he thought. "I am stuck at this spot, and if something major doesn't happen, I will be here all of my life!"

This is where so many of us stumble and struggle. Even though we've become adults capable of carving our own path through the boulders on our path, we still feel and act like the little boy stuck on the path. We're still waiting for someone else to remove it for us even though we hope and even know deep down that we ourselves now possess the strength and ingenuity. But because we couldn't remove the obstacle as boys, we continue to doubt our ability for the rest of our lives. We're afraid that we'll fail, so we don't even try.

One of the hardest struggles of youth is the fear of not having what it takes to make your mark in life. It is a real challenge because you have so much potential, but there are so many obstacles. These obstacles, or rocks, if you will, become harder to cut when they are made out of rejection and set in uncertainty about one's own identity. Many young men succumb to peer pressure not out of weakness but out of desperation to find some place, group, or person who says, "Yes, this is who you are and where you fit." Even for men who have a sense of who they are, as David surely did from his time alone on the hillside praying and writing poetry as he tended his sheep, we all need validation of that identity. But it must start within us. Self-discovery is a vital part of human development. How my heart has ached as I ministered to men who were incarcerated or otherwise on a path of destruction. Not all of these men were truly wicked. Most of them were boys who grew up and never found the king inside the kid.

Whether you are ten or sixty, it is never too late to touch the king inside of you. David, in spite of hardships, abandonment, and hurdles, must have had some consciousness that beneath his mediocrity there was a man of might lurking within. You see, David, despite his youth, his lack of experience, and the absence of his father's recognition, must have harbored some awareness of his own greatness. And when the opportunity to birth his greatness came along, his heart must have leapt that the time had finally come to throw off the guise of his shepherd's cloak and don the royal robe of his destiny. Finally, he could be himself!

INCREASING YOUR RANGE OF MOTION——FOR MEN

What is the dream inside that needs to be birthed?

What's been holding you down? Mocking you? Keeping you from your dreams?

How much fight (or fright) is left in you?

If you have children, how would your son/daughter describe you?

What could you do for fun that you haven't done for a while?

INCREASING YOUR RANGE OF MOTION——FOR WOMEN

Do you know his dreams? His deep inner desires?

Are you afraid of his dreams? Afraid they would upset your life—and his—if they were more out in the open?

Could it be possible that he is being taken for granted in the relationship and not being appreciated for what he brings into it?

Could you share any part of his dreams as an exciting adventure for you both?

Does your Samson have a safe place to lay his head? Are you better at criticisms than you are at compliments?

Now to be sure, all of us don't have a Samuel at our disposal to tell us we are kings. But I believe David's dilemma is a common one for many men: There is a king inside the kid just waiting to be recognized and anointed. Maybe not a literal king like David, but a man of greatness waiting to overcome and succeed if given the right variables and opportunities. However, most of us don't believe it ourselves. Too often men today remain so fixated on the kid within them, on the lack of recognition from their fathers or from other authority figures, that they can't manage to become the kings they were meant to be.

All the more reason to come to your senses and realize who you are and what you're capable of accomplishing. You may be a great musician, but because no one recognized your talent and paid for guitar lessons when you were a boy, you've given up on yourself. Or maybe you have an entrepreneurial gift but have always been dissed for your "foolish" ideas about how to do business. Perhaps you have compromised your character and given up the dreams of your youth, the hopes for cultivating the potential greatness within you. Now is the time to reclaim who you are. Spend some time with yourself. Read through this book slowly. Pray for God to open your eyes, to bring you to your senses, to place a Samuel in your life right now to confirm what He is bringing forth in His creation of you. Discover who you were meant to be and embrace this man, exploring your own facets like the precious work of art God calls you to be. Unleash the king inside you!

TWO

---〜〜〜---

PURPOSE OR PERISH—
FINDING YOUR PLACE IN
THE WORLD

The thing is to understand myself, to see what God really wishes me to do . . .
to find the idea for which I can live and die.

—Søren Kierkegaard

After September 11, 2001, I was summoned to the White House as part
of a small corps of religious leaders. We were such a diverse group, with
every possible belief system represented: Presbyterians and Hare Krish-
nas, Catholic priests and charismatics, Buddhists and Baptists, men and
women from various races and backgrounds. President George W. Bush
convened us and charged us with helping to heal the masses of people
grieving and struggling after such a terrifying violation and catastrophic
loss. As news coverage surveyed the massive destruction that had not
only toppled two towers but had toppled the sense of security of the
entire country, we all knew that only our faith could see us through
this dark time. As we all gathered in the White House, the president revealed to us how he was handling the situation, not so much as a matter of national policy but personally. He shared his prayer life, his
exercise routine, his own attempts to return to normalcy. And most of
all, he conveyed his passion for leading the individuals who comprise
our nation into a secure and healthy state of existence.

Out of such a diverse group, I can assure you that there were many opposed to Republicans in general, others who did not agree with the president's politics and policies, and there may have been others who didn't particularly care for his personality. However, I was awed by the fact that in spite of the obvious diversity of political alignments and even theological differences, there was an overwhelming concern and support that is seldom achieved in forums like that. The other thing that was riveting was the deep sense of passion that was obviously transmitted through the room as the president spoke with resolve and tenacity. Our consensus was clear: Here was a man who had found his purpose. With a flame burning in his eyes and tightness in his jaw, the president exuded a clear sense of a man in sync with his destiny. It was clear to me that this was a defining moment for which he seemed prepared to act with precision and determination. He almost seemed called to a task that I'm sure none of us in the room would have wanted to assume. The manner in which he spoke seemed to give direction and leadership in a critical moment. Perhaps he was born for this moment. Here was a man who had come to himself with a full awareness of how his life had led him to this specific moment, for handling such an unprecedented tragedy. He now had a challenge befitting his journey—an all-encompassing commitment of purpose into which to pour all his past experiences, all his gifts and talents, all his wisdom and knowledge. His combination of energy and calmness was contagious and inspired us all to want to do our best in our own communities and churches.

MAN ON A MISSION

The principles that I observed there are, in fact, transferable truths, not limited to tragedies or presidents. We get the same sense of deep resolve from watching the world's truly great performers. Take Pavarotti, for instance. You don't need to know Italian, or even like opera, to witness the greatness of this man when he opens his mouth to sing the notes of an aria. It's what he was born to do, and the music flows effortlessly from his being, like a stream from a mighty river. Or consider Tiger Woods on the golf course. Have you ever watched this man? His level of concentration, his expressions, the fluid grace as he arcs the golf club into that little white ball and sends it sailing like a missile over the sand traps and water hazards and onto the green. It's what he's meant for, and he knows it and takes pleasure in it for its own sake. There's a kind of athletic poetry that emerges from such a man, a combination of talent harnessed by discipline, of passion paired with hard work, of love united with commitment to being the best he can be. In some ways, the man becomes so associated with his purpose, and his response to this gifting, that the two become synonymous. Who can think of basketball without considering Michael Jordan? Who can think of great writers without including James Baldwin or Ernest Hemingway? Who can think of scientific accomplishments without mentioning George Washington Carver or Albert Einstein?

People who fulfill their calling exude an enjoyment and connection to their gifts that transcends the recognition, fame, and fortune they may receive for performing or expressing their talents. Most have simply discovered the secret of finding a way to get paid for doing what they love. Money never replaces purpose. When a man has found that thing which he would do for free, simply for the fulfillment of doing it, he has found his calling. I believe that realizing all you are capable of doing and then pursuing it is what we as human beings are called to do. Since we are created in the image of our own Creator, we have a built-in drive to create ourselves. This doesn't mean that you necessarily have to have an artistic or creative temperament to find your purpose. But I would venture that every man who is aware of his calling is in the process of giving birth. It may seem obvious that those who are songwriters and artists, poets and actors are birthing their dreams. But so are any one of us who discovers who he is and answers the calling God places on his life through his unique gifts. He may be birthing a new business, or inventing a technical device that will benefit us all. He may be discovering a cure for multiple sclerosis or finding new patterns of efficiency in his corporation.

DIGGING FOR GOLD

You may likely agree that if a man knows his calling, then he's well on his way to fulfilling his destiny and living a satisfied and God-pleasing life. But how to know that calling? How to discover your purpose? That may be the million-dollar question, for it relates inherently to who a man is and how well he knows himself. So many men are willing to remain on the surface of their lives, to accept what their upbringing, their environment, and their culture dictate regarding who they should be and what they should do. However, there's nothing more miserable than a man trying to fit into a part for which he is ill suited. It's like trying to stretch the fabric of someone else's jacket to cover your body—when clearly the garment was designed for and belongs to someone else.

Ideally, a man would discover who he is and what he's called to early in his life. He would have parents who understand him, who have a vision for him, who encourage and support a life direction for which he is well suited. However, in my experience, those situations are rare. More likely, he is the son who attempts to fulfill his father's dream for the father's sake—becoming a star athlete because the father was cut from the team, attending law school because the father was stuck as a bus driver and never had the

> *You can't be a success if you don't know who you are.*

chance. Yes, more times than not, a man must wade through the expectations and deferred dreams of his parents and discover his own identity and purpose.

Identity and purpose—the two are certainly married in a unique coupling that provides the foundation for the man's entire life. A man's identity is inextricably interwoven into the fabric of a man's purpose, and it's so difficult to separate the two. One is who he is, and the other is what he is about, but so much of what comprises a man affects what he does with himself. If he doesn't know what's inside himself and who he is, then it's impossible for him to fulfill his calling. If a man is unaware of the tools, talents, and abilities he possesses, then he will not know they are at his disposal to use.

Despite the close relationship between the two, I believe that the man's identity must be discovered, explored, and celebrated before he will be able to hear his life's calling. It's as if he must first have an awareness of himself—his net worth as we called it in the last chapter—before he can begin to birth greatness. If Clark Kent didn't know that he was capable of more than the menial tasks he was assigned at work, he would never have discovered the real identity of his "superman" soul. You must at least believe in the possibility of your success with the endeavors you attempt. Yes, it may be a great risk, but if you aren't aware of something in you that gravitates toward the endeavor, that's willing to learn even if you fail, then it won't be something you will even be willing to consider. This is what causes many men in the middle of their lives to jump ship and leave the task or life that seemed to define them for years. Often I have noticed that in the middle of our lives we have a tendency to need to reevaluate ourselves, to separate the things we did for others from what we always wanted to do but were afraid to try. Is it a crisis? Maybe so. But sometimes it seems a deeper crisis to have lived and died and never done what was in us to do.

As we explore and discover more and more of who we are and, just as important, embrace and accept all of who we are, then we also begin to solve the scavenger hunt of finding our purpose. Do you remember going on scavenger hunts as a kid? You'd have a list of things you were looking for, usually wacky and off-the-wall type things like old newspapers, fashion trends from bygone years, or some small token from a nearby landmark or establishment. And then often the items would serve as clues that revealed a larger, overall puzzle, which could only be solved by putting the pieces together. Such is the search for our identity, and similarly the quest for our purpose. While we will never arrive at our final destination in this lifetime, we can get on the right path, with the right tools, making the right choices along our journey.

I want to encourage you today to consider your awareness of purpose in conjunction with your awareness of who you are and who you want to be. Here are some practical questions you might ask yourself as you consider where you are in relationship to your purpose:

QUESTIONS FOR DISCOVERING PERSONAL PURPOSE

1. Return to the personal inventory (net value) you completed in Chapter One. What strengths stand out? What are you good at? What do you enjoy doing most?

2. What accomplishments make you feel good about yourself? When do you feel most alive and "in the zone"? List five moments in your life when you were acutely aware of this sensation. What else might they have in common besides how they made you feel? Does this reveal anything about your purpose?

3. If money were not a consideration, what would you want to do to fill your days? How does this compare with where you are now? What's one small step you can take right now— one phone call made, one letter written, one email sent—to move toward your true life's calling?

4. What have you learned about your purpose from your failures in life? In other words, are some areas clearly not a part of your calling at this point?

5. Who do you admire and envy for the way they've applied their talents? How are you like these people? What can you learn from seeing the way they fulfill their calling?

6. How would you describe your vision for yourself this time next year? Five years from now? Ten?

7. As morbid as it might sound, a wonderful exercise for exploring how you want to expend your life's energies is to write your own obituary. That's right—imagine that you are penning a description of your own life after you pass seventy or eighty years on this planet. What would you want to be remembered for? How are you presently pursuing smaller goals to fulfill being this man in motion?

8. Who are the people in your life who really "get" who you are? Have you asked them what they think your purpose might be? Have they given indications of how they think you should use your talents?

BURIED TREASURE

So what keeps so many men from pursuing their calling? It's tempting to say that many men haven't discovered what they should do when they grow up, that they're still searching and ignorant of what they are most gifted at doing. However, I would argue that this is generally not true. Most men, I believe, are aware at some level—maybe one they've never articulated or dared to share with another person—of what they love and what they would do if they allowed themselves. So what is the barrier? What is the obstacle that looms like a large granite boulder across the path of their dreams? Too often, it's fear, plain and simple. Fear of risking, fear of failing, fear of changing, and fear of succeeding often imprison a man's sense of calling so that he remains locked within himself, claustrophobic and contained.

Certainly there are circumstances that hinder and drag us down and unravel the tapestry of our calling. However, the truly great ones, the men who are so aware of who they are and what they must do, find a way to persevere, to transform their circumstantial barriers into stepping stones for achieving their destiny. No, I believe the daily grind of surviving life and all the rocks thrown into our path only compound the fundamental fears of failure, of disappointment, and of loss. What if I risk my 401(k) to start this new entrepreneurial adventure and lose all my retirement savings? What if I finally start writing and recording the songs that constantly stream into my mind and heart and no one wants to hear them? What if I never win the Academy Award for my dramatic performance? What if I never sit on the state hospital board? What if I give my all to what I love to do and I never make it to the big leagues? "Who will I be then?" many men ask themselves. "No one but a big loser," they answer themselves.

But I vehemently disagree, my friends and brothers. For I believe the real loser is the man who never attempts to fly with the wings that he's been given, the man who never dares chisel the marble and release the beauty he sees within, the man who never launches the ship he's spent his whole life building upon the beautiful and tempestuous seas. The only real loser in life is the man who never risks challenging his mind and committing himself wholeheartedly to the endeavors for which he was made.

Lest you think I'm being harsh, let's consider how Jesus explains this same truth in his parable of the talents:

For the kingdom of heaven is like a man traveling to a far country, who called his own servants and delivered his goods to them.

And to one he gave five talents, to another two, and to another one, to each according to his own ability; and immediately he went on a journey.

Then he who had received the five talents went and traded with them, and made another five talents.

And likewise he who had received two gained two more also.

But he who had received one went and dug in the ground, and hid his lord's money.

After a long time the lord of those servants came and settled accounts with them.

So he who had received five talents came and brought five other talents, saying, "Lord, you delivered to me five talents; look, I have gained five more talents besides them."

His lord said to him, "Well done, good and faithful servant; you were faithful over a few things, I will make you ruler over many things. Enter into the joy of your lord."

He also who had received two talents came and said, "Lord, you delivered to me two talents; look, I have gained two more talents besides them."

His lord said to him, "Well done, good and faithful servant; you have been faithful over a few things, I will make you ruler over many things. Enter into the joy of your lord."

Then he who had received the one talent came and said, "Lord, I knew you to be a hard man, reaping where you have not sown, and gathering where you have not scattered seed.

"And I was afraid, and went and hid your talent in the ground. Look, there you have what is yours."

But his lord answered and said to him, "You wicked and lazy servant, you knew that I reap where I have not sown, and gather where I have not scattered seed.

"So you ought to have deposited my money with the bankers, and at my coming I would have received back my own with interest.

"Therefore take the talent from him, and give it to him who has ten talents.

"For to everyone who has, more will be given, and he will have abundance; but from him who does not have, even what he has will be taken away."

(MATTHEW 25:14–29)

Part of fulfilling your calling is taking appropriate risks to maximize the potential of the gifts and talents with which you've been entrusted. I believe this is why Jesus tells this parable and makes it clear to his disciples and those listening that playing it safe is not commendable, avoiding risk is not to be rewarded, and living out of fear of what others will think—with their approval and disapproval—should not be what motivates us. Many men work so hard to excavate their identities from beneath the layers of pain and disappointment, from beneath the expectations of others and approval of loved ones, but then once they have a clear sense of who they are, they bury their treasure again. They bury themselves. But it is never too late. Like Lazarus being called out of the grave, our Lord calls each one of us to come to life in the fullness of who God made us to be.

Our personal loss is not the only one suffered when we avoid fulfilling our calling and bury our talents. Everyone loses out when we don't pursue our dreams. There's a domino effect, a trickle-down effect of loss, in which everyone around us suffers because they are cheated of the greatness lying dormant inside their husband, father, son, brother, uncle, and friend. If you are a wife or mother or girlfriend reading this book, realize that you not only benefit when the men in your life fulfill their purpose, but you also can play a role in helping them pursue their calling. It is an invaluable gift when a woman believes in a man's dream. We all need someone who helps facilitate the dream inside, even if the facilitation of the dream is nothing more than a listening ear and a gleam in a watchful eye. Ladies, please remember that the torch that burns in a man's soul is but a mere ember flickering in the wind. Keep fanning the flame of his greatness, even if his ideas of success may be different from what you had in mind. Manipulation is not facilitation.

A man tends to cherish forever a woman who helps him be all that he can be inside. He will also ultimately resent the one who denies him a chance at self-discovery. Ladies, this self-discovery may benefit you, but this is his challenge; if you love him, help him get there. Most men (especially those raised by strong mothers) define love by what their mothers did for them. No, ma'am, I am not asking you to mother him. I am only suggesting that you be to him what you are so good at being to your children—a strong resource of support and understanding.

To my brothers, my fellow travelers who are searching for the one thing, or in some cases several things (many of us have more than one dream), that gives them a sense of vitality and purpose, let me say this: A real man knows when he's not living out his calling, not fulfilling his true identity, and not moving toward his heart's destination. Whether you communicate your disappointment or concern overtly or implicitly, you know, and those around you know, that you're not being true to who God made you to be. As a result, you often end up even more frustrated, angry, and eventually bitter that your life didn't turn out the way you hoped and wanted it to go.

I'm afraid I've seen these expressions on men at all ages and seasons of life. It crosses all lines of race, religion, age, culture, economics, and education. I've sat with teenaged boys who couldn't imagine themselves as any bigger, any brighter, any better than what they saw in the 'hood. Their listless eyes shift downward as they desperately long to believe that there's something more to who they are and what they can do than what they've experienced so far. I've seen these looks of bitterness oozing out of the hard faces of well-educated, middle-aged men who have a beautiful home, a fat bank account, a prestigious job and title, but who are dying inside because it's not what they were made for. I've seen healthy gentlemen die shortly after their big retirement party, because all of a sudden they no longer have a sense of purpose, or they realize that they've wasted their years on the wrong pursuits. Yes, if you postpone your life's purpose, you will wither and your heart will die.

Men who bury their talents, who are not actively pursuing their dreams, who put their lives on hold while days, weeks, months, and years pass them by, suffer an empty existence. They are not following the path God has set before them; they are simply not living life. Instead, they go through the motions, never getting anywhere, only getting bitter, disillusioned, and their dreams just wither away.

LABOR PAINS

Even after you feel in your bones that you know why God put you on this earth, and have determined to pursue your purpose, it often remains a challenge to keep your passion alive and your feet moving in the direction of your dreams. Just because you discover your purpose doesn't mean that life circumstances and the attitudes of others will change. This is where you must have a long-term view, a vision that sustains you beyond the daily grind of small annoyances and trivial problems, which will attempt to accumulate like barnacles on the bow of a moving ship. The key is often to remain in motion toward destination.

Another key is reminding yourself of the truth about who you are and what you're about and finding ways to remind yourself of this. You may need to change priorities, change jobs, change locations, or change lifestyles. You may need to surround yourself with objects or mementos that remind you of where you're headed and how you're only going to get there by focusing on getting through today before you tackle next year. Gentlemen, this is more than a decision. This is a process.

Your imagination and perseverance will be paramount. "Without a vision, the people perish" we're told in God's Word, and this is so true.

Passion is key to purpose, to facing life effectively. And living purposefully brings joy and peace in new dimensions you may never have experienced before. When you have a sense of purpose, your vision is enlarged and you don't mind the small sacrifices that are part of the journey. When an apprentice knows that he will be the master some day, he doesn't mind doing the daily chores and tedious tasks that he's called to fill. I recall from my own experience, even after God had extended his call to me to enter the ministry, I still had to work at jobs that seemed far from the church. I worked as the manager at a paint store, as a cashier, and as an operator at the local utility plant.

While none of these jobs fulfilled my sense of calling, they each gave me an opportunity to earn a living, to learn and practice character building, and to move toward my calling of full-time ministry. Though there was absolutely nothing wrong with these positions, still I knew that I would not be a cashier or a factory worker for the rest of my life, and therefore I didn't mind the present season of inconvenient challenges

Reevaluate your goals and don't be afraid to modify them when needed.

and uncomfortable responsibilities. I knew that this was only a stepping-stone, a stretch of road along the highway, and that I would move beyond it according to the Lord's timing. I knew I must keep my eyes on the prize of discovering who I was and what I was to accomplish. And in the meantime, I was grateful for His provision and for the lessons of patience, dependence, and diligence that came from each of those opportunities.

I later learned that all things work together for the good of those who are seeking the Lord and His loving purpose for their lives (see Romans 8:28). You must use everything you have ever learned about anything as fuel. No time is wasted if you convert each experience into fuel to get to the next destination. The principles I learned managing the paint store helped me later with my own companies and businesses. The production of chemicals at the utility plant gave way eventually to establishing the production of tapes and videos in our ministry. What I am attempting to say to you is do not waste anything you went through on your way to getting to what you feel you were meant to do. It is all part of the process of greatness.

David certainly learned not to waste any of the parts of his process. In the last chapter, we looked at how his identity as a king lived inside his kid-like exterior, and how no one around him recognized his potential for greatness until God found him and had His prophet Samuel anoint David. He must have grown impatient and wanted to expedite the process of becoming the king, but he was forced to endure the birthing process of his own potential.

Most men assume that birthing is only for women, but the truth is that God birthed His creation, and then Adam, since he was created in his Master's image, contributed to the creation of Eve, his helpmate, through an actual part of himself, his rib. It could safely be said that God birthed Adam and Adam birthed Eve. Every man since then has been called to birthing. Every man must reconnect with what it means to birth the greatness within himself.

David, singing psalms and writing poetry on the hillside, was as pregnant as any woman has ever been. You see, there was a king inside this kid. How to unlock that royal power inside the lonely shepherd boy stuck on a hillside? That was David's challenge. In each one of us there is a king, struggling for power. We're called to birth the king within.

We see this is true for Moses, and the way God called him to birth a great leader out of a murderer. With Joseph we see the same birth process in place as he labored to believe in the power of his dreams from the inside of a cold prison cell, charged with a crime he didn't commit. Could he dare to believe in the power of his dreams? So far, they had only gotten him in trouble. After he shared his dream with his brothers, they sold him into slavery and told their father he was dead. His coat of many colors was tattered and smeared with goats' blood, but his dreams didn't die. Or consider Job in sackcloth and ashes, desperately wondering why he should muster the strength to get up again. He had no support from friends, wife, or children. He was forced to birth out of his despair. This is the essence of faith—taking action to birth your greatness against overwhelming obstacles.

TOOLS OF THE TRADE

Within the process of birthing your greatness comes the formidable task of facing the giants that will attempt to block your path. Like President Bush facing the formidable task of protecting, securing, and salving the wounds of our country after 9/11, we see David facing his legendary giant, the behemoth known as Goliath, a brute so savage in his spite that the entire Israeli army cowered before him—even King Saul. I encourage you to read the description of David's adversary (1 Samuel 17:4–7) and see for yourself—this ugly brother was massive.

However, what's even more impressive than the daunting description of David's opponent is the description of the weapons and tools that David chooses for his fight.

> Then he took his staff in his hand; and he chose for himself five smooth stones from the brook, and put them in a shepherd's bag, in a pouch that he had, and his sling was in his hand. And he drew near to the Philistine.
>
> (1 SAMUEL 17:40)

The courageous David took only five smooth stones and a sling to challenge Goliath. Can you imagine? And this massive monster, who towers over David, comes into battle with a sword, a spear, and a javelin. It would seem that the odds are certainly stacked against our hero. But David is undeterred; he is confident. He defiantly faces his opponent and advances toward victory.

> Then David said to the Philistine, "You come to me with a sword, with a spear, and with a javelin. But I come to you in the name of the LORD of hosts, the God of the armies of Israel, whom you have defied.
> "This day the LORD will deliver you into my hand, and I will strike you and take your head from you. And this day I will give the carcasses of the camp of the Philistines to the birds of the air and the wild beasts of the earth, that all the earth may know that there is a God in Israel.
> "Then all this assembly shall know that the LORD does not save with sword and spear; for the battle is the LORD's, and He will give you into our hands."
> So it was, when the Philistine arose and came and drew near to meet David, that David hurried and ran toward the army to meet the Philistine.
> Then David put his hand in his bag and took out a stone; and he slung it and struck the Philistine in his forehead, so that the stone sank into his forehead, and he fell on his face to the earth.
> So David prevailed over the Philistine with a sling and a stone, and struck the Philistine and killed him. But there was no sword in the hand of David.
> Therefore David ran and stood over the Philistine, took his sword and drew it out of its sheath and killed him, and cut off his head with it.
> And when the Philistines saw that their champion was dead, they fled.
> (1 SAMUEL 17:43-51)

Despite overwhelming, near impossible odds, David kept his hope alive. Perhaps it was the combination of his boyish naiveté, his faith yet undaunted by life's dents and dings, and his willingness to hope for a miracle in the face of an unyielding enemy. Perhaps it was his righteous anger so focused on this Philistine, who embodied everything that violated David's life and faith and identity. Whatever it was, it was enough to fuel his willingness to take action, to come toe-to-toe with the foe who had felled his countrymen, to select smooth stones from the riverbed and channel the strength of his body into a mighty sling toward the giant's head leering above him. The Scripture emphasizes again that the young man killed the giant and "had no sword in his hand." In fact, after David has felled the giant, he uses his enemy's own sword to behead the bully, a cultural practice that would ensure the surrender of the remaining Philistine army. He had faith in his God and in himself to attend to the task at hand, no matter how daunting or impossible it seemed to those around him.

It's the same challenge that men are called to face today. Often the giants are the expectations of others, the prejudices and biases because of your race or looks or lack of education. Sometimes they are our own weaknesses grown up into mutant problems against us: addictions, past failures, and lost relationships. Like David, we must be willing to know what the true battle requires of us. We must be able to strip off the armor foisted on us by others, even those who love us and are well intended, and to be true to our own strengths and giftedness. We must look to the simple, unadorned tools that will serve us best, the ones we have tried and tested, even if others laugh at their simplicity or lack of sophistication.

David's tools may not be your tools, but the principles are transferable. His life spent as a shepherd taught him an appreciation for simple tools of the trade, techniques that might seem unconventional to his fellow soldiers but that proved more than effective to accomplish his goals. Responsibility, resourcefulness, and relentlessness were tools he developed with sheep, but it helped this kid become the king. Yes, he used a rag and a rock, but these were tools that were proven to him. I believe that the answer you need for the fight you face is always close at hand.

NOTHING VENTURED, NOTHING GAINED

It's amazing how easily we are distracted from the core conflict of a problem when there's a giant problem in our life. Perhaps it's our fear or insecurity, but sometimes it seems easier to focus on getting the girl, or advancing our career, or keeping up with the rat race in the never-ending quest to acquire the right car, or address, or designer wardrobe than to take a long look inside our hearts at the real battle. I think it often takes years of our lives to separate the distractions from the destiny one has inside. And while we may busy ourselves with these distractions for a time, the real giant of a problem looms before us, waiting patiently to devour us day by day. Is there a giant in your life right now that you are terrified to face? Or are you trying to take him down for the wrong reasons?

Sometimes we overcome obstacles and obtain coveted goals only to discover that it doesn't really address the larger problem of who we are and what we're about. We earn the degree, get the promotion, afford the sports car, or win the beauty queen only to discover that we're still who we are. In other words, we equip ourselves with what we thought we needed but that has little if anything to do with who we really are called to be.

One way that we get caught up in this trap is by trying to become who other people want us to be. Surely, David must have thought twice before he told the king—the king, mind you—that he wouldn't be needing the royal armor and sword. "I haven't tested these," he tells

Saul very matter-of-factly when the king offers him his personal armor. David didn't worry that Saul might think he was being insolent or arrogant. He didn't want to try to be what the king wanted him to be— what the king wished he, himself, could be. How often do we dress up in the suits or uniforms that our fathers handed down to us? How often do men accept someone else's weapons to fight someone else's battles instead of picking up their own tools and facing the enemy who stands before them?

Many women do not realize that your husband, after years of marriage, may just now be gaining the courage to strip out of Saul's armor and become who he feels he was meant to be. Some are trapped in the armor of a career they do not enjoy, a life that gives them no happiness, and sooner or later he will ultimately reject the armor and face the giant of being a man dressed in the strength of his boyhood tools. It may be a sling shot, but if it is who he is . . . it will work!

Regardless of your stage of life, most of us continually have giants we face. The hurdles may be those things that happened to us that shape our self-perception and the opinions of others. It may be the color of our skin, the character and reputation of our community. It may even be our body build or facial features that become a giant towering over us. Some men struggle with these things, many of them struggling silently without the benefit of anyone to discuss them with. Drugs, sex, or other pursuits become a way of validating who we are or anesthetizing the pain. These things seem to make some men believe that they have gotten over the hurdles, but in reality they are still there.

> *Obstacles don't have to be boulders in our path; they can be stepping stones to a higher purpose.*

The giants may be those external enemies that threaten to devour us. Unsafe surroundings, toxic home lives, at-risk environments. (Notice I said at-risk *environments* and not at-risk *children*. I don't think it is healthy to tell a child he is at risk when in reality it is his environment that is at risk.) Hurdles may require the assistance of others, and you may benefit from the counsel of those around you, but when it comes right down to it, you must slay your own giants in your own way.

With a giant, it is kill or be killed. Generally, giants are killed by right choices, and choices are something we generally have to make alone. They can make or break you. After years of working with inmates incarcerated at early ages, I realized that many of them really are good young people who had tough giants to face and failed to shoot first. The result of their timidity to make the wisest choice led to destructive cycles, which ended in sad consequences. All of us, believe it or not, are only one choice away from sad consequences. It is not always easy to make good choices, but if we have faith in ourselves, we more often than not make the right decisions.

David knew that he must be himself. He couldn't try to be the king, or his brothers, or a tough bully like he was facing. He simply needed to be himself and bring an awareness of his purpose to the situation. David was committed to being himself and knew that if he was actually going to have a chance at taking down the giant, then he had to stick with what he knew and what he knew best. It's so hard for many men to remain authentic today. We get caught up in those roles that society and culture dress us up in. We're uncomfortable and know we don't belong in such roles, but we don't have the courage to hand them back and say, "I haven't tested these. I must use my own equipment that I know by heart."

Based on David's utilization of his natural weapons, as well as my own experiences and observations with the giants I've encountered, here are a few ways to overcome the obstacles in your life:

FIVE SMOOTH STONES FOR THE GIANTS IN YOUR LIFE

1. **Confront what is threatening you.** Don't pretend that it will go away just because you don't think you can bear to

face it. Don't be intimidated by it just because it's bigger than you are.

2. **Level what you've learned in the past against what you face in the future.** Don't look to be rescued by others or to find a secret somewhere beyond your reach. Recall yesterday's trials and how you've slain the giants from your past.

3. **Don't let the spectators and speculators break your focus from the real villain.** It's tempting to look away from the eyes of your problem and seek advice, counsel, and solutions from others. While there's certainly a place for the wisdom of your friends and colleagues, when you're in the midst of a fight, don't lose sight of the real problem and its source.

4. **Never assume a problem is dead just because it's dazed.** Make sure you kill your giant and don't simply leave him unconscious to return and sneak up on you another day. Conquer the problem with a permanent solution and not a short-term fix.

5. **Use the enemy's sword against him. Kill him with his own sword!** Without stooping to unethical practices or immoral behavior, you should be willing to fight with the same intensity level as your opponent. Learn what you can from your enemy and then apply it to his weakness.

If we are to ever know who we truly are as men, then we must be willing to face the giants in our lives. We must be willing to carve steps into the rocks that attempt to obscure our paths. Whether there's a giant looming right now or not, and I suspect that for most of us there is something that we need to face down, I encourage you to take that look in the mirror and see who looks back. Even if there's fear, keep

---

INCREASING YOUR RANGE OF MOTION——FOR MEN

What did you learn about yourself by answering the questions on pages 45–46?

How would you sum up your purpose in a short phrase or motto? How are you presently living it out?

What's the greatest obstacle to discovering and living out of your purpose right now?

INCREASING YOUR RANGE OF MOTION——FOR WOMEN

How is he doing? Depressed? Anxious? Fearful?

List and talk to him about five happy/precious times you've had together.

What will help (and what can you do) to bring back the passion and purpose in his life?

---

looking. Even if there's insecurity, don't stop. If we are to embark on this journey of self-discovery and forward progress, then we must be willing to know and to exercise our purpose.

And we must not overlook our dependence on God for an awareness of what He calls us to do and when to exercise our gifting. I encourage you to ask Him what He sees in you and be prepared to be blessed by His response. Commit yourself to prayer and to studying His Word to learn who He says you are and to discover why you're here. You are His child, created in His image, made to be a man, imbued with unique gifts, strengths, talents, and worth unlike anyone else. And you are created for a special destiny that He wants to help you live out.

Hold yourself up to the light of who God intends for you to be, and look for the steps He has carved into the rocks of life for you. Look yourself in the eye and dare to hope again that your dreams are still alive, still attainable. Uncover your buried treasure chest of talents and risk them in God-honoring ways. Be prepared to use the unique tools of your past with which He has equipped you. And always, always persevere toward the vision of what you were made for. Keeping this hope alive and pursuing it with every ounce of your strength is what fuels your journey as a man in the process of fulfilling his manhood.

Part Two

A MAN'S
RELATIONSHIP
WITH TIME

*"I don't want to be immortal by leaving something behind;
I want to be immortal by not dying."*
—WOODY ALLEN

"Discontent in your life isn't all bad—it could be the mother of invention."
—BOB BUFORD, *Half Time*

*"Eighty percent of all suicides in the U.S. are men. Male suicides
at mid-life are three times the rate versus other times; and
for men over 65, it is seven times higher."*
—ARCHIBALD HART, *Unmasking Male Depression*

THREE

~~~·∿·~~~

AGES AND STAGES

As for man, his days are like grass;
As a flower of the field, so he flourishes.
PSALM 103:15

Airports are wonderful places to people-watch. There are folks of all shapes, sizes, colors, and cultures. Not long ago, I was in the airport and I noticed an elderly man walking with his son. His son looked to be about my age. Walking side by side, they looked like a split screen of the same man at two different ages of his life. I couldn't help but think of my late father, and I wondered what it would be like to have him still by my side. Momentarily lost in my reverie, I was brought back to the moment by a tug on my hand, and I smiled as I was comforted by the warm hand of my youngest son gripped tightly in mine.

As we continued through the airport terminal, I noticed men of various ages bustling through the crowded corridors busily moving toward their destinations. I wondered where they were all going. I knew that some had reached their final destination, while others were just beginning their journeys. I'm sure that some of them were merely on a layover, with many more miles to go ahead of them. And I realized that this scene in the airport mirrored the lives of men. We are all traveling, moving rapidly through the stages of our lives, racing toward eternity. We may have different flight routes, we may be on different legs of our trips, with different itineraries. Some experience delays and turbulence, and some are temporarily grounded, unable to take off until flying conditions improve. Although my estimated time of arrival may be different from yours, ultimately we all have the same final stop.

This set me to thinking about the stages of men's lives as we develop from infancy to puberty to adulthood to midlife and beyond. Each leg of our journey has distinct characteristics, and to successfully maneuver through each part of our trip, we must adapt to the inherent changes that we are sure to face. Undoubtedly, moving from one stage to the next requires adjustment, but sometimes transitioning doesn't occur smoothly. So often we speak of the midlife crisis as if one's forties are the only decade when you have a real crisis of identity, purpose, or passion. But each of the different stages includes its own crisis. Consider yourself when you were a teenager, too old to be a child and too young to be a man, struggling to free yourself from what you considered the stifling restrictions of youth but unable to totally adapt to the freedom of adulthood. Transitions are difficult for men of all ages.

I cannot tell you the many mothers who walk up to me with some teenager in tow behind them. His face is scowling and his look is obstinate. He is disinterested as she shares with me how her son suddenly went from being a good student to an angry young man, whose odious remarks and belligerent disposition make her wonder if her once cute and cuddly little boy has been possessed by demons. But you know what? It is not demonic influences that have possessed him. It is the fear that accompanies him in the throes of adolescence while he's struggling to gain some sense of identity. The young man, often fatherless, is trying to fit in, figure out life, manage his sexuality, and live up to standards his mother taught him that now don't seem applicable to his situation.

He is betwixt two stages, not quite fitting in either. He found comfort in his mother's arms as a child, but he has seen glimpses of adulthood, and it is difficult for him to be her little boy again, but he is not yet a man. He is a boy with mannish tendencies. He is, no doubt, one of those young men who says he is a man because he can drive a car but is so much a boy that he can't afford one. He wants money but is not prepared to work. He is in transition and is confused.

As his mother tells me of her distress caused by her son's behavior, he takes on a look of annoyance, clearly perturbed that she is discussing his changes with me. He stares at me as if to say, "How can this dumb old preacher know anything about me?" He looks at my graying beard and the crow's feet gathering at the corners of my eyes and assumes that I could never understand what he is going through. But, boy, is he wrong! I have been this young man. I have been in his skin. I can relate to his uncertainty. Oh yes, I have been there and done that. I know his emotional roller-coaster ride too well. And what he doesn't know is that he will have this lost-in-space feeling again and again, every time he transitions from one stage to another.

Just waiting around the corner for him is the crisis at midlife, when a man is too old to be young and yet far too young to allow the creeping signs of age to bind him prematurely. Similar to the perils of adolescence are the maladies facing men at midlife: concerns about sexual prowess, performance, career, identity, and much more. The teenager is trying to find out what he can do and be. The man at midlife questions what he has done and who he has become. The young man has a false sense of immortality and mental focus that keeps him transfixed in the moment. His mother keeps telling him to think of his future, but he lives in the moment and finds it hard to conceive of a time beyond today. When a man is older, he is so aware of the future and his mortality that it screams in his ear. He is in the middle of his life and wonders about the choices he made and if he has served a purpose. Both he and his younger counterpart are confused and angry, and both are often in need of some support but don't know where to find it.

BAR MITZVAH OF THE MASCULINE SOUL

From street gangs to Indian tribes, most cultures celebrate the transition from childhood through various rituals and rites of passage. Many of them include a formal ceremony during which a child is recognized as an adult and expected to assume the responsibilities and privileges of adulthood. In Jewish culture, this tradition is called a bar mitzvah for boys and a bat mitzvah for girls and takes place when the child is thirteen years old. Bar mitzvah means "son of the com-

Face the changes in your life by allowing yourself to change along with it.

mandment" and reflects the commitment that the young man makes to uphold the Ten Commandments as well as other rules and customs of his religion and its community. In light of the magnitude of such a passage, boys are trained and educated about what it means to be a man in their culture, what it means to uphold the history, ethics, and morality of their people.

Unfortunately, in our contemporary and secular society, many men must face most of the transitions they go through without much ceremony or formal lessons to help them navigate their new terrain. They find themselves driving along a rocky road in the dead of night without any lights to guide them or a map to show them the way. It's dark, it's bumpy, and there is no one to ask for directions (although even if there was, most men would never dare to ask!). It's not uncommon for a man to veer off the road, drive into a ditch, and get stuck. He can press on the accelerator all he wants, but his wheels will just be spinning and he won't be getting anywhere.

Many men often feel stuck, paralyzed by the transition from one stage to another. They know they can't go backward, and they don't want to, but they are having trouble moving forward. Men tend to be performance-oriented, and when they fail to move smoothly from one stage to the next, they get angry at their inability and they feel lost. Men also have the need to feel in control. Control is a *major* issue—as if I need to tell you that. Being in transition represents a loss of control. Men who have mastered everything in one stage may become depressed to find that they have a whole new set of issues and roles to master in a new stage.

Unlike the female, who processes her life by communicating, the male, both younger and older, deals with his predicament in total silence. Like a mole, he goes underground to try to sort through the secret thoughts he keeps locked deep within himself. He'll grapple with his emotions in silence, and his wife or girlfriend or mother will ask him what he's thinking about. "Why won't you talk to me?" she asks. But he isn't sure she can handle what he'd really like to say. Sometimes he isn't sure he, himself, can handle what he would like to say. It's a lonely place because a man finds it difficult to admit that he's lost his way, that he doesn't know who he is, that he's uncertain about where he's going. He's embarrassed to admit that he needs guidance because he sees his need as a weakness. So he wrestles alone with his fear and feelings of inadequacy.

I have counseled many men who responded to all this by backing further and further into a dark hole, where few can reach him but God. This dark place is decorated with silence and filled with inner anger or sexual sedatives. It is a place of helplessness and hopelessness, and it is not uncommon for depression to take over. Six million men suffer depression every year in the United States, and 20 million men will experience depression at some time in their life.

To successfully manage the transitions of life, I believe we must cul-

tivate humility and patience and actively look for guidance. There is
nothing wrong with seeking counseling and mentoring. Most men see
it as an admission of weakness to get help, but I do not. We must seek
out others who have passed through similar stages and reached the shore
on the other side. Many men I counsel tell me they take great comfort
from knowing that I've gone through most of what they've gone
through in their lives. I've lost both my parents. I've been depressed.
I've questioned my calling. I've struggled in my marriage. I've worried
about my children. I've lost a job. And I've lived through these events
and moods and storms of the soul and continue to move forward, knowing that I'll encounter new trials and transitions ahead.

We must also realize that each stage we go through has different requirements, and we must embrace each stage and our role in it. In Ecclesiastes, the Preacher says that there is a time and season for every
purpose. A time to be adolescent . . . a time of wisdom . . . a time to be
stable . . . a time to change . . . a time to grieve . . . a time to celebrate like
there's no tomorrow . . . a time to die. The role we filled in one stage may
not be suited for the next. Often, we are no longer needed for this or
that, so we must search for significance.

We must also ask ourselves the crucial question: How should I live
my life? Certainly that answer will be different at different times of
our lives.

In a mature male, there are changes in his needs and feelings. It is important that couples are aware that relationships change. People change!
Their perspectives change and their needs do too. Countless marriages
fail when one of you is giving the other what he needed or she needed
years ago without doing an update. What seemed true to us at age nine-
teen may shift 180 degrees by the time we're twenty-five or turning forty.
The carefree single life that seemed an endless parade of fast friends,
beautiful women, and easy money makes us think we should do what
feels good. Soon, however, we become lonely and want some substance

in our lives: a relationship that's more than just a physical attraction or sexual encounter; a job that offers meaning and purpose, not just a well-earned paycheck.

What a man needs when he is trying to build his career and provide for his family in the early years of marriage may differ drastically from what he needs when these early giants are eradicated. Many times, these changing needs go unnoticed and often not mentioned. Busy schedules, work demands, and survival instincts distract men from inner needs. But eventually, his motions slow to a pace where his emotional, personal, and relational needs resurface.

This is often disturbing for the family because they are sure they know who you are, but in reality they know who you *were*! Couples, while you may know each other, the truth you know is not an absolute! Many people become angry and confused, resentful and sullen, feeling betrayed by the changes in their mate. But these changes are often as unavoidable as sunshine giving way to rain. You can't make it through this without a willingness to learn and go back to the school of love and date again. You have a new person coming out in the old one.

Ultimately, we realize that our truth is limited, as all human perspective is, and that we need our Father's guidance and a connection to our Creator, and to His wisdom and truth that transcends our own. He knows how to navigate you through the changes, the ages, and the stages, and He can keep you from losing each other in the changing seasons that are an inevitable part of a prolonged love and life together.

THESE ARE THE TIMES THAT TRY MEN'S SOULS

When I was a young boy, I recall hearing older folks saying that time is more precious than money or any accomplishment a person might achieve, for its supply is limited and cannot be restored once it is spent. How true this is! Time, my friend, is a forward-moving, linear commodity that waits on no one, changes course for no reason, and refuses to be recovered or reclaimed. It is a commodity you must utilize with utmost care, for even the minutes you have just spent reading this page will not be returned.

When we are young, we lose sight of the value of time. We get so busy with our day-to-day lives that we don't notice the hours pass into days, into weeks, and into entire pages on the calendar. The sand spills out of the proverbial hourglass and slips through our fingers and gets carried away on the wind. Occasionally, a significant event such as a birthday or major health concern jars a man into recognizing his own mortality and realizing his days are numbered.

> *Depression thrives in privacy. Break the silence and you will weaken its grip on you.*

It is the brevity of life that makes time so significant. It is by understanding that life is but a vapor that is soon expended that increases its value. But this realization also increases anxiety, as the shocking reality emerges that the young man who was an adolescent yesterday has aged in a flash. When did this happen? What happened to my hair? Doctor, what do you mean I have diabetes?

When a man starts to age, he realizes that something is happening to him that he cannot control. This is difficult, especially when he is used to being in power and authority. There is no check he can write for this. There is no phone call he can make to take care of things. Most men like to fix things, but life is not like a car that needs a new carburetor. The passing of time is not something that can be fixed or even altered. Life moves forward, and there is nothing we can do about it. Our time here is limited, and when our days run out, we are done.

Our man David was well aware of such transience:

As for man, his days are like grass,
he flourishes like a flower of the field;
the wind blows over it and it is gone,
and its place remembers no more.
(PSALM 103:15–16)

Like a snowball rolling downhill to start an avalanche, this personal awareness finally walloped me when I was in my late thirties. As my life changed and I watched friends and relatives pass from this life, I began questioning who I was, second-guessing what I'd accomplished, and pondering my purpose as if for the first time. I knew that I would someday die and no longer have the opportunity to fulfill my life's calling.

Has this realization sunk into the center of your soul yet? I encourage you to think for a moment about how you've faced this awareness of your own limited time in this life. Have you ignored it because you're young and healthy enough that you still feel invincible? Is it creeping up on you as you establish yourself and watch the days carry you along like a flooding current? Or are you in the midst of a full-blown midlife crisis wondering what it's all about and how you're going to go forward? Perhaps you're beyond that point and have owned and even embraced the knowledge that you don't have as much time left as you once thought you did.

When such an awareness bears down upon your soul, many of us seem to go to extremes. We study ourselves in the mirror and find new lines around our eyes, a few more gray hairs (if we have any hair left!), and the profile of our parents pressing against our sagging flesh. We run to the indulgences of youth in a desperate—and if you've ever seen a grown man with hair plugs driving a new red convertible, then you know what I mean by desperate—attempt to reverse the clock and recapture that which eluded us in our quest during our first adolescence.

Some men try to attain the feeling of being alive they had when they were single with less responsibility. So they flirt or maybe even consider having a fling to reignite the waning embers of a dying passion in their soul. Some switch careers, abandoning a life's work just as it's beginning to reap the rewards of success for them, because they are bored or frustrated or burned out. Viagra is sold by the cases and Rogaine is poured into the scalp. Fresh tattoos are cut into the skin and pierced ears abound as we all try to turn back the clock and return to our days of youth. So many wives tell me they feel like they're living with an aging Elvis look-alike, who spends more time in front of the mirror and uses more hair care and skin care products than they do!

Now, brothers, there is nothing wrong with taking care of yourself, trying to be healthy and look your best, but there are so many men who spend half of their lives in the gym, sweating it out in weight rooms, making horrible faces as they lift barbells and contort themselves into poses that make them look more like Gumby than Schwarzenegger. They are perpetually in motion, with the imprint of a stationary bicycle seat etched into their behinds and a water bottle clutched in their fists. You know the type: those perfectly manicured men whose teeth are always white as snow, their chiseled bodies like a Michelangelo sculpture. They make quite an impression outside of the gym as well; their dress pants look like they have marble columns imported from Venice beneath them and their chests resemble the Himalayan Mountains encased in designer shirts.

Okay, I will admit it. I am a little envious—not jealous, mind you—just slightly envious of how marvelously they are made. But I came to terms with reality a long time ago. While I may admire the ideals to which these men are committed, I will probably never join their ranks. Most of us won't. Most of us are simply lacking the genes to achieve Adonis-like looks. And quite frankly, many of us have too many other responsibilities and priorities than to spend hours each day working on our physical form. Tyson Beckford gets paid to look that good, and when you sign a multimillion-dollar contract with a professional sports team, conditioning your body *is* your job. But I, for one, have too much going on to devote an excessive amount of time to the pursuit of male perfection.

But truth be known, there are benefits to exercise. Nothing else fights off the carnivorous effects of aging quite like it. Like water eroding the banks of a river, time takes a toll on us as men, although most of us don't like to admit it. You don't have to talk about it if you don't want to, but let me tell you, as sure as the sun will set tonight, the closer you get to the twilight of your life, the more you will start to break down. But exercise and healthy living can delay the aging process and can help you avoid many of the dreaded symptoms that go with it.

Now I'll admit that going to the gym isn't one of my favorite things to do, but I do it. To be sure, the goal for me is not to pose in my underwear or prance around the beach in a Speedo (although it might be nice to have the option). No, what I'm seeking is a healthy body that functions like a well-oiled engine that propels me through my life so that I can live it to the fullest.

I want to encourage you to find something healthy to do and do it as often as you can. Not only does it relieve the stress that lurks in the shadows of a man's life like a stalker, seeking opportunities to rob you of the quality and sometimes the quantity of your life, but it also restores vitality. One of the things I quickly learned from being middle aged is that if a man doesn't fight back, being out of shape will rob you of your energy, your agility, and if that was not enough, your sex drive! As you get older, your metabolism starts to creep at a snail's pace, your muscle mass begins to deteriorate, and your hair slowly starts to vanish into some dark hole. But I have good news. Although there may not be a Fountain of Youth, exercise can combat against the ravages of time. So, my brothers, I want to encourage you to fight hypertension, diabetes, stress, heart disease, and erectile dysfunction with just one hour three times a week. Jogging, walking, weight lifting, or even walking up stairs instead of taking the elevator will help you get more out of life.

I know I will never become one of those guys who ends up on the cover of a romance novel or on a poster in some young girl's room, and I'm okay with that. But I'm not just going to sit here and let death creep in early by not taking care of what God gave me. In the past few years I've managed to melt off one hundred pounds and keep most of it off—except after vacations, near holidays, and sometimes when I just fall off the wagon! Okay, okay, I will admit that it is a lifelong struggle for me. Prayer may be a great tool for developing spirituality, but I've learned that praying for weight loss just doesn't work. The battle with the bulge is like a wrestling match. One moment I have it down, and the next it has me trapped in a full-Nelson, screaming, "Uncle!" But I am starting to enjoy the exercise and the routine that adds more "life" to my life. Working out makes me feel better. Sure, there are still mornings when my knees sound like a drummer warming up for band rehearsal, but it would be much worse if I didn't fight back.

Men, you need to do something for yourself. Right at the age when most everything you do seems to be for someone other than yourself, working out or taking up a sport has an uncanny way of giving you something back, which can be exhilarating and even rewarding. I beseech you, therefore, to arise from your couch. Drop your remote

> *Taking care of yourself is the best gift you can give those who love you.*

control and fight back. You'll be amazed by how much better you feel. No one is going to do this for you. This is something you have to do for yourself. Age is not as much our enemy as apathy is. For many of us, fighting the good fight of faith means arming yourself with weapons like treadmills and stationary bikes. Trust me. Your wife will love it. Your knees will thank you. Your food will digest better. Your blood will circulate better, and your rest will be far more rejuvenating. Exercise is so

---

INCREASING YOUR RANGE OF MOTION——FOR MEN

Take an inventory of your life and honestly tally your achievements and your goals.

Can you find an older man you admire who can serve as your role model? What questions can you ask him about the stage of life that you are currently experiencing?

What sport or activity did you enjoy as a younger man that you can pick up now? (Remember to check with a doctor before starting any type of new exercise program.)

INCREASING YOUR RANGE OF MOTION——FOR WOMEN

What can you do to show your husband that you're happy with him as he is—gray hair, wrinkles, and all?

Is the man in your life suffering from depression that has gone undiagnosed for some time?

What can you do to help your man stay healthy?

---

important to the body, but what might surprise you is how much more in control you feel over life and aging when you do something to build up what time is trying to tear down.

If I can do it, so can you. Neither of us may become body doubles for Jean-Claude Van Damme, but it will allow you not to run out of breath when you walk up a hill, to be able to finish a sermon without collapsing on stage, or to do whatever it is you need to do with adrenaline and enthusiasm. You can sit there in denial and let your life evaporate, or you can watch what you eat, exercise more frequently, and spend more years being the spiritual, life-loving, stud-muffin you were meant to be!

Age isn't something to be afraid of. Don't run from the aging process into the throes of a midlife crisis. Do what you can to ward off the negative effects of time and embrace the wisdom and spiritual maturity that a life well lived brings to you. Yes, time never stops and our days here are limited, but don't let this panic you. Instead, live with no regrets. Do not use this as a license to indulge sinful whims and selfish desires, but live with a fixed purpose and an engaging manner that maximizes every moment of your life. Like the adolescent seeking transformation and trying to acclimate himself to a new stage, we also must recalibrate ourselves to what I call a "new normal." Your past is behind you. Do not seek to recapture what is now history. Your power is in your destiny. Make the necessary adjustments for where you are now in life. Maintain your focus, brother, and for God's sake, keep moving.

FOUR

———◈———

SURVIVING THE
SEASONS OF LIFE

To everything there is a season,
A time for every purpose under heaven.
ECCLESIASTES 3:1

Many of us make the assumption that the seasons of our lives pass us by never to return. However, just as we experience the four seasons of weather year in and year out, so, too, do we go through the seasons of our lives repeatedly. These seasons may have some slight variation due to our current circumstances and external forces, but there are distinct characteristics and expectations that mark them. Please allow me to explain.

It's easy to think about our youth and adolescence as the green springtime when we are impressionable, impassioned, and invulnerable. We are new to the world, and it holds all the potential of an open field, newly turned and just waiting to be seeded. Our vigor and stamina and determination outweigh our wisdom and maturity, but our resilience allows us to bounce back from life's stretching like Silly Putty.

My grandmother used to say, "Youth is wasted on those too young to enjoy it." And I think this is often the case—that without experience and a basis of comparison, it's challenging to recognize the gifts that come during this season of new life. But it's not only in youth that we can experience a springtime fresh with new possibilities and budding life. There are many seasons of new beginnings that each of us undergoes as we mature and develop. You can be an old man chronologically but just now be discovering new aspects of yourself, new areas of growth, and the beginning of new relationships. Or you can be in midlife and just now embarking on the beginning of a new career, a new journey into fatherhood, or a new passion for a hobby or sport previously undiscovered. You may have only recently placed your faith in God and experienced a spiritual birth. Spring is not just a season for the young but a season for all of us who seek to continue growing by planting seeds in new ventures.

Typically, we think of our life's summer as a time of watching the temperature go up as life blooms around us. In summer, we have begun to establish ourselves, to seek and find a mate, to make decisions concerning parenthood and our career path. We learn to take care of ourselves and grow in wisdom, watching roots take hold and new buds flourishing into green maturity. And this summer season recurs in our lives in ongoing ways as well. We don't have to be in our twenties or thirties to watch with great pride as some of our investments grow into strong and healthy products of our time, energy, and resources. Whether it's our children, our home, our ministry, or our career, we begin to see and taste some of the fruit of our life's journey.

Summer is also a season of hard work. I can recall long, sweltering days under the West Virginia sun as I'd help neighbors weed their gardens when I was a boy. I'd roll up my sleeves or abandon my shirt altogether, as sweat beaded and trickled down my neck and back. Even though my arms would be sore and my back would hurt from bending, hoeing, and pulling weeds, I took immense pleasure in the satisfaction of my labor, relishing the feel of dirt on my hands and the awareness that my efforts would have a direct effect on the quality of the corn, beans, and squash later harvested from Mrs. Johnson's garden. Similarly, many of us find ourselves in seasons of hard work and demanding schedules, time often spent away from our families and friends. I believe the key to a profitable and gratifying summer is keeping in mind the relationship between your labor and your vision of the harvest. But one must also maintain a satisfactory balance between work and play. The summer of life is a time when a man is in the heat of it, in the heat of life's test, trying to stand up to its demands, live up to his vows to God, his wife, himself, and so on. These times pass quickly, almost in a blur. It is so easy to become so preoccupied with the season that one forgets to enjoy the budding fruit and some of the special moments with children.

In the fall seasons of our lives, we experience the outcomes and consequences of many of our fruitful, and sometimes fruitless, actions. And these realizations don't necessarily occur in the autumn years of our lives. No, instead we taste the fruits of our harvest each time we recognize and accept responsibility for using our talents wisely, along with each time we taste bitter fruit and learn from our mistakes. Don't be afraid to fail, my brother, if your labor involves a worthy endeavor and honest labor. Not all seeds produce the harvest we desire or grow crops that look like the picture in the seed catalogue. Learn from your mistakes and carry this harvest with you into a new venture, the next new spring of your life. It is here that we have to accept that something might not have been meant for us to do in the first place. Some crops may have been lost. It is important that we, as men, accept the fact that none of us can do everything correctly. Still, we have to appreciate success, learn from the failures, and garner the strength we received from both to prepare for winter and to impart the lessons to our sons.

David learned later in life that he could not continue to kill giants like he did in his youth. Doing what he used to do almost killed him, first at the hand of Saul and then with various other tribes. Even his own son

Absalom tried to destroy him. He had to realize that his strength was now in other areas. The Bible said that his sons and soldiers killed the new giants and David's wisdom was more important than his physical strength (2 Samuel 21:16–22). In his poetry, David repeatedly shares this valuable lesson he's learned—to rely on God's strength more than his own: "O Lord, the king rejoices in your strength. How great is his joy in the victories you give!" (Psalm 21:1). As he embraces the autumn years, David accepts his new role and rests in his kingly graces.

And finally there's winter, a season of hibernation and rest, a time for burrowing underground and waiting. As related to our life's span, winter is usually depicted as old age, as a time of bitter cold and decline into our final days. But I believe winter gets a short shrift as far as seasons go. The winter seasons throughout our lives are those times when we need to rest, to regroup, to recharge our batteries and wait before starting new ventures or harvesting old crops. This can be the most difficult season to embrace for many men, perhaps because it feels like we're being passive and dormant, like a bear retreating to his cave for his hibernated state of suspended rest. But this is also one of the most necessary seasons to accept and embrace, for it offers one of the largest returns.

I have noticed that as men get older they get more relational. Some men become more sensitive and affectionate; others tend to want their grandchildren around them. I do not want to suggest that they become less masculine. This is certainly not the case. Men may seem more emotional, but there are good reasons for that. They are less busy, having some accomplishments under their belts. They may have faced the loss of their parents, which is a tremendous wake-up call regarding their own mortality. Real values become more important to them. Businessmen start thinking about leaving a legacy. Workaholics become family-oriented; they try to regain some of the special times that life and busyness have stolen from them. They become more emotionally expressive and physically demonstrative. Often this new behavior throws family members for a loop. They're not accustomed to this attention. Some families, wives, and others have become disinterested, tired of waiting, and by the time Daddy comes home to roost, they're no longer waiting for him anymore.

He has unknowingly conditioned them not to give him in one stage of his life the affection that he now needs desperately. He was too busy when he was young for something that he cannot seem to live without now. It is challenging for the family around him because they are not used to the desire he now has for family outings, games and activities, romance, and walks in the park holding hands. But allow me to explain: Dad has become terribly aware that something is missing, something that his job has never given him. He may have damaged some relationships that he is now hungry for. Men, please avoid damaging people with thoughtlessness or by scoffing at their tenderness and sensitivity— you will later need them. Keep the family and friend door open in the summer and fall so that when winter arrives you can enjoy your family and embrace your wife without them having become frozen from the cold aloofness to which they had become accustomed from you.

To the women reading this and saying Amen!, this may confirm your suspicions about where he is right now. But the question I need you to address is, Do you have the elasticity to readjust to this newer guy who is what you wanted at first and have become accustomed to living without? If you can switch to the sound of the new music, you could waltz your way into the bliss of old age connected to a soul mate for a lifetime.

Winter doesn't have to represent age. It can represent a time of resting, so that when you recoup, you are refueled and ready to start again. Without rest and renewal, there is no new life in the spring. If a field is not allowed to lie fallow after producing successful harvests, then it will not have the nutrients and replenished deposits of minerals to feed new seeds to be planted. You don't have to be old to appreciate your body's limitations. Adjusting to new "norms" is simply common sense. You can do most of what you always did, but with a little more planning and a little more rest, you can stay in the game all of your life. I've mentioned before how important it is to take good care of yourself, but I would go so far as to insist that you allow yourselves seasons of rest, periods of time when you take a sabbatical, lay low and enjoy what you have before you start new ventures and continue your journey. We will explore this in more detail momentarily.

Even when winter marks the final season of a man's life as he approaches death, there is still ongoing life—in his children and his legacy to them. At this time, a man shifts his focus from his own rewards to what he can bestow upon those who are heir to his throne. He now wants his sons and children to carry on his lineage, to take comfort in knowing his seed lives on beneath the snowy ground of his own imminent demise. All good things must come to an end. So it is with life itself. It is the brevity that enhances the days we do have. It makes you grateful and careful, conscious and respectful. Every day is to be enjoyed, and when there are no more days, there is always eternity, for which there is no season and no end. In other words, life is a commercial that will soon be over, but stay tuned. The best is yet to come. Heaven is the main event, and I have read that it is a wonderful way for the story to complete itself.

KODAK MOMENTS

Despite the fact that time is a limited commodity and is marked off in regular intervals, there is one way to slow time down and control it for ourselves. It sounds clichéd and corny, like some Kodak film commercial or one-liner from a Hallmark card, but we must learn to transform moments into memories. Too many people miss the moments of their lives. As I said earlier, it's very easy to get so caught up in the busyness of day-to-day living that we fail to notice what is going on around us. Others miss their moments because they have their heads deeply buried in the past. Could-haves, should-haves, would-haves preoccupy their thoughts. They're so mired in a bog of "if onlys" that they're stuck as if in quicksand while the rest of the world passes them by. And we all know people who ignore the present because they're so worried about the future. Someone once said life is what happens when you're busy making other plans. Don't let life happen without you noticing! Pay attention to the moments and preserve them in your memory. If we're paying attention to our lives, to the various seasons of our soul, then we will live with fewer regrets and transform the ticking of the clock's hands into a priceless treasure.

Think about some of your very best moments. What would you include on your top-ten list of all-time joyful moments? Meeting your wife for the first time? Being there when your son or daughter was born? A fishing trip with your best friend? Getting a new bike for Christmas when you were ten years old? Graduating from college with your degree in hand and your parents in the auditorium watching? Maybe the best moment in your life was one filled with love and affection, intimacy or accomplishment. Even if my list and your list contained some of the same events, each one would be different in myriad ways, for they are personal and richly imbued with the distinct colors of our unique experience, personality, and shading of memory. And they are timeless, able to leap outside the confines of the fifteen seconds or forty-two minutes or three days during which they occurred to last a lifetime. You would do well to stop once in a while and pay attention and to savor the moment that you are in. Even God stopped in the midst of the creation to acknowledge things He had done well. He says over and over, "And that was good."

When my mother was alive, she used to say, "Take your happy moments and save them in a box. When life is really hard, take them out and rehearse them again and again." Mom was right. You can feed off of things that were moments of ecstasy in your past. If negative past experiences can be a source of ongoing pain, then positive ones can be a source of strength. Often when I minister to inmates who are physically trapped in a small space, confined to limited areas and controlled for months and years, they tell are me that they able to withstand the regret, the obvious remorse, and the continued reminder of events out of their painful past. Many of them say that they transcend walls inside of their own mind by reminiscing on good days, happy moments, and pleasurable thoughts. Maybe this is what the Apostle Paul means when he says, "Whatever things are true, whatever things are noble, whatever things are just, whatever things are pure, whatever things are lovely, whatever things are of good report, if there is any virtue and if there is anything praiseworthy—meditate on these things" (Philippians 4:8). You have to choose what you feed on if you are going to survive life's many storms.

We can probably recall moments that seemed unbearable and lasted far longer than what the clock or calendar revealed. These are probably moments we would like to forget, to bury and suppress as if they never happened. But they are there, my friend, and unless we acknowledge and confront their anguish and embrace what we can learn from them, they will continue to haunt and undermine us. Have you ever been playing in the pool and tried to push a beach ball beneath the surface? If you do manage to forcibly submerge it, I'm sure you know that it doesn't stay there for long but bounces back to the surface like a man gasping for air. Our most painful memories are the same way, floating outside of time's boundaries, often draining us of so much energy as we attempt to press them below the surface of our consciousness, beneath the tide of memory.

But they are there and deserve to be acknowledged just as much as their pleasant counterparts. If we do not remember the past, then we are doomed to repeat it. Whether these dangerous fragments include memories of abuse, molestation, betrayal, weakness, humiliation, or shame, we can learn much by allowing them occasional time to air out before us. What can we learn from such devastating moments? I believe we can learn to know ourselves better, our weaknesses and limitations, our wounds and scars. We also can learn to take care of ourselves and know what we need, forgiving ourselves and others for their mistakes and transgressions. Finally, we can learn something of God's goodness to sustain us through these hardships and to see some of these redeemed by His own hand. As Joseph declared to his brothers, "You meant evil against me, but God meant it for good, in order to bring it about as it is this day, to save many people alive" (Genesis 50:20).

CONDITIONAL LIVING

Too often, what prevents us from making the most of our moments is conditional living, acting as if there's an imaginary state of existence in which we will finally arrive. "If only I made this much money, if only I met the right woman, if only my kids would graduate and get out of the house, then I'd be happy and could get on with my life" we say, always using some future event or condition as the prerequisite for our success. And then, of course, when and if the event passes or the goal is fulfilled, we're on to the next big thing, the next benchmark for a nonexistent state of bliss that remains forever elusive, just out of grasp. It's as if our plane is always arriving, just about to land on the runway when it swoops back up into the sky chasing after another goal. This kind of thinking is so dangerous, so debilitating to a man in motion on his journey. We must be engaged with the present even as we know the past from which we've emerged and glimpse the future to which we're called.

It's not that I don't want you to have multiple goals that you're in the process of fulfilling. It's simply that I want you to enjoy the success that you've achieved this far, to be accepting of what has brought you to this present point in your life—all the mistakes and missteps, the small sacrifices and large decisions, all the mundane moments and larger-than-life minutes when you took a step forward. If we are to make peace with our relationship to time, then we must be willing to accept that life is dynamic, not static. Each day we think we know what we're going to do, and often we do follow through our routine as planned without interruption. But in our ultramodern world of digital technology and e-nnovations, we're lulled into thinking that we can have total control over our time. I know some men who book every ten-minute interval between five in the morning and ten o'clock at night. They schedule everything and get upset when they run behind, which inevitably happens because of traffic, the weather, or the domino effect when one of their clients runs late.

Once again, it's not that I'm discouraging you from planning and scheduling—no, I am all for thoughtful organization and allocation of our most valuable resource. However, if you do not leave margins in between your appointments or if you're not willing to improvise when meetings run over and spontaneous plans develop, then you will drive yourself crazy. And if you are more committed to fulfilling the agenda on your Day-Timer than in engaging your work or the people around you, then you are sadly deceiving yourself in an attempt to control time. My encouragement is that you prepare yourself and make a plan but then exercise the flexibility to go with the current of each day's tide.

Such adaptability is what you often see in the great artists and musicians, the dynamic teachers and pastors. I'll never forget what one of my high school teachers told me when I complimented her ability to flow with the material, to allow for spontaneous interactions and exciting discussion in her classroom. "How do you prepare for such a class?" I asked her. She looked at me and replied, "I make sure I know the material so thoroughly that I'm free from having to follow my outline. In other words, I overprepare my lesson plan and then rely on the class to help me determine our needs and what will work best. I like to think I'm creating each class as a unique learning experience." I remembered her words because I think it's what we're all called to create: Each day should become a unique creation where the material is familiar but our approach is interactive, spontaneous, and innovative.

A recent exchange with a friend of mine illuminates what so many men encounter as they reach a certain stage in their lives. We can call it midlife crisis, burnout, a dry season, or going crazy, but its reality hits us all, often several times during our lifetime if we live long enough. Below the surface of our lives, many of us are constantly fighting the fires of a burnout or blowup.

My friend, I'll call him Frank for our discussion here, literally had all the trappings of success. Starting out as an accountant for a major oil and gas firm, Frank became bored and switched careers around age thirty-five, entering the ranks of a Hollywood production company as a numbers cruncher. But the reason my friend switched careers in the first place was to leave behind his bean-counting mindset and utilize his vast creativity and imaginative powers. He felt called to write, produce, and direct videos, television programs, and feature films.

So Frank patiently made the transition, leaving the accounting behind and proving his creative giftedness in small steps as those around him grew to appreciate his insight and value his direction. In fact, he and I first met up a few years ago when he was recommended to me as a consultant for my program, *The Potter's Touch*. I was impressed by Frank's easygoing warmth and thoughtful professionalism; his direction and insight indeed created a positive impact on some changes I made in our tapings.

Recently Frank and I began emailing and chatting by phone as he shared the storm swirling at the center of his calm exterior. "Believe it or not," he began, "after ten years, I've simply lost my passion for the film industry—all of it, writing, directing, producing. Right after I finished shooting this last cable movie, I felt like someone had deflated me like a balloon. I feel like I've been attacked in the very area that has always energized me the most, being creative. I'm in the middle of a project now, with bigger stars and the largest budget I've ever worked with before, and I have to force myself to get to the set in the mornings. I can exercise more creative control on this project than any I've ever worked on, and yet I feel like I'm trying to squeeze creative juices out of an old, dried-up sponge."

Can you relate to my friend's dilemma? Perhaps you are in the midst of such a lost passion yourself, whether it is your marriage, your relationship to your kids, or your interest in your career. Frank went on to explain, "I know this is crazy because I'm in the best situation of my life, doing what I thought I enjoyed most. But I don't have seventy-five percent of myself to give, or even fifty percent; I have zero—no passion whatsoever. Constant thoughts of 'I've wasted my life,' 'What will I do with the second half of my life?,' 'Nobody appreciates what I do anyway' bombard my mind. Moodiness, daydreaming, and feeling sorry for myself seem to consume me. I keep trying to jump-start the creative flow by going back and watching old movies, my favorite shows from when I was a boy, but they don't help. When your whole life centers around movies, and then all of a sudden you lose your drive and passion to make them, your life seems to have no value or purpose. I feel like I must be going crazy, Bishop!"

After assuring Frank that he wasn't crazy for what he was feeling, I proceeded by asking him a few simple questions to help him get at the heart of his dryness. I would ask them of you as well. Even if you are not currently struggling with burnout, these questions can provide you with a good pulse reading on the overall balance, or lack of, in your life.

QUESTIONS FOR RESTORING BALANCE

1. What hobbies do you have that are outside of what you do, i.e., fishing, golfing, para-sailing, etc.?
2. When were the last times you spent any significant quantity of time doing these hobbies?
3. How many friends do you have who are outside of your family and co-workers for whom you obviously feel responsible and in some ways provide for or work with?
4. Tell me about your vacations. How many, how often, and with whom?

ALL WORK, NO PLAY

Frank's responses are very common, and you may relate to them as you read through these and contemplate your answers.

"Bishop, your questions are so simple and direct but very incriminating! I'm almost embarrassed to answer them. How often have I advised others in these same areas and yet have ignored it for myself? I guess I'm always thinking that there's some profound answer or hidden issue I need to uncover. I really just need to take some time for myself."

In response to questions one and two, Frank shared that he works out three times a week in a gym close to the studio where he works. He acknowledged that he often sees co-workers, celebrities, and other directors and producers there and ends up talking around the water fountain or in the locker room about work projects. The other hobby on his list is going to the movies. Unfortunately, he's rarely able to enjoy the movie experience like you or I might enjoy it, hunkered down in a cushy seat in the dark, munching popcorn or Junior Mints. Frank confessed that he usually takes notes during the films he sees so that he can create new scenes for his own films.

His hobbies, as he and I both realized, were nothing more than extensions of his work life. While the potential exists for both working out and enjoying movies to be good outlets to relieve stress, I recommended that Frank try starting something new and different. Something that takes him out of his normal Frank-type activities. I often say that a vacation from being me is a vacation for me!

I want to do things that are so outside of my normal scope of activities that it gives me the feeling of freshness, adds depth to my life, and avoids the feeling of being robbed by my life's work or consumed by its strict limitations and demands. Bear in mind this is only a suggested option for renewing your soul. Meeting people outside of what you do and developing interests within a new hobby or business venture can divert your attention and stimulate underutilized parts of yourself. You can become engaged with a new direction and part of yourself without sacrificing the other, older parts of your life. Ultimately, as your life begins to regain balance, your passion for other areas of your life will return. This loss of passion in Frank's career, like all losses of passion, is generally temporary and will reignite again. You don't want to throw away something that is still valuable.

PEN PALS

Regarding question three about his friends, Frank acknowledged that he doesn't have any friends who are outside the film industry. Many of his family, including his son, his brother-in-law, and his cousin work in some capacity related to the business. Like finding new passionate diversions and hobbies, having friends that are unrelated to your career is crucial for a man's well-being and balance. You must allow yourself diverse connections with men who seem very different from you and your world.

In a later chapter we will explore friendships in greater depth. They have been such a vital resource for me. Such interactions provide new stimulation that can be so helpful. I have a friend in my network who is a medical physician. It's so refreshing for me to have a friend who is not a preacher or parishioner. His passion for people is similar enough to my own that I relate to his need to help them, but he is also different enough from me that his issues are fresh and intriguing in discussion. I am not such a resource for him that it starts to be a mentoring relationship. I am not an expert in his arena, nor is he in mine. We can use our friendship as a passport into each other's private nations where our citizens clamor for our attention and leadership. When we get together, there's something refreshing and vastly different as I gain insight into his world, much like the effect of traveling abroad and seeing the sites and tasting the exotic food of another culture. It reminds me of having a foreign pen pal and exchanging information and customs about each other's culture. He doesn't need me to help him do his job. He just likes me. And that is so good for me, and so good for all of us to have people who simply enjoy us and want to know us apart from our field of work. Anytime we work where we worship or work with our friends or family, we have no real escape.

Frank shared with me that he had never really considered himself someone who needed guy friends just to hang out with. He said he had plenty of friends at work, but he didn't like to socialize with them much after hours. "I just want to leave work at work." I counseled Frank that maybe the reason he didn't want to bring friendships out of the work arena was because those relationships weren't about camaraderie but were relationships of responsibility. His co-workers depended on him; their success was tied to his. I told him to look beyond work for friendships and to not be afraid to enjoy them just for camaraderie. When you only associate with people with whom you are doing business and in some ways helping to support, undergird, or enhance, you have a sense of responsibility that can be crippling when you are mid-lifing (my term for this kind of season). When your relationships make you weary, it can be an indicator that you are carrying too many people across the water. You must remember that you are ultimately responsible for yourself first, because if you cannot walk across the bridge yourself, you will never help anyone else across it.

KEEPING THE SABBATH

Finally, regarding vacations, Frank, like so many men, was sorely in need of one. If we think about this word "vacation" for a moment, we realize it comes from "vacate," meaning to leave, depart, abandon. We must leave behind all the old burdens that we are carrying, set them down and leave them in our inbox, on our desk, in our unanswered email, unreturned phone calls, and incomplete chores. Don't worry, they will still be there when you return. But if you don't set them down, then you will not have "vacated" at all. You will simply have strung yourself out even more by trying to add another item—"relaxation"—to your to-do list.

Frank told me he was in the habit of taking some long weekends occasionally. This is a good start, but if he is like most of us, by the time the weekend is over, he's just beginning to wind down and all of a sudden he must crank back up and get motivated to pick up all his burdens again. I recommend vacations of at least a week so that you have a couple of days to "detox" from your everyday world of hectic work and constant responsibility. By the third day, you're finally relaxing and catching up with yourself. You've barely unpacked your bags—not just your suitcase but the bags of stress you're carrying around inside—before it's time to load them up again. Some stress levels require more than a week, depending on what you do for a living and what you deal with in your life.

If possible, create a season of rest and renewal in the midst of your midlife burnout. Consider the many precedents for such a need in the Scriptures. God commands for His children to keep the Sabbath day holy by honoring it with rest, just as our God rested on the seventh day of His own creation of our universe. The Israelites would also honor a year of jubilee, an annual event held every fifty years when debts were forgiven, fields lay fallow, and restoration was mandated. Recall how Jesus at the beginning of his ministry retreats to the desert for forty days for a period of prayer and fasting, and how he would often retreat to a quiet place for solitude and renewal. In our modern culture, we've lost sight of what it means to even know what rest feels like sometimes.

If we do not heed the signals from our bodies and the weariness from our souls, then we will pay a much greater price, losing our passion, making foolish choices for immediate gratification instead of long-term satisfaction, and throwing away good parts of our lives. We burn up and burn out like a candle at the end of its wick in a puddle of hot wax. We begin to question the future direction of our lives. One of the definitions of "weary" is to have your sense of pleasure exhausted. This simply means that you no longer enjoy what you once did. My friend Frank had helped countless people, including myself, was respected and well liked in his field, and had produced many thought-provoking and heart-wrenching films. He has inspired businesses, spawned creativity, and nurtured talents to aspire to new heights of accomplishments. But in his state of soul-weary depletion, he could not see any of that. Most people pursuing greatness cannot see their own accomplishments clearly. They lose sight of both their contributions and the cost.

To regain our perspective and replenish the supply of energy and creativity, we must learn to take a sabbatical. At times like these, you must allow for frivolity and maybe even a little "selfish" indulgence. We must

INCREASING YOUR RANGE OF MOTION——FOR HIM

What change do you need to make in order to embrace your current season of life?

Write out your "If only" list. Now throw it away and start living your life today!

What steps can you take to rest and recharge your soul?

What is your passion? What brings you life?

INCREASING YOUR RANGE OF MOTION——FOR HER

How would you describe the current season of your man's life?

It is sometimes too easy for a man to become completely task-oriented and to forget to enjoy the fruits of his labors. Voice your appreciation of his labors and suggest ways for him to take the time to acknowledge the things he's done well.

How would you evaluate the gap between your husband's dreams and his achievements?

What can you do to help him bridge the gap between success as the world judges it and significance as God would define it?

relearn what it means to be still before our Lord and allow Him to fill us as well. God restores your soul. He gives you what was taken away, what has been drained out of you. And a lot has gone out of you over the years—a lot of passion, a lot of support, a lot of endurance, and now your soul says, "I am tired, I am unappreciated, and I am not fulfilled." My friend, no one is fulfilled or filled full when they have been depleted. Now it is give-me-back time. Go get a massage, a pedicure, sit in a steam room, take a hike, make a road trip, go on retreat. You've worked hard. Let's have a Sabbath season for a while.

Finally, from a biological perspective, a midlife crisis often means that a man is getting less testosterone. As he ages and as stress depletes his body of this hormone, his drive lessens in many ways. In some men this occurs professionally; for others it may be in the bedroom. Sexually, it may simply mean that he needs more coaxing to get in the mood. It doesn't mean that he can't perform well, but that he finally needs the emotional intimacy his wife has desired all along; he may find he now needs tenderness, affection, a new kind of stimulation.

Similarly, when his drive lessens professionally, he needs a new kind of stimulation as well. He may need new inspiration in order to create and to produce. Men like Frank need to find new ways to inject the passion back into their careers—think of it as professional Viagra! I recommended to Frank that he consider a safari in Africa to restore his creative vision, or a ministry working with prison inmates who want to write screenplays and develop acting skills to rediscover the passion a novice brings to his field. These suggestions may not be right for you, but find something to bring excitement back into your life and give you the spark needed to reignite your passion. Honorable, scriptural, and reasonable stimulation may be just the solution to light the fire back into your life.

My friend, regardless of which season you presently find yourself in, you must be willing to remain as flexible as the willow and grow into the circumstances of your environment even as you bend toward the goals set before you. Life is all about change and adapting to change. The key to dealing with change is the willingness of those involved to adapt to a new normal, a fresh baseline that allows them to reinvent themselves by keeping what works and finding new methods for what doesn't. So, my brother, find your new normal. Your outdated ways are like old shoes you've outgrown; they cause the soul to ache. Isn't it time you tried some new steps, slipped on a pair of loafers or cowboy boots or running shoes and picked up your pace? Isn't it time to make the most of your time in this life by dressing for the season and wearing shoes that keep your step firm? Embrace the season and allow yourself to grow into the man no one else has ever been before or will ever be again—you!

Part Three

A MAN'S
RELATIONSHIP
WITH HIS FATHER

"Masculinity is bestowed. A boy learns who he is and what he's got from a man, or the company of men. He cannot learn it any other place. He cannot learn it from other boys, and he cannot learn it from the world of women. The plan from the beginning of time was that his father would lay the foundation for a young boy's heart, and pass on to him that essential knowledge and confidence in his strength. Dad would be the first man in his life, and forever the most important man. Above all, he would answer the question, Do I have what it takes? Am I a man? for his son and give him his name. Throughout the history of man given to us in Scripture, it is the father who gives the blessing and thereby 'names' the son."
—JOHN ELDRIDGE, *Wild at Heart*

"Tonight . . . about 40 percent of American children will go to sleep in homes in which their fathers do not live."
—DAVID BLANKENHORN, *Fatherless America*

"One of the greatest underestimated tragedies of our day is the psychological and physical distance of fathers from their children. This distance is contrary to the explicit teachings of Scripture which defines the roles and involvement of the father with a child."
—H. NORMAN WRIGHT

FIVE

FINDING OUR FATHERS

When a father and son spend long hours together, which some fathers and sons still do, we could say that a substance almost like food passes from the older body to the younger.
—ROBERT BLY, *Iron John*

Elisha screamed as the chariot took Elijah up in the clouds. His face contorted in pain and tears flowed freely as he watched his father disappear into heaven. "My father, my father!" he cried without any comfort, his shoulders shaking and his heart breaking. His grief was so intense, he ripped the clothes off his body (2 Kings 2:11–12).

Whenever I read of Elisha's anguished screams, I find they harmonize with my own and perhaps with the screams of other men who have seen life, death, work, jail, and even success carry their fathers away from them. His voice sounds strangely like my own echoing in the canyon of my manhood, billowing out of my past like smoke from the chimney of my memory. Even now I occasionally release a whimper as I remember the ache that started me to search for the missing part of who I was and what I would inevitably become.

The smell of upturned soil, glimpses of tombstones with the names of my ancestors etched in gray granite, the bright green artificial turf around this new grave, the small flash of a pale red salamander's tail scampering up from the darkness as I peered into this socket of fresh earth. The four metal posts, the gurney unwinding to lower the casket into the ground. The preacher saying "Ashes to ashes, dust to dust, into the earth we commit the body of this departed soul." These sensory details are indelibly tattooed on my soul and form a pattern of bittersweet memories evoking one of the most devastating losses I ever faced.

I was sixteen years old when my father died. We lived in West Virginia, but my family's people were from Mississippi, and that's where my father was to be buried. He had been either busy or sick most of my life. I had endured his busyness in hopes that eventually he would slow down and I could catch up to his pace and finally get to know him. Then renal failure snatched that opportunity away from me. I watched and helped and tended to him as best I could, taking him to dialysis, cleaning up after him, doing whatever I could simply to be close to him. I shaved him and learned how to run the kidney dialysis machine for him, determined to catch as many crumbs from my father's table as possible.

Then I found myself standing beside his gravesite in a black suit, blue shirt, and yellow tie, silently screaming out a barrage of questions into the red-clay dirt. "Who am I? Did you like me? What should I do with my life? Who were *you*?" It was like a conversation on a cell phone in which the signal is abruptly terminated and I was left in mid-sentence holding the rest of my thoughts inside.

I wept over many losses that day: the lost battle for his life, the small losses snatched away daily by his disease, the cumulative loss of all that my father's life encompassed. But another loss ached in my soul that day just as powerfully as any other. It may sound selfish, but as much as I mourned the loss of my father on that day, I also mourned the loss of me. Standing in that Mississippi cemetery as a young man on the threshold of full manhood, I realized that I had lost the personal battle to get what I needed. I felt like I had failed to get what was desperately required for my journey from the only man who could give it to me. How would I ever find my way? How would I go on? There was so much to ask and to discover. I wondered, "What did I look like to him? What did he see when he looked at me? What did he think? Was he proud? What were his hopes and dreams for me, his tips for life, his advice and wisdom? Who was he *really*?" I wanted to ask him what it was like being married, how he knew what job he should do, what it felt like to become a father, and whether he was scared when he died. With my father's passing I felt like I had been given an Incomplete in the only course I needed to graduate. And I watched my diploma going down into a hole in the ground with his remains, with no chance of my ever completing the course for graduation and receiving the degree that he could pass on to me.

I was haunted for weeks and months and would see his image on the bus, at school, everywhere I looked. And then gradually his face began to fade. With time, my memory slowly began to erase the sharp clarity of the image, leaving me with a soft-focus frame of this man. And the pain? I kept waiting for time to ease that acute feeling, but that deep sense of loss remained. So much had been left undone. He never gave his blessings for me, his seal, his hands on my shoulder, telling me words my soul was parched to hear. I was left in the wilderness without my personal Lewis and Clark to help me navigate the paths of my journey. I recall much later asking my grandmother, "Did he like me?" As I sobbed out this so important question, she seemed surprised that I didn't know the answer to it, and tried to console me with words that her son never spoke to me in his lifetime.

THE FIRST MAN I NEVER MET

He was the first man you met . . . and didn't meet. The first man you knew . . . and didn't know. Your relationship with him affects every other relationship. It sets up your relationships with your mother, with other men, with the way you view other women, your own children, and on and on. A man's relationship with his father often causes all kinds of complications with his relationship with his Heavenly Father. So before we proceed, it seems imperative that we discover why this relationship has so much potency in a man's life, and why it's sorely lacking in so many men.

Part of the answer may seem like common sense: We long to be loved and to connect with our parents, particularly the same-sex parent who serves as a model to us. Psychologists and sociologists consistently emphasize the significance of the father in affirming and nurturing his children in ways that are distinct from the mother's contribution. Fathers can speak to a child's sense of identity and purpose in ways that challenge the child to move beyond the security and comfort of childhood. Fathers can provide models for masculinity that influence who their sons become and whom their daughters marry.

Unfortunately, many sons and daughters grow up reacting against the impressions of manhood they received from their fathers. If he was not all that you wanted him to be when you grew up, then he was probably your template for what you did not want to become. This reminds me of a story a preacher told me once. It seems that a town drunk had twin boys. They grew up in the house with an abusive, thoughtless father. Once they were grown, one of them became an alcoholic. But who could be surprised? "After all, look at how his father was," people would say when he stumbled down the street. But the other son was sober all of his life. Oddly, both of them said they were who they were because of their father! My point is, life often hands us the same sad story, a horrible plight, but how we react to it is unscripted and remains a matter of choice.

For men in particular, it's often an extra challenge to navigate between discovering your unique self and individuality, and learning and reacting to what you experienced in relationship with your father. Perhaps you wonder if you're truly non-confrontational or if that's simply the style you've adopted because your dad was such a hothead. Maybe you're pursuing a career in law enforcement because of your own strong sense of justice—or is it your desire to fulfill your father's dream that he never attained? It's a difficult and often ongoing process of sorting through the messages and our motivations. We can spend a lifetime trying to determine the boundaries between who we are and the man who was our first and most influential role model. We constantly question what it means to be a man in relation to our father, and we have a constant need to connect with this man so we may discover who it is we really are.

Think back on your childhood and your attempts to get your daddy to notice you. Perhaps you performed and worked and strove to be a star athlete or a straight-A student. Perhaps you acted out and rebelled and tried to get his attention through angry words and illegal activities. But regardless of where you fall on the spectrum of action and reaction, you must begin to acknowledge the truth about your relationship to your father. You may feel like you're a grown man and don't need your daddy's approval. You do. You may have experienced the absence of your biological father and struggled to find a worthy surrogate who could show you the way to your manhood, and you're still searching now. Even if you grew up with the extraordinary blessing of a good father who poured into you powerful streams of confidence, wisdom, faith, and humor, my bet is that you will continue to crave connection with your father throughout your life. Certainly, this longing for connection may not be as acute if a firm foundation was established between father and son, but the desire for a role model, a mentor, an older man who knows the road ahead of you, who is there to listen to your fears about your marriage and to advise you on asking for a promotion—this desire lingers from cradle up until the time you are taking your last breath.

And if a man didn't experience the goodness of a father's love, then he will often suppress that wounded part of himself even as he continues to search for another man with a father's genuine interest in him. That's why so often men are willing to settle for far less and attach themselves to whatever is available. So often men seek it out in drugs and gangs, in behaviors that will get them noticed, in activities that allow them to emulate their fathers or father figures in some way. Men want and need the approval, attention, and the affection of their fathers. Most men didn't get enough of it then . . . and they don't know how to get it now. They remember growing up with moms and grandmothers, tossing the ball alone, spending hours on the basketball court by themselves or with other fatherless boys. They looked across the dining room table to see an empty chair. They looked up in the stands at the big game and saw their mothers and girlfriends cheering them on, but there was always someone missing.

The fatherless rate seems astronomically high, particularly among black men. But this epidemic is not caused merely by the color of our skin. After making several trips to Nigeria, Ghana, and South Africa, it became increasingly apparent to me that while each of these areas has its own challenges, African men by and large do not seem to have as many struggles with the father-son relationship as we do. This seems to give some validity to the assertion that some of our misery is locked into the complexity of our history here in America and not some genetic predisposition based on our skin tone. For African Americans, fatherlessness can be traced to slavery, to dividing up families often before a child was even born by selling individuals to different owners. This division of families, in this case of separating sons and fathers, set up a terrible domino effect of loss perpetuating loss. Black men had children who were sold, and often they never were allowed a chance to experience parenting. Their children grew up never having known a father or the value of a family. There was a scarcity of teaching, of tenderness, and of time together, simply because fathers and sons were ripped apart and forced to live out their lives removed and unaware of each other's daily existence. This separation created an incredible void of identity and purpose, which these men were forced to endure. Even after slavery yielded to the prodding forces of emancipation, a terrible scar remained. The men were free, but free to do what? How can you offer a son or daughter what you never experienced?

Today we live in a free society with mobility and the pursuit of happiness. And yet the scar remains evident in many of us as we struggle to develop and maintain strong family units. Freedom does not heal history quickly. Generation after generation of men have grown up fatherless, without exposure to male role models. They don't know what it takes to be a father, so they abdicate the role. Like their very own fathers before them, they are absent or invisible.

By discussing the prevalence of fatherlessness in the African-American community, my intent is not to assign blame but to promote understanding. It is imperative that we, as African Americans, have the cathartic experience of being able to discuss our history as well as our destiny. And for those who do not share our historical trauma, you too might find it helpful to understand the plight of one group of American brothers of a different hue.

> *A father's love is a vital part of a man's development throughout his life. Don't pretend you don't want it or need it.*

Without the legacy of fatherhood, many men today are at a loss as to how to fulfill that role. The mere passage of time takes a boy and makes him grow, but he has no guidance in how to become a man. Biology enables him to make babies, but he has no idea how to father them. "You may kiss the bride," the minister announces, and the man looks up wondering about the journey he is about to embark upon. How can he master marriage when he has not witnessed anywhere in his recent or distant history any healthy illustrations of how to keep vows so easily recited?

What will he do later when he hears, "Honey, we're going to have a baby!" He wonders if he has what it takes to be called Daddy by this new little life. He knows he certainly never got it himself, so he's naturally terrified that he won't know how to father his legacy. In fact, just the thought of fathering this child and being there for his own son or daughter makes him a little uneasy, because it touches the nerve of his own wound.

WOUNDED WARRIORS

I'll never forget the tragedy of a friend of mine. He went to his father's house and discovered that this elderly man he knew as his daddy had shot himself. There was no note, no explanation, just the terrible evidence that his father had given up the fight to face life's many challenges. Later, after the ambulance was gone and the house was quiet, a confused and bewildered young man found himself cleaning up the remains of his father's self-inflicted wounds, scrubbing at blood stains splattered on the walls. As horrific as this scene is, it is unfortunately not so uncommon. The blood of all our fathers, from slavery to contemporary agony, has left an indelible stain that many young men find nearly impossible to remove from their hearts. I have witnessed the stain in the lyrics of young poets, rappers, and even in some preachers. I see it displayed daily in the tragedies reported on the evening news.

Later on, I preached the funeral, and when my friend could not bear the weight of the loss any longer and burst into wrenching sobs of anguish and grief, I almost carried this grown man out in my arms. He screamed and cried like a wild animal. He was hysterical over what happened to him, but I suspect part of him was grieving what now would not happen. Silently, I walked back to my car, drained and empty, and as I drove home, a tear silently built up momentum and slid down my face.

My tear was for the father's life ended too early and too tragically with a single bullet—a bullet I knew would affect those who remained behind.

The bullet that took the father's life remained lodged in my friend's own heart. Similarly, we all carry the wounds of our fathers. We can't go back in time and prevent those bullets from being fired any more than we can undo history, but I plead for what the Scriptures say is paramount, "In all thy getting, get understanding" (Proverbs 4:7). Wisdom is the principal thing; therefore, get wisdom and with thy getting get understanding. We must seek to understand the wounds our fathers bear and the weapons they may have crafted to defend themselves. You may see your dad as the tired body slumped at the kitchen table at dinner before he dozes off on the couch with the newspaper in his lap, but he is a man with a secret life, a sex life, a prayer life, a married life, a work life. And he may be hurting. I beseech you to strain your ears and listen for his silent screams. It is only in the understanding that we may learn to heal our own wounds.

Men are aching inside, our souls trembling with anger and hurt and sorrow, our hearts yearning for our father's embrace, the scent of his cologne, the spotlight of his attention. And for many of us it is too late in that relationship. The clock has run out and we are left to find comfort in surrogate fathers and other male relationships, in the process of being there for our own children and for the orphaned sons and daughters of other men missing in action.

How do men begin to cleanse and heal this wound? Foremost, we must talk about it. We must look at the wounds of our paternal warriors and examine who our fathers really were and why it was so hard for us to receive their blessing. We must examine our own wounds and be honest about what we needed and never received, no matter how wrenching such an examination might be. If we cannot bear to uncover the wound and assess its shape and size, its depth and intensity, then it will be difficult to know how to approach our needs for the healing process. A doctor would not treat a burn victim the same as a man with a bullet lodged in his side or a patient hemorrhaging in his chest cavity. And so we must learn how to treat ourselves by knowing the extent of our pain, disappointment, and anger toward our father, along with its causation.

Before we continue on, please let me add a disclaimer: Such an investigation is by no means a license to blame or adopt a victim mentality. "If only my father had loved me as much as my older brother." "If only my father had been there for me instead of working late and running around on my mother." "If only my father hadn't abandoned me when I was a kid, then I'd be okay now." At the center of stanching the flow of your life blood out of your father-wound is the acceptance of its contribution to your present strengths and giftedness. This is often the great irony of life's circumstances and the great mystery of God's goodness working in our lives. I'll explain more of this momentarily, but for now, please embark on this journey of reflection about your father not as a witch hunt for a scapegoat but as an archaeological dig, reconstructing the fragile structure of a relationship that began changing and cracking so long ago.

And there are myriad reasons for the fractured relationships and disconnected conversations between fathers and sons. So many fathers worked extensively—they had to work to support their families—and were not home or available to their children when they were home. We can call them workaholics if we like, but that doesn't invalidate their tireless efforts and hidden fears. Nor does it excuse their absence. They were often rigid, hard, rough, non-expressive men who were double-shift weary. The reality for so many of us men today is that our fathers were the unavailable strangers in our home. This isn't blaming, just explaining. Their work ethic was strong, but their heart connection flickered and dimmed like a candle in an open window.

Besides workaholism, many other variables continue to divide men from their fathers. Disease and illness claim the lives of many fathers who wish they could be present for their children but whose lives are taken prematurely from the home. My own father's death due to kidney disease robbed us of unknown precious years together. Cancer, hypertension, and heart disease continue to claim a multitude of men's lives and, interestingly enough, many of these diseases are compounded or brought on by stress. Many of these ills, especially hypertension and prostate cancer, occur more frequently and with more deadly consequences in the black community. Too often the cost of insurance, prescription medication, and advanced treatment options inhibit many men from getting the effective help they desperately need to survive.

Alcoholism and drug use also play a part in the high incidence of fatherlessness. To numb their own wounds or to escape the confusion of not knowing how to fulfill their responsibilities, many men succumb to these seductive substances that promise easy answers, artificial fortitude, or oblivion. Caught in a web of addiction, these men can't be there for their children because they're lost in the bottom of a bottle or trapped in the burning bowl of a crack pipe. Sadly, as if being held prisoner by an addiction isn't enough, too many men wind up in prison, serving time for engaging in their habits or, worse, committing crimes to foster them.

Many fathers simply go AWOL, leaving behind women and children who wonder at the disappearing act. Some men storm off in an avalanche of angry words and accusations; some quietly leave, never to return. And still others slip away gradually, spending less time at home and more time "out with the boys" or finding company with another woman. Some of these men may actually establish a second family, and have more children whom they fail to care for and eventually abandon. These fellows go back and forth between two separate homes until one day they vacate the premises completely and renounce their role as father.

Too often this issue of fatherlessness gets even more entangled and complicated by divorce. Many a divorced mother slays the father for their kids, using him as a scapegoat, a doormat, a scratching post, a firewall for the disappointments and losses in her life. Too many men responded to their ex-wives with the same weapons of blame, anger, and loss, and they take it out on their children, or use their own sons and daughters as pawns in a dangerous and tragic game in which there are no winners.

BREAKING THE CHAIN

Where are our fathers? Homeless, in the office, in prison, in hospitals, or just in denial. They're missing in action, and the search party has long given up hope of bringing them back. But we can't give up the fight. We must start now, today, to break the chain of abandonment. All of us have reasons—many justifiable ones—that can explain why it is difficult for us to be to others what we didn't get ourselves. However, the vicious cycle must be broken in your generation and not passed on. Perpetual dysfunction makes new victims from each new son. One of my favorite Scriptures simply says, "What do you mean when you use this proverb concerning Israel, saying: 'The fathers have eaten sour grapes, and the children's teeth are set on edge'? As I live, says the Lord God, you shall no longer use this proverb in Israel" (Ezekiel 18:2–3).

We must stop the legacy of leaving and make some attempt to set an example for our sons and daughters. Here are some ways that men can resist their impulse to flee and can play a more positive role in the lives of their children:

Men must remain actively and intimately involved in their children's lives. In the animal kingdom and the world of insects, it's not unusual for the male to instinctively avoid or abandon his offspring. In fact, the mother is often so protective that she pushes fathers away. Many men may experience a similar dynamic in which their natural instinct is to withdraw and detach, which is then compounded by their women's resistance to male involvement in the parenting process. So sometimes men must fight to maintain their place in their children's lives—they must battle themselves and their own inner struggles with what's required of them when they're with their children. Many men are afraid that they won't do it right, that they won't be a good father because they themselves never had a positive role model. But children are much more gracious and accepting of their fathers than we are of ourselves. They simply want our attention and our love. They simply want us to be present with them, to listen eagerly and participate in their lives, to help with their homework, watch the movie with them, include them on our trip to the store. They just want us to be there.

Men must take the risk of being transparent. Many men may think they have to be Superman for their kids. I admit that I thought my father invincible when I was a child. But I also watched him crumble. When he got sick, I watched his body break down and his organs fail him. How I wished he would have spoken to me about his suffering, about his pain. Maybe then I would have had the chance to get closer to this man who I never really knew. Maybe he could have shared with me the invaluable lessons that time and experience impart to a man. As much as I hated to see him sick, how I would have embraced an honest testimony about what he was going through.

Too often men fail to express the deepest parts of themselves to their children for fear of disappointing them. But holding back certain things means not giving yourself completely to those who could benefit the most from your experiences. Sharing your weaknesses is one of the surest ways of strengthening the bond between you and your children.

I'd also like to address the women at this time and implore you to be mindful of the power you wield over how your children see their father. It is one thing for a man to expose his weaknesses to his children, but quite another for their mother to tear down their father right before their eyes. Ladies, your anger toward your husbands bruises your children. It assaults your son's masculinity when he hears you tear down his father, criticize the male gender, and wonder why you ever hoped his father would be any different from any other man. Think about the message this conveys to an impressionable heart, already eager to find his place in the world. Young girls are also affected; their hearts harden and they become ever distrustful of men. Or else they become victims to abusive men, for they never expected anything more.

Men must fight to stay fully present in their home. For many men, their father may not have physically abandoned them, but his absence penetrated the family like a gaping hole nonetheless. Dad may have shown up, but his sons didn't know him. The father kept to himself and anesthetized his pain by watching television or drinking or working in the garage. And when his son would charge after him like a bull in a china shop, eager for engagement and interaction of any kind, the father would dart and dodge like an experienced matador, almost as if he were saying, "I'm right here son, physically present, the provider of the roof over your head. But I'm not here, son; my emotions and heart are wrapped up and put away. You can't reach me." So many men feel cheated, at least in part, by this mixed message of their father's presence, wondering if there's something wrong with them for wanting more than they had in their father's physical presence. But boys need much more than just a male body in the house. We need to see a man in touch with all the facets of his identity, who can feel and express the range of his emotions. We need a man who interacts with us, engages us, really nurtures us.

> *Being a father is not about being Superman. It's about being there.*

It has become so easy for fathers to run from the responsibilities of their calling at the first provocation. But they must be willing to face their fears and insecurities and stand their ground. They must persevere regardless of their confusion or uncertainty, and if all they can do is simply be present, they will have gone a long way toward breaking the cycle of pain.

OVERLOOKED AND UNDERVALUED

A father's influence on his son's development, and his daughter's for that matter, is not optional. It is critical, every bit as essential as the mother's role. Young men and women who grow up without their father's attention, his engagement in the essence of who they are and what they're becoming, suffer the loss of something they've never known, something that aches like the loss a parent feels when a miscarriage occurs. There's a feeling of emptiness and sadness that shrouds the soul with the unknown possibilities of "what if?" In both cases, the individual asks himself, "Who was this person who exists but who I do not know? Who am I in light of this person's absence?"

In its worst extreme, the result of fatherlessness can be life threatening. Young men without the guidance of a father to lead them along life's path can get so utterly lost that they never come back. Looking for acceptance and family, a boy might be drawn to the gang lifestyle, seeking identity in the "colors" that he wears, finding self-worth in the crimes he commits. The lure of belonging may entice a boy to try drugs for the first time, but the feeling of euphoria or the numbing of the pain keeps him coming back. It saddens my soul but does not surprise me that several studies, including one by the National Fatherhood Initiative, have shown that approximately 70 percent of juvenile and adult inmates were fatherless. That's almost three-quarters of all felons behind bars! Astounding.

Surely David experienced feelings of fatherlessness even though his father, Jesse, was very much a presence in his life. The problem was that David did not hold such prominence in his father's life. David is the eighth son, the baby, the gofer who waits on his brothers and remains invisible within the family. Instead of being spoiled like many babies in the family sometimes are, David seems to be an afterthought, just another boy born into this household of boys, merely the latest and last child to enter a household already bustling and running along its course. So this young man with the tender heart, the brilliant mind, the poetic imagination, and this passionate soul gets swept up in the rapid current of a mighty river already in motion. This presents a swirl of conflicting emotions in the young man, a vortex of longing and anger, of resentment and yearning, concerning his relationship with his father. It casts him in the role of the black sheep, the overlooked and undervalued, always striving to be noticed, to be helpful, to do whatever it takes to get attention and belong.

We see this so often today in men who feel like the stone that the builders have rejected. Their fathers ignored them or ridiculed them, and it's arguable which of these has the harsher effect on the fragile growth of a man's developing identity. Understandably, this abandonment creates a smoldering cauldron of hurt and hatred toward the father, an open wound caused by the father's indifference.

This wound can fester and destroy a man with the poisonous gangrene of bitterness and blame. Or, as we see in David's life, this wound can become a portal to worship, an opening in the soul crying out for God's presence to stanch the pain and bind the broken heart. Out of his woundedness, we see David write poetry that speaks directly to the heart of loss and grief. Out of his heartbreak, we see David worship on the hillside, dancing in the darkness of a starlit night in Bethlehem before the God who sees.

The LORD is my light and my salvation;
Whom shall I fear?
The LORD is the strength of my life;
Of whom shall I be afraid?

When my father and my mother forsake me,
Then the LORD will take care of me.
Teach me Your way, O LORD,
And lead me in a smooth path, because of my enemies.
(PSALM 27:1, 10–11)

God, who knows David's heart and hears his cries, announces, "I've found Me a man!" And God eagerly accepts the lifelong task of fathering David. Nobody fathered David but God. And so many of us know what that is like. It reminds me of the book by Paul Crouch, the founder of Trinity Broadcast Network (TBN), *I Had No Father But God.*

How is such a relationship forged? So much of it happens through transparency and communication. David talks to God, worships Him, complains to Him. The many Psalms reveal a man in touch with the full range of notes in his emotional symphony.

Whether it's grief and fear, anxiety and sleeplessness, joy and praise, peace and security, David captures all his emotions in the incredible poems, many of which were likely written out of his loneliness beside his sheep.

FEARS AND SPEARS

Even as he senses God's presence, David still searches and hopes for an earthly father figure, someone who will embrace him and affirm him, see him for who he is, and give him the encouragement and support he craves. So when David goes to the house of Saul, it seems natural that he's excited at the prospect of having someone appreciate who he is and what his gifts are. David is hungry and expects to find the feast of a father's attention inside the palace—after all, he's already proved himself by slaying Goliath and redeeming the king's army. Notice the way things begin smoothly and then deteriorate when Saul becomes jealous of David:

So David came to Saul and stood before him. And he loved him greatly, and he became his armorbearer.

Then Saul sent to Jesse, saying, "Please let David stand before me, for he has found favor in my sight."

And so it was, whenever the spirit from God was upon Saul, that David would take a harp and play it with his hand. Then Saul would become refreshed and well, and the distressing spirit would depart from him.

Now it had happened as they were coming home, when David was returning from the slaughter of the Philistine, that the women had come out of all the cities of Israel, singing and dancing, to meet King Saul, with tambourines, with joy, and with musical instruments.

So the women sang as they danced, and said:

"Saul has slain his thousands,

And David his ten thousands."

Then Saul was very angry, and the saying displeased him; and he said, "They have ascribed to David ten thousands, and to me they have ascribed only thousands. Now what more can he have but the kingdom?"

So Saul eyed David from that day forward.

And it happened on the next day that the distressing spirit from God came upon Saul, and he prophesied inside the house. So David played music with his hand, as at other times; but there was a spear in Saul's hand.

And Saul cast the spear, for he said, "I will pin David to the wall!" But David escaped his presence twice.

Now Saul was afraid of David, because the LORD was with him, but had
departed from Saul.

(1 SAMUEL 16:21-23; 18:6-12)

I see this kind of expectation and the ensuing consequences in many
men I encounter. It helps explain men's attraction to certain jobs, their
willingness to serve their church, their desire to volunteer for certain or-
ganizations. Men follow opportunities when they are looking for a father. If another man, particularly someone who is older who reminds
the man in some way of his own father (even if the shared characteris-
tic is abusive or demeaning), then he will seek this man's attention and
approval. We can see the positive effects of this father hunger in young
men who sign up for sports just to have their coach notice them and encourage them. And many coaches have enjoyed the rare privilege of
bringing these young men alongside them into the maturity of manhood. When we older men have this opportunity, we must seize it and
give humbly to those who serve us and serve alongside us. You never
know what kinds of subtle and symbolic touches of a father you are providing to the men around you.

And we can see the negative effects, the way David came to experience Saul, in the way drug dealers and gang lords prey on these vulnerable and insecure young men in their neighborhoods. While Mom
works a double shift at KFC, these boys long to find men who want them
around, men who want to teach and train them, even if they're teaching them how to sell crack and training them to kill or be killed. David
was almost killed by his surrogate father. Even after he dodges Saul's
javelin, David stays in the man's house, still hoping to be affirmed.

Without defending Saul here, perhaps we should recognize that in
many of these situations, the fathers or father figures are not entirely to
blame. Many men do not always know how to be good sons either. They

need to respect that their father has his own weaknesses and struggles, his own needs and desires. We see this in the relationship between Noah and his sons. In his weakness, Noah gets drunk and undresses himself—certainly not the best parental behavior to display. But his sons don't know how to handle their father's shame. His son Ham even takes advantage of his father's state and ridicules the older man, looking on his nakedness and mocking him. There comes a stage in most every man's life when he begins to see his father coming down off the pedestal and being an ordinary mortal, a man with flaws, who is struggling in many ways similar to his son. Sons must learn to allow their own fathers to have fears and disappointments, to have all the same flaws and fragments as any other man. And both fathers and sons must learn to trust each other. Can a son know his father's secrets and still trust him? Can a father be vulnerable with his son and trust *him*?

There's so much power to be gained from men allowing other men to witness their lives—the good and the bad. True mentoring is in showing someone your strengths *and* your liabilities. True hope emerges when a young man can glimpse not just another man's successes and achievements but also the discipline, disappointments, and diligence needed to attain them. This allows those younger men room to take risks, to fail, to learn and grow from the missteps and mishaps that invariably occur even to those who are most gifted and accomplished. It's no coincidence that Jesus showed his wounds first after his resurrection.

REVERSE THE CURSE

The curse of having a father is simply wanting more of him than you probably experienced and living with this longing through the various stages of your life. The way we begin to reverse the curse is to turn the garment of our father-wound inside out. We must be willing to break the silence, examine the wounds of our relationship with our father, and learn what we can about this man who so often remains a mystery. In order to see our relationship with our fathers transformed, we must begin where we are right now, not where we were as boys or where we want to be.

I can't tell you how many men have confided in me that so much of the shape of their lives has been carved by the blade of their longing for a father. Inmates in maximum security prison have wept like baby boys as they lowered the walls of their own machismo and bravado and admitted their longing for a father who was not there. Successful businessmen who serve as deacons in my church have shared their pursuit of their father's approval long after their fathers have passed from this life. Teenaged boys, sullen and too cool for school, have confided to me that if only their fathers would want to spend time with them and see them for who they are, they could make it through the labyrinth of drugs, gangs, and temptations with dead ends.

Men must come clean about their need for their father if they're going to begin to assess the wounds of their own manhood. Again, the purpose is not to blame but to explain. And explaining alone will not change who you are and unleash the full potential of becoming the man you were meant to be. However, it will help you carve steps into what is often one of the greatest barriers blocking a man's path. In order to reverse the curse, let's

> *We must clean out the wound before it can begin to heal.*

continue this journey as we venture forward into the next chapter and learn about what it means to forgive our fathers, learn from his mistakes, and rely on the love of our Heavenly Father.

But before I close, we must offer a huge thank-you to all the fathers who have stayed, who have fought through the fear and the pain, and who have served their sons and daughters well. We must celebrate the men who continue to impart wisdom to their children and grandchil-

---

INCREASING YOUR RANGE OF MOTION——FOR HIM

What is your happiest memory about your father?

What is your saddest memory of your father?

When do you miss your dad the most?

What was the last conversation you had with your dad?

How do you feel on Father's Day?

If you asked your dad, "Tell me one thing you would do differently as a man or as a father," what would he say?

INCREASING YOUR RANGE OF MOTION——FOR HER

What is your best memory of times with your father?

What kinds of stories does your husband tell about his father?

What has your father-in-law passed on to his son?

What legacy do you want your children's father to pass on to them?

---

dren and great-grandchildren. We must celebrate the fathers who did pour themselves into their children, who gave them all they could give them. And truly the reality for most men is a combination of some rich moments with their fathers intermingled with times of disappointment or frustration. It's so important that you don't overlook the good times as you assess what you don't have.

I know we didn't focus on the fathers who were there in this chapter, but I dare not end this chapter without telling you how much we need to see you. Even those of us who have never had what you so lavishly gave your families thank you. You make us believe that it is possible, and in some way you restore our faith. Thanks for showing up at all the ball games. Even if you were not our fathers, we saw you. We admired you, and in those moments when you touched your sons, it touched us too. Thanks for standing by us. Because of you we can believe that we can heal the wounds.

SIX

---∿---

WRESTLING THE ANGEL— RECLAIMING YOUR FATHER'S BLESSING

He who forgives ends the quarrel.
—AFRICAN PROVERB

Recently a good friend of mine called and asked me if I thought he should attend his father's funeral. You might imagine that I would be stunned by such a question, and normally I would be taken aback by the absurdity of such an inquiry. But I knew the details of Brent's relationship with his father from various conversations we'd shared, the violent and tempestuous dance of father and son set to the tempo of disappointment and abandonment. His father was an alcoholic who terrified Brent's mother and siblings, as well as my friend, before finally leaving the family when Brent was ten. As Brent's mother began to put their life back together by moving her family to another state, Brent was both relieved and saddened. As frightened and upset as he was by his father's drinking and violent behavior, Brent missed him.

"It's funny," he told me once. "I felt like I couldn't live with him and yet I couldn't stand to be without him." After a faraway look and a moment of unbridled pain crossed his brow, he continued, "Sometimes I was even willing to put up with his drinking and punches just to know he was around."

Though my childhood was far different from his, I did understand the conflict that comes in the heart of a man who struggles to sort through grief when it is contaminated with unresolved issues. Additionally, I knew that Brent loved his father. You see, I had lived long enough to know that love is often totally unreasonable.

Throughout Brent's teenaged years, his father darted in and out of his life like a recurring character on a bad soap opera, one of those predictably unpredictable villains who never seem to go away for long without turning up again. Just when Brent would convince himself that he never wanted to see his father again, his dad would show up, three days' sober and begging to make a clean start. If Brent gave him the chance, then it was only a matter of another three days before his father started drinking again. If Brent refused to see him, then his father cursed and complained that Brent was punishing him for the past and wasn't willing to forgive. It was a no-win situation for the young man so eager to know and receive a father's love but so tired of repeatedly being let down.

Finally, as a young man, Brent found a mentor in his church and began to set firm boundaries around his father's attempts to pull his son back into his orbit. While it saddened Brent that his father was drinking himself to death, he knew that he needed to maintain his distance and get on with his life. Yet now he'd lost his father for good and felt more ambivalent than he'd ever imagined. He knew for sure that he'd lost something that he could never regain. The relief he felt sparred with a sense of guilt over wishing he'd reached out to his dad and wrestled with his longing to have connected with this man in a meaningful way before his passing.

SOUL SURVIVOR

In the weeks and months after his father's death, Brent found himself grieving harder than he had expected. Since he was a successful businessman just entering midlife with his own family, Brent expected to move back into his life quickly. "I had grieved my relationship with my father already—or so I thought. But in that first year or so after Dad's death, I felt several different kinds of loss at once. I grieved for the father I never had growing up as well as the one I did have. I grieved for lost opportunities. For times when maybe I should have taken a chance and tried to have a relationship with him. And I began grieving my own life, wondering if anything I was doing had real meaning. What would my children have when I was gone?"

The death of his father triggered a full-blown midlife crisis in my friend. But I didn't worry so much about how he would come through this desperate storm of the soul because of his willingness to talk to me and other men in his life. He is what I call a "soul survivor," someone who's willing to open up and examine the pain in order to lance the wound and perforate the power of the past. It's the same phenomenon of keeping the windows open during a tornado, allowing the harsh winds to pass through—not without some damage, but at least not toppling the edifice that's locked up and unable to "breathe."

Indeed, it's the many men who shutter themselves and board up their hearts that trouble me far more, those who suffer in silence, who simmer inside with a slow-burning grief and toxic anger that drains their hearts and drowns their souls. These are the men whose silent screams go unheard and unheeded until it's too late. Instead of moving in the powerful current of he-motions, they become pulled under by a vortex of their own woundedness. You can recognize these men by their brooding looks, a constant scowl on their faces, an underlying sense of hostility caused by unexpressed pain and suffering. When counseling them I have found that these bitter men often hold their anger inside until it comes oozing out somewhere else in their soul, much like a cancer that starts in one area and metastasizes to the other.

Sadly these men feel trapped and are often caught in a "damned if you do and damned if you don't" dilemma. They are criticized if they leave the home and desert their family, and although this criticism may be warranted, they are not treated much better if they stay and fight through their feelings. I have found that many men who work hard to make their marriage and family relationship work often go unrecognized. They may struggle to deal with their feelings and remain in the relationship, and when there is no positive reaction to their efforts, they become disheartened.

It is sad that most men who win the battle and stay the course do not get the proper recognition they need and do not feel rewarded with the love and appreciation they crave. In reality, maintaining relationships should not be taken for granted by either the man or the woman. Not today, when people leave easily and move on without any justifiable provocation to the greener grass they think they see somewhere else.

> *You must acknowledge that your father has a profound influence on your life even if he was absent from it.*

I believe that Brent was losing momentum in his own life, battling with mid life and all of its symptoms partially because he was playing a role for which he had little mentoring and no script. In the absence of a role model, it eventually becomes difficult to defy the urge to run and hide, as pressures in life mount and appreciation dissipates. While I understand that women also carry a great deal of stress, men often have little-to-no support system, friends, or confidants around them. Few men's magazines focus on anything more than biceps and triceps and sexual staying power. The news articles focus on investments, and the slick glossy sport magazines show more female thighs then male solutions for their predominantly male readership. Even church has little to offer men in terms of responding to the torrent of issues confronting them today. Most men's groups at church are weak, if in existence at all. Those that are strong are focused totally on overcoming sin issues, but little is said about the dysfunctions that create some of the sin issues in the first place. Men are seldom the focus of talk shows or self-help books. Instead, mass media puts all its energies into targeting the female consumer, who has everything marketed to her, from help with menopause to relationship advice. This lack of media attention is partially responsible for the escalating despair we see in men.

This lack of attention leaves men without the tools they need to become aware of their feelings and handle them effectively. There is no material that helps men work through their pain and maintain their relationships. Those men that do keep it all together do so without instructions, trying to figure out on their own how to build back what grief, pain, or perpetual loss may have depleted from them.

Many men simply don't have the help they need to effectively deal with their emotions. Most men are ashamed to admit that they even need the help. Consequently, they turn to destructive behavior as a cry for help that generally doesn't evoke sympathy but further damages their own credibility, as most see the behavior not as a plea but as a dereliction of duties and a childish infatuation with irresponsibility. Brent's father, like many men today, had succumbed to his weaknesses and was a "quitter" who resigned himself to his plight and gave up on the struggle. His occasional visits were futile attempts to wake from the coma of indifference he had allowed to numb his senses. Now Brent is left trying to avoid falling into a similar rut as his father did before him.

ATTITUDES OF GRATITUDE

If reading this book causes a newfound respect and appreciation for men and the struggle they face, I will be proud. If it causes one son to call his dad and say, "Thanks for staying the course and fighting through the many pains of life," it will be a success. If it causes merely one woman to recognize that she is not the only one who needs emotional support, gets frustrated, faces struggles for which there seems little cure and stands relentlessly and gallantly in spite of personal loss and pain, then this time invested will be well spent.

To all those men who weathered storms and stayed home even when being there didn't always result in the jubilant enthusiasm you felt your sacrifices warranted, we all should say thank you. We know that fathers and real men in general are an endangered species. Even to those men who lost the battle for the marriage but kept the connection to the children, we also say thank you. Thanks for sending the check to the kids even when it meant that your whole month was tight and your own bills were backed up. Thanks for phone calls placed, notes left, emails sent, and any way you tried to mend the hole in your child's heart to let him know that you would always be there for him. It is only through applauding you that we will shame the others into a more interactive relationship with their sons and daughters. An attitude of gratitude is not too much to ask. These are the words that men often crave. It isn't from me that they really want to hear it but from those that they love and have served.

You would be surprised that real appreciation, heartfelt thanks poured on a weary man, is like watering a neglected plant whose greenery has withered to a dark brown. I know we act as if we do not need any affirmation, but, alas, I must tell the real truth, we really do. As most of us work with, play golf with, and interact continually with men like Brent or his father, it is not hard to see a need for implementing teaching that builds fire walls. These truths may help insulate the strong men from falling prey to decisions they will ultimately regret. And will give others the tools for damage control needed when one makes poor family choices as a result of feeling overwhelmed.

The process of being a man is sometimes difficult. Life is often a maze, filled with pressures in the workplace, responsibilities on every side. Many men face performance anxiety at work, at home, and, yes, even at play. From the bedroom to the boardroom, men feel like Gomer Pyle with Sergeant Carter screaming in his ears, "Keep it up, keep it up!" They are often afraid to admit and unable to adjust to the disappointment when they let anyone down, and in the process they inevitably let everyone down.

> *Stop reading from your father's script. Be the author of your own destiny!*

Being a man is often like playing the role of a soldier in an armored suit on an August day in Texas. You may look admirable in your glistening silver suit on the outside, but you are about to faint on the inside! So fellows, let's take off the hot tin suit, strip down to the nuts and bolts of manhood, and get real for a minute.

SINS OF THE FATHER

In light of these confessions of the masculine soul, we come face to face with some critical issues. We will continue the process of assessing the old scars and fresh wounds from our fathers, and we must be willing to look at the extent of what was needed and not given, but we should not be looking to place blame or heap on criticism. Instead, our goal is to make a fair assessment with appreciation and encouragement to those men who showed up and stayed, while assessing the damage done to all involved when men like Brent's dad leave sons and daughters. Even with them my intent is not to blame but to explain, and to move forward into the freedom of who we are and how we were made.

However, I'm convinced that the only way we can really avoid playing the blame game is to see our fathers as men—fallible and flawed like all of us—and to forgive them. Easier said than done, perhaps. I know how hard this can be from experience, as well as from countless conversations with men from every point on the demographic spectrum. I've spoken with many men incarcerated for a laundry list of crimes, including murder, and when issues of their family come up, I usually try to inquire about their fathers and the important men in their lives. Inevitably, the inmates seem to shut down and get an edge of anger in their voices at the mention of their fathers.

You may have heard about the greeting card companies such as Hallmark who donate cards at certain holidays to inmates at various prisons around the country. Mother's Day certainly outnumbers all other holidays as the time when inmates send the most cards—virtually every incarcerated man who has a mother living wants to send her a note, a card, a reminder that no matter what he's done, he still loves her and appreciates her. On the other hand, Father's Day is last on the list—in fact, some companies have quit sending cards for this holiday altogether because only a handful out of thousands of men want to send their daddies a card. When we look at the statistics and see how many inmates were fatherless, it is clear why they would not be extremely excited about honoring their fathers. But I am concerned that this tightly kept bitterness against the ones who left is just as dangerous as the denied appreciation of the ones who stayed, or at least in some way represented themselves in the lives of their children.

When fathers are absent, or when they are present and inflicting overt or indirect wounds on their sons, it's natural that mothers attempt to fill the void. And this can be a healthy supplement that allows a young boy to know he is loved and complete his journey to young adulthood. But ultimately, he is looking to another man—even if it is a surrogate father, a pastor, a coach, any man he admires—to validate him, to tell him that he's made it and is indeed a man among men. As much as we want to believe that the love of a woman can prove our manhood, most men realize at some point that this only expresses the masculinity that is already present in them—it doesn't create it or fuel it or validate it the way we might prefer. Nonetheless, many men continually move from relationship to relationship, woman to woman, sexual conquest to sexual conquest, wondering why they don't feel any more secure in their manhood. Our culture certainly reinforces this notion as well—that all you have to do to be a man is have sex. But most of us are capable of reproducing long before we know how to operate the equipment and exercise true masculinity. We're looking to another man to show us the way, to provide instruction and insight into what it means to relate to women, and when the father is absent or fails in this capacity, then it's often another offense the son holds against him.

Many men who are trying to make their lives at home functional find it difficult to do so, particularly at certain seasons in life when they are more vulnerable to the weariness they face. That, coupled with all these father/son wounds, leaves many men feeling at a loss as to how to go about the process of healing and getting on with their lives. While I pray that there are more men than I am aware of who had strong nurturing fathers who offered incredible support and direction, my fear is that many men are looking for something to alleviate their painful issues with Dad and may not consciously know that it is the Dad issue that is handicapping them along the way. I have learned that before a man can go forward, he has to be prepared to finish his unfinished business in the past.

The solution is incredibly simple and yet a remarkably difficult endeavor. We must forgive the sins of our fathers. If we don't practice forgiving our fathers, then our old wounds will remain infected with a bitterness and silent rage that will eventually spread to our entire lives. Perhaps we are seeking appreciation from those we serve while not giving any appreciation for the man who tried to give us what we needed. Now I know some of you had fathers who did a miserable job, others had fathering that was mediocre, and some lucky ones had fathers who were absolutely stellar. In spite of our diverse experiences with our fathers, one thing is sure. I now know what I couldn't understand as a boy. Being a father is not as easy as I thought. In short, if we don't learn to love what our father gave us and let go of what our father failed us, then we run an incredibly high risk of repeating the melody of his mistakes in a new key.

How many times have I seen men reaching the boiling point of a crisis in their lives, their careers, their marriages, because they continue to live off of an old script. And perhaps you've witnessed it yourself—it's often much easier to spot in others than in ourselves. The man who's the first in his family to have a college degree but can't hold a job because of his problem with authority. The man who jumps from one woman to the next as if he is playing connect the dots on a page from a coloring book. The man who can't commit and is always running, always moving because he can't allow himself to risk loving someone. I've counseled and conversed with numerous men, and so often as we plunge into the stories of their lives, their fathers hold a crucial piece of the puzzle. Despite seeing themselves as more enlightened or educated, despite making ten times as much money as their fathers made in their lifetimes, despite living in better houses and driving nicer cars, being Christian or whatever other distinction, so many of these men continue to play out their fathers' drama simply recast on a different stage.

It reminds me of seeing the musical *West Side Story* on Broadway a number of years ago. The genius of this classic musical drama is the way it retells Shakespeare's *Romeo and Juliet* by extrapolating the relational dynamics and recasting them into a gang war in New York in the 1950s. Yes, the setting is very different, but the feuding families and star-crossed lovers' fates remain the same. Similarly, many men live lives that are remakes of their fathers'. They play the same parts, fall into the same patterns, and perpetuate the same problems. It's the same story, just a different time, a different place, and a new cast of characters.

If men aren't willing to examine their father's life and connect it with their own, forgiving their father when needed and honoring him when appropriate, they will find themselves stuck on a treadmill chasing an elusive dream, avoiding fears, and repeating mistakes, all of which are coming from an unresolved relationship with your father. Without forgiveness there is an irrevocable connection between his sins and your own. His mistakes become your mistakes, and the cycle continues from generation to generation. It is simple, actually. He sowed his wild oats, but they keep coming up in your garden! Now, I may make mistakes, but at least I want to make them my own so I can learn and grow from them rather than my father's regurgitated issues, or anyone else's for that matter.

Another benefit of seeing your father through a lens of forgiveness is the effect it has on your relationship with other loved ones in your life, particularly your wife and your own children. Many men discover that they have much more emotional energy to lavish on their families once they've released the festering wound of their anger and hurt over their father's failures. They can be present with themselves, the special woman in their life, their children, and their male friends in new, authentic ways because they experience a freedom, a cleansing. For you see, it's not just the one who's forgiven who undergoes a change; it's equally powerful for the man who's doing the forgiving as well.

4 GV 2 4 GT

I'll never forget the license plate of a large SUV in front of me on the interstate: 4GV24GT. Forgive to forget, I thought to myself, even as I disagreed with the equation being offered. I've seen enough people freed by the powerful experience of forgiving their abusers, their cheating spouses, their crack-addicted parents, and their deceptive business partners to know that forgiveness doesn't cause a kind of amnesia that washes over and erases the memory of the offense and its consequences. I think we all know that some kinds of emotional pain have a chronic quality to them that evolves with us over our lives even as we change, much like arthritis settling into one's joints and causing an ebb and flow of pain based on the weather, the temperature, the transition from one season to another.

Rather than forgiving and hoping that we can forget, I like the definition I heard a pastor share at a church I visited a number of years ago. He said that forgiveness means that we let go of the belief that the past will ever turn out any differently. As I turned that thought over in my mind at the time, I appreciated the relationship this pastor made between what we harbor from the past and its effect on the qualities of our future. For when we cling tightly to our wounds, to being victimized by absent fathers, to experiencing disappointment over his failures, whatever they may be, then we limit our ability to reach ahead and grasp what lies ahead for us. If we hold firmly to the banister of the stairway of the burning house and refuse to let go, then we can't reach for the ladder leading out of the dangerous inferno. How do we pry loose our scorched fingers and reach for relief? In other words, once we're willing to do the hard work of forgiveness, what's next?

Perhaps you're like so many men who are earnestly willing to forgive but simply don't know how to facilitate the process. You agree that the benefits to forgiving our fathers are numerous but wonder what this process looks like on a day-to-day basis. And I wish there were some cookie-cutter formula that worked for all of us, some prayer or verse or something we could do that would work every time. But the truth of the matter here is that forgiving our fathers is usually individual work, a process over time that we must attend to on a regular basis—in some seasons of our lives, even daily.

Certainly the best example of forgiveness in action comes from Jesus on the cross, who prayed—even as He was being hung on the cross— for his captors and abusers to be forgiven their ignorance. "Forgive them, Father, for they know not what they do," He cried out. However, I'm afraid that too often many men hear this example and overlook its power and view Jesus as someone who's capable of being perfectly passive, not perfectly forgiving. Such an attitude is often perpetuated by some people in the Church, especially by those who want to castrate the anger, even rage, they see and fear from men in the Church. Such a response only fuels more rage that we feel we must suppress instead of giving us an outlet and an escape from the internal smoldering.

> *Don't let your paternal blessing be your curse; ask your Father for His blessing.*

Perhaps examining another story Jesus tells about forgiveness will help us find a model we can follow. When asked by one of His disciples how often we should forgive others, Jesus told him seventy times seven, and the parable He tells to illustrate His answer is even more illuminating:

Peter came up to the Lord and asked, "How many times should I forgive someone who does something wrong to me? Is seven times enough?" Jesus answered: "Not just seven times, but seventy time seven!

This story will show you what the kingdom of heaven is like: One day a
king decided to call in his officials and ask them to give an account of
what they owed him.

As he was doing this, one official was brought in who owed him fifty million silver coins.

But he didn't have any money to pay what he owed. The king ordered him
to be sold, along with his wife and children and all he owned, in order
to pay the debt.

The official got down on his knees and began begging, 'Have pity on me,
and I will pay you every cent I owe!'

The king felt sorry for him and let him go free. He even told the official
that he did not have to pay back the money.

As the official was leaving, he happened to meet another official, who
owed him a hundred silver coins. So he grabbed the man by the throat.
He started choking him and said, 'Pay me what you owe!'

The man got down on his knees and began begging, 'Have pity on me, and
I will pay you back.'

But the first official refused to have pity. Instead, he went and had the
other official put in jail until he could pay what he owed.

When some other officials found out what had happened, they felt sorry
for the man who had been put in jail. Then they told the king what had
happened.

The king called the first official back in and said, 'You're an evil man! When
you begged for mercy, I said you did not have to pay back a cent.

Don't you think you should show pity to someone else, as I did to you?'

The king was so angry that he ordered the official to be tortured until he
could pay back everything he owed.

That is how my Father in heaven will treat you, if you don't forgive each
of my followers with all your heart."

(MATTHEW 18:21–35)

Jesus makes it clear by this parable that his initial response of seventy
times seven isn't an attempt to give us a formula for saying I forgive you
four hundred ninety times. No, if we look at the context, we can realize

the true intent of His words. The Pharisees of His day would often focus on praying for God's forgiveness seven times a day.

Their teaching also provided for their forgiveness of a transgressor's sins but limited that forgiveness to three times. Hence, Peter is quite generous in actually doubling the number for forgiveness. But Jesus goes on to teach that forgiveness must be unlimited in its scope. I believe the main point that Jesus makes in his story has to do with seeing and relating our own weaknesses and shortcomings with those of others who have harmed us. We see this message in the Lord's Prayer as well: "Forgive us our trespasses as we forgive those who trespass against us."

Now please don't hear me asserting that God's ability or willingness to forgive us of our sins is contingent on whether or not we forgive others. But I do believe that our ability to accept, embrace, and experience God's forgiveness is often revealed in how willing we are to extend the same grace and mercy to others who have harmed us. To the extent that we're honest about our own flaws and failures and our need for God's mercy and grace, then to the same extent we'll be able to relate to others in the same boat as we are. We must learn to apply this standard of forgiveness to our deepest wounds, including those from our fathers.

SOUR GRAPES

If we don't learn to pursue and practice forgiveness, then we're setting ourselves up for our own bitter harvest. However, we can experience a new level of freedom in the fruit we produce if we're willing to forgive. God's Word reminds us of this powerful possibility:

> " 'The fathers have eaten sour grapes, and the children's teeth are set on edge.'

"'As I live,' says the Lord God, 'you shall no longer use this proverb in
Israel.' "
(Ezekiel 18:2–3).

It may be hard to absorb and act upon, but the truth of Scripture resonates: The harmful consequences of your father's actions do not have
to be perpetuated in your life. Unfortunately, so many men harbor
anger and unresolved bitterness toward their fathers and unwittingly repeat his mistakes in their own lives, doubling the power of his original
mistakes.

Take Isaac, for example. Here's a man who repeated the same incredible sin that his father, Abraham, had committed years before his
birth. You may recall the story about how Abraham and his wife Sarah
were traveling into Egypt to escape the famine in their native land. When
the Pharaoh and his princes commented on the beauty of Sarah, Abraham became afraid that they would kill him and take her from him if
he told the truth that she was his wife. Instead of trusting God to protect him and fulfill the covenant that He promised to Abraham, the
man caved under pressure and lied that Sarah was his sister. God became
so angry that He sent plagues to Pharaoh's house and forced Abraham
to reveal the truth, both about his lie and his fear (Genesis 12). They were
then sent away from Egypt and forced to sojourn in another land.

Then we shift the time to the next generation and, as Yogi Berra said,
It's déjà vu all over again. For Abraham's son Isaac finds himself in a
near-identical situation as his father. There's a famine in the land, and
the Lord directs him and his household to dwell in Gerar with a promise of blessing and the favor of the Philistine king, Abimelech. However,
fear must be a genetic trait in this family's DNA code, for Isaac notices
the attention his beautiful wife, Rebekah, receives and lies that she's his
sister. The king catches on when he looks through their window and
spies the couple being romantic. He's furious because he realizes that he's

been lied to and that if he or one of his men had lain with a married woman, even unknowingly, they would have committed sin and brought the Lord's wrath upon them (see Genesis 26)

This acorn certainly did not fall far from the tree that produced him, that's for sure. Like father, like son. Both men lied about their wives and almost got the women raped in order to protect themselves. It seems ironic that Isaac wasn't even born when his father, Abraham, pulled the same stunt and likely didn't know what his old man had done before him. It just occurred naturally to him because that's the kind of vibe he grew up with, a father who was willing to deceive and hide behind others to protect himself. Isaac acted just like his father even though he hadn't witnessed or likely even heard about the incident from his father.

The progressive power of this pathology continues on within one family as Isaac's son Jacob perpetuates deception as a relational style. With his very name meaning "supplanter" or "trickster," Jacob has two sons who cheated the men of Shechem. Simeon and Reuben were instruments of cruelty in their devious plan to trick the men who raped their sister into getting circumcised and then killed them while they were too sore to fight (Genesis 35). Jacob cursed them at his deathbed for their behavior, but in reality he had already cursed them with his own pattern of similar, if not worse, behavior. He himself had been a con artist who tricked his brother Esau out of his birthright and then conned his father, Isaac, out of his blessing (Genesis 25 and 27). Jacob's mother was herself a con woman, who lied to her husband about many things, including her conspiracy with Jacob to secure Isaac's blessing. This is a pattern that had to be broken.

Can you relate to this family, who seemed to give new meaning to "dysfunctional"? Many men tell me that their struggles with their tempers, or with alcoholism, or with domestic abuse can be traced to the kind of behavior they witnessed growing up. I have known men who were physically abusive to their wives, many of them acting out what they had seen in their homes while growing up. It's been documented by many psychologists and social scientists that child molesters were often molested as children themselves. It's believed by most conservative estimates that at least one third of abusers were themselves abused. And when the focus is exclusively on incestuous fathers, the percentage skyrockets to 70 percent being abused themselves by a parent.

FIGHT OR FLIGHT

The temptation, my brothers, is to turn and run away from your father and all the issues between you and him. But it's worth fighting for forgiveness in order to overcome your father's sour grapes so that you can rinse out any lingering bitter taste that might set your teeth on edge. To the extent that our issues with our fathers continue to haunt us, we will be unsure of who we are and uncertain about where we're going. We must be willing to wrestle, to choose to fight instead of taking flight or making light of this battle. Lest we think that there was no hope for Jacob's family, I'm reminded of his own battle, his own attempt to overcome his family's weaknesses so that he could find a better way. He is still a weak man, a deceiver and trickster, yet when he encounters an urgent battle for his future, for his destiny in the grappling holds of an unknown assailant, he's willing to fight.

> Then Jacob was left alone; and a Man wrestled with him until the breaking of day.
> Now when He saw that He did not prevail against him, He touched the socket of his hip; and the socket of Jacob's hip was out of joint as He wrestled with him.
> And He said, "Let Me go, for the day breaks."
> But he said, "I will not let You go unless You bless me!"

So He said to him, "What is your name?"

He said, "Jacob."

And He said, "Your name shall no longer be called Jacob, but Israel; for you
  have struggled with God and with men, and have prevailed."

Then Jacob asked, saying, "Tell me Your name, I pray."

And He said, "Why is it that you ask about My name?" And He blessed
  him there.

So Jacob called the name of the place Penuel: "For I have seen God face to
  face, and my life is preserved."

Just as he crossed over Penuel the sun rose on him, and he limped on
  his hip.

(GENESIS 32:24–31)

It seems so striking that Jacob is placed in a situation in which he can't
trick, can't manipulate, can't deceive his way out of the struggle. He's
forced to go hand to hand and risk hurting himself permanently, which
he does, because he so desperately wants this worthy opponent's blessing. And it seems to me that Jacob also wanted something more, something he didn't ask for directly, but which God's messenger bestows
upon him nonetheless: a new name, a fresh identity, a clean slate. Such
a christening seems worth the limp that it costs Jacob, seems to be the
source of his new name and new humility in many ways.

And the same is often true for us, especially regarding how we view
the wounds we experience in relationship to our fathers. These wounds
can limit us and falsely identify us, or they can empower us and invig-
orate our sense of purpose and identity. Yes, I suspect that we all have
our wounds that we limp around with in this lifetime, but we must ask
ourselves if we're fighting the right battles. Are we wrestling with the
angel, seeking God's presence in our lives, striving after the incredible
goals He sets before us, or are we pinned to the mat, waiting for the
final bell to ring? Do we know our new names, or are we clinging to boyish nicknames that we outgrew long ago?

INCREASING YOUR RANGE OF MOTION—FOR HIM

If you could go back, what would you want from your dad?

How are you like your father in his best attributes? How do you differ from him in his worst attributes?

Have you forgiven your father for any lingering pain or sorrow?

Do you believe your Heavenly Father has a specific blessing for you?

INCREASING YOUR RANGE OF MOTION—FOR HER

Have you really considered the influence your husband's father has had in his (and your) life?

How do you honor your partner's father? Your own father?

Has your father influenced your relationship with other men?

Do you honor your husband as the father of your children?

I encourage you, my brothers, to fight the good fight in regard to any unfinished business with your fathers. Free yourself up to love them with the same love that you experience with God and with the men He provides in your life to fight alongside you. Which brings us to the place where we examine the way that men relate to one another and how they can assist one another in pursuing what matters most. Let's continue on our journey by exploring the ways that men relate to one another, and more important, the ways they can experience the kind of Jonathan-and-David friendship for which we all long.

Part Four

A MAN'S

RELATIONSHIP

WITH OTHER MEN

"Men talk, but rarely about anything personal. Recent research on friend-ship . . . has shown that male relationships are based on shared activities; men tend to do things together rather than simply be together."
—BETTINA ARNDT, *Private Lives*

"A friend is someone who knows you as you are, understands where you've been, accepts who you've become, and still invites you to grow."
—STU WEBER, *Locking Arms*

"A simple friend thinks the friendship over when you have an argument. A real friend knows that it's not a friendship until after you've had a fight."
—UNKNOWN

"You can make more friends in two months by becoming interested in other people than you can in two years by trying to get other people interested in you."
—DALE CARNEGIE

SEVEN

⟨ornament⟩

LOOKING FOR A FEW
GOOD MEN

One of the joys of my adult life has been discovering male friends.
—STEPHEN AMBROSE, *Comrades*

Remember with me two little boys in an apartment building watching the black-and-white television and dreaming of better days. The theme song of *The Jeffersons,* the slick melody of *Happy Days,* along with the lyrics of other popular shows rang in their ears. Cartoons like *Fat Albert* were the order of the day. The boys were left at home while their mommas worked. Skateboards, roller skates, and go-carts that never ran right were their only modes of transportation. These boys were friends, spies and crime busters, villains and instigators. They played jokes on each other, then called "snapping," "ratting," and "playing the dozens." They did everything together imaginable, shared their secrets, swapped their marbles, covered for each other, and played spin tops. These were the guys who were dragged to church and made fun of the old ladies in the service. These guys skipped school together, cheated on tests together, and came home dirty from school playing games along the way.

Through it all, they were friends, the kind of friends that were bonded and inseparable. One boy got a BB gun, and they had fun for many days to come until his mother made him put it away for breaking a neighbor's window. Then they were back to the ragged, jagged slingshot that an uncle made from a branch and a big rubber band swiped from Mother's bill drawer. Giggling to each other behind the house, they swapped stories about a neighborhood girl whom they swore gave them a kiss. Both of them knew it wasn't true, but that didn't matter at the time. It was the entertainment afforded kids whose imagination had to provide them for the life across the tracks about which they had no way of understanding.

Can you relate to this scenario? Do you fondly recall a childhood filled with friends who you played kickball and traded baseball cards with, challenged to a new video game, or worshipped the same sports hero with? Perhaps you played on a Little League team together or lived next door to each other and had adventures in your neighborhood as you rode your bikes carefree through the streets, racing to see who could get to the tire-swing at the park first. Maybe you went fishing together and never caught much more than an old tennis shoe or a rusty can, but you laughed and shared some of your dreams and conveyed what it was like for you at your house with your family. You didn't have to be anybody but who you were, and you felt comfortable and contented in the presence of your friend. You likely didn't even realize how special this relationship was at the time.

This may sound like nostalgic, wishful thinking—a Hallmark card commercial depicting something you wished for but never had. I understand that there are countless men whose boyhoods lacked the luster and brilliancy suggested in the scenarios above. In reality, some lived with concrete jungles instead of camping retreats, street gangs instead of Boy Scouts, and as you reflect on your childhood you recall it was anything but tranquil. It was a place filled with boom boxes, street parties, waking up to breaking glass and screaming sirens. But even in these environments, friendship managed to survive and gave many young boys some sense of camaraderie. These relationships with the boys you called your "homies," "road dogs," or your "main man" were the street equivalent of the Huckleberry Finn–type relationships that others had.

Regardless of your experiences with male friends growing up, I believe that men can benefit from that kind of connection with other men in adulthood just as much as, if not more than, they did as children. To put it bluntly, we men need one another. And the sad reality is that most of us aren't in touch with this need because it makes us feel so uncomfortable, so needy, so afraid of being vulnerable and ending up hurt—like being the last one picked at recess for the team—that we bury it and suffer our masculine journeys alone in silence. As we grow up, we grow apart, believing that autonomy is part of masculinity. But the sad truth is we live our lives in a solitary confinement that imprisons the masculine soul.

I'm more convinced than ever that if men are to overcome the numerous and various obstacles of distraction and destruction in their paths, then they must embrace this need for healthy male connection and cultivate it. Perhaps the solution lies in us men climbing out of our cocoon, where we have incubated in isolation for years, and coming to grips with who we are and what we need to feel more complete. Men must learn to overcome their fears of what others will think of them, and express their genuine need for the trusted heartfelt friendship of other men. We can't overcome these obstacles all at once, mind you, but for most of us I believe that we must start by admitting to ourselves just how lonely, how disconnected, how eager we are for a comrade who is enough like us to relate to and relax with, and different enough to engage and encourage.

IN TO ME SEE

One of the most sacred human relationships is between a man and his wife, but even the holy union of matrimony doesn't replace a man's need for male friendship. Many times men cannot relate to a woman's way of seeing things and her views on various issues. This doesn't mean he doesn't love her, cherish her, and need her in ways too numerous to list. I want to dispel the myth that one person can fill the entirety of another person's life for fifty years leaving no need for extended relationships, brotherhood, or times of frolicking shared by men on a boy's night out. I have seen cases where a woman in love feels obligated to be all things to her man: his mother, his friend, his wife, his counselor, his buddy. This isn't realistic for any person to try to do.

The truth of the matter is that in spite of his deep trust for his wife, the fulfillment that he gets from her presence and the comfort he gains from her touch, he still may need other relationships. Not extramarital ones, but platonic, intimate relationships with other men that supplement the great life you have together. While he loves you, he may not always—nor should he need to—relate every concern or interest to you. Nor should he have to relate to every feminine interest that you have in order to be a good husband and a great source of rich companionship. As awesome as your relationship may be, it doesn't mean that he wouldn't deeply benefit from a close friend with whom he can share some of the bruises and bumps he incurs along the way. No one is more adept at sympathizing with the plight and understanding the concerns and fears of a man than another man who has been or is currently entrenched in similar experiences. Ladies, please don't allow insecurity to create a relationship that ultimately asphyxiates the love you share because you do not allow him to have the friendships he needs. You need to know that none of us can be all things to anyone, no matter how much we love them.

I know there are some brothers who may be saying to themselves, "Intimate relationships with other men? What in the world is he talking about?" Just the use of the word "intimate" is enough to stir up fear in most of us. Often, as men grow from childhood into manhood, they begin to distrust male friendships and other men. This suspicious distrust of men can stem from a bad experience or can develop because of the negative implications male friendships have in our society. While this distancing will provide some insulation from disappointment, it also alienates them from sharing and friendship they enjoyed as boys.

Certainly most men have numerous friendships—coworkers at the office, guys at the gym, and your buddies you play golf with—but from my observations and input from a variety of diverse men, the usual ways that men connect are okay but often don't facilitate real friendships. The focus remains on the externals, the opponent's strategy, the weather, the playoffs, the latest gadgets or improvements for a sport or shared hobby. It's easier for a man to talk about the new GPS in his SUV than to risk the greater, deeper subjects of pressures at work, frustrations at home, communication with family, and sexuality.

Many of us find it difficult to become transparent with other men. It is our nature to be competitive, and being open makes us vulnerable. There is the uncertainty and the fear of being misunderstood, appearing weak. God forbid that anyone know that we don't have everything together! This fear often keeps us to ourselves and our deepest feelings locked deep inside us. Even ministries such as Promise Keepers and Man-Power, which offer a large crowd atmosphere of support, do not provide the one-on-one relationship, the honest sharing and understanding that can change men's lives over the course of their friendship.

What is real male bonding and what prevents it from occurring between men today? From boyhood, and particularly during the teenage years, a man is conditioned by peers, the media, and other cultural factors to want to be seen as 110 percent heterosexual, studly, and macho, the king of conquests with women. (The perception lingers that there's a direct correlation between a man's number of sexual exploits with women and his masculinity. This is not necessarily the case at all, since a man who cannot control his sexual desire often battles insecurity, fear, and anxiety over his manhood.) Even though he may be totally free of any homosexual desire, interest, or tendency, that doesn't mean that he doesn't have some insecurity or anxiety about being misunderstood when it comes to same-sex friendships.

Many men do not seek friendships with the guys they work with or even men with whom they worship, because they do not want to be labeled homosexual. They may feel that people will call into question any same-sex friendship. Certainly, a lot of recent media attention has been given to homosexuality and men crossing the line with other men "on the down low" (which is just a new term for bisexual behavior). While it is obvious why such attention is warranted given the spread of AIDS and the declining morality issues, it does not negate the fact that this attention plays on the already existing fear that many men have that others will misconstrue their friendships. We will discuss homophobia and the sexualizing of male relationships later in this chapter, but this fear is a real impediment to forming significant relationships for some men. Imagine what would have happened had Timothy allowed such fears to keep him from Paul. Or think of what would have happened to Elisha had he avoided traveling with Elijah!

Another barrier that prevents true male bonding is the conflict between our need to belong and our desire to maintain our individuality and be our own man. We want to be close and know we fit in, but we don't want to be consumed and lose our identity. We may be reluctant to seek advice or guidance for fear that this somehow compromises our sense of self. Over the years I have noticed that when counseling couples, it is generally the man who resists the idea of counseling. His need for privacy and his tendency to feel that asking for help is somehow not masculine leaves him in turmoil and silent frustration. Men who struggle with depression and other emotional disorders often avoid getting the help they need. Many men are unable to allow anyone into the struggles they have with grief, rejection, divorce, or the many issues that can arise to cripple a man's emotional well-being. Too many men will not admit or allow anyone into their struggle and instead remain alone and angry.

However, there is no greater education we can receive than the lessons learned at the knee of another who has been there, done that, and can offer us the map to navigate the terrain that he himself has already maneuvered. A fortunate man is one who can learn from both the accomplishments and mistakes of another and benefit from the knowledge that only experience can bestow.

Many men are also reluctant to share what matters most to them—their hearts, their feelings, their relationships. The perception remains that real men don't talk about their feelings for fear of showing weakness or giving a fatal opening for someone else to exploit. And the enemy loves it when we struggle along, afraid and uncertain, thinking that we're the only ones wrestling with the current issue brewing in our souls. The devil can tempt us and pull us away if he can isolate us. All the more reason that men must break the silence of their own individual prisons and communicate with other men.

Most men hide behind what they do, not who they are. How often do we ask another man what he does right after he introduces himself? It's as if we want to go back in time to the dawn of our country and identify the man by his profession the way early American colonists often did. John the tailor became known as John Tailor and George the ironsmith became George Smith. Can you just imagine if men were named by their professions in the same way today—Ken Quarterback, Bob

Plumber, Wesley Engineer? And perhaps at times we might as well be based on how others perceive us and miss us in the process. From the aching depths of our loneliness, we long to be seen for more than the roles we perform, the jobs we hold, the relationships we maintain, but it so rarely happens and it involves risking part of ourselves that our culture usually doesn't want to see. Our social interactions reinforce this alienation by rating and identifying men based on performance alone—the salesman who makes the big deal, the quarterback who delivers the winning touchdown, the doctor who saves the life, the soldier who successfully wins the battle.

> *Male friendship is essential to men on the move.*

This constant need to measure up has placed many of us into a cocoon, emotionally embalmed and spiritually entombed. Instead of engaging in a friendship as brothers, we see it as a contest between rivals. Secret rivalry corrodes pure friendships and decays the covenant that could be attained.

When we use our success, our position at work, our education, or anything else to keep score and determine who we are, we shrink emotionally into an abyss of shame when things are not going well. Or, at the other extreme, when we are flourishing, we develop an inflated ego and a need to feel superior to another who may be facing a different season or stage in his life. Defining yourself by what you have is a dangerous habit. It can make a man swing from mood to mood like a monkey jumping from one vine to the next. If you want to stop the madness and stabilize your emotions, you must define who you are apart from what you may be going through. Here is where a close friend becomes vital. They are neither drawn to you by what you have attained nor repelled by what you have not accomplished. Every great man needs a friend who is secure enough in his own accomplishments to acknowledge who you are and affirm your worth as an individual. This is not a fan but a friend!

You are not what you do, my friend. What you have may change, just like David's circumstances changed when he moved from the sheepfold to the exotic, palatial surroundings of Saul's kingdom. Things will change over the course of our lives. The guy who is down today may be up tomorrow. You will never be stable until you can experience bad times and good without losing your focus on who you are.

I have spent countless hours with athletes, serving as a pastor, a confidant, and a friend. Although I would never share intimate details of any of their lives, I think it is important to share that even these guys, who are often admired by everyone because of their accomplishments, still struggle sometimes to adjust to changes in their lives. Many of them struggle to focus themselves when they are having a bad season. It is a challenge for some to adjust to life outside of the uniform. Often they allow press releases and game reviews to make or break how they see themselves. Many who are traded or face the end of their careers are inwardly devastated, as they have for so long drawn identity from their occupation and accomplishments on the field. I have repeatedly shared with many of them that there is life beyond the goal post, the court, or the ball field.

Similarly, police officers, as well as ministers, have a propensity to become entrenched in what they do and lose their sense of who they are outside of their calling. Anyone of us who works in a field where you give all find it difficult to get back what you put into the position. That is why you need relationships outside of your job to help balance you when you are too consumed.

When a man allows himself to be measured totally by his performance, he is apt to drown emotionally when those variables change. He has to find the strength to redefine who he is without describing what he does. Balance is the name of the game, and that means there has to be enough on the other end of the scale to keep you from tilting into overload.

I remember meeting Bill McCartney, the former National Championship—winning football coach at the University of Colorado, who founded Promise Keepers. In light of the phenomenal success of his ministry, I had wondered, as I so often do about many successful ventures in the public that seem to be spearheaded by the passion of a particular man, "Who is the person behind the personality?" In this case, I wondered, "Who is the real Bill McCartney? What is he like?" I was eager to meet him and see for myself. I had the chance to come face-to-face with Coach McCartney when I was invited to speak at a Promise Keepers conference. As he and I conversed at the event, I was struck by his warmth, his transparency, how in touch with himself he seemed. We shared our common goals for touching men's lives and uniting them in the pursuit of more authentic, faith-filled lives. In this case, the man matched his public persona. He seemed distinguished yet open and transparent, in a way that left me inspired. It was obvious that he was a man who had managed to maintain balance even as his success grew. The same guy who was on *Larry King Live* was able to have an honest, friendly exchange with me. He was balanced. That is the goal, men—balance.

Which brings me to another barrier that often looms between men, one in which a man is often split between how he looks on the outside and what he's experiencing on the inside. When it comes to personal relationships, you have to leave your image and your ego at the door. But some men are afraid to reveal their true inner feelings and conflicts because they believe they have to maintain a certain image. The football player may be wary of admitting his fears; the pastor may believe he cannot disclose his battle with temptation; the professor may be unwilling to say he just doesn't know the answers. This problem emerges especially in the Church and involves men relating to one another in terms of accountability. Too often today, accountability among men, especially men of faith, amounts to a "warden" mentality that sets us up to keep our secrets to our self and our self defined by our secrets. Since we already know that what we've done is wrong or that our weaknesses compel us to seek out less-than-godly pursuits, why do we need to share this with someone else? We already know what we should be doing. Who needs more police in their life? And who wants to police someone else's life when you know you've got your own issues simmering inside? How can you fix anybody if you yourself are broken?

But true friendship is not only about accountability, and it is certainly not about trying to "fix" someone else's problems or having them fix yours. True intimacy is not necessarily solution-oriented; it's not about making sure everyone is following the rules. Break down the word in•ti•macy, and you get in•to•me see. Intimacy involves listening to and really seeing the person, not fixing or providing answers. That's why I prefer the term "covenant relationship" to describe the kind of intimate and abiding friendship that has the power to connect men as they strengthen one another upon their journeys. In covenant relationships there may be, and should be, accountability, but there's more—a deeper sense of caring about a brother who's struggling without trying to punish him or shame him for his misdeed.

AS HIS OWN SOUL

Perhaps there's no better model for this type of relationship and the incredible power it can have on a man's life than the covenant friendship between Jonathan and David. For many of you reading this, just naming this famous pair brings to mind a longing for a soul brother, a best friend, a man whose kindred spirit is knit from the same cloth as your own. How can we experience this level of healthy masculine intimacy? Let's examine some of the intricacies of their friendship and purpose to glean insight into this relationship:

> Now when he had finished speaking to Saul, the soul of Jonathan was knit to the soul of David, and Jonathan loved him as his own soul.
> Saul took him that day, and would not let him go home to his father's house anymore.
> Then Jonathan and David made a covenant, because he loved him as his own soul.
> And Jonathan took off the robe that was on him and gave it to David, with his armor, even to his sword and his bow and his belt.
>
> (I SAMUEL 18:1–4)

The opening of David and Jonathan's friendship and the intensity of their connection often troubles many men, especially if you already struggle with homophobia and fear of being in a healthy intimate relationship with other men. This passage has also been used by some to justify sexualizing the closeness between male friends. I believe it's essential that we address this controversial and sometimes uncomfortable issue directly. I do not believe that Jonathan and David were involved in a homosexual relationship, although there may be a minute group of people who would take issue with this and perhaps disagree. The language makes it clear that this is a soul tie, not a flesh tie. However, even if theirs was a sexual relationship, their example would not justify homosexuality any more than David's relationship with Bathsheba justifies adultery. The Bible is clear on such matters (1 Corinthians 6:9 and Romans 1:27).

While I find no biblical justification for this lifestyle, it is nonetheless quite clear that many sincere young men have this struggle in their lives, even some who have come to Christ and find their past trying to attach itself to them again. These men, like all of us, have the challenge of controlling themselves and not allowing their past to define their future. As you might know, conquering one's old nature isn't always a seamless series of perfect victories. Hang in there if homosexuality is a part of your past, and please understand that heterosexual men often have no less of a struggle in being who God wants them to be. Sin of any kind is sin!

There is no justification for homophobia. The church should not recoil and retreat from anyone who seeks the presence of the Lord and the mercy that the Scriptures promise. We cannot dispense mercy only to people who struggle in the same areas as we do. In reality, from Adam till now, men have struggled against sin and the sin nature in various forms. Though many would have you believe that they themselves have no struggle, it is simply not true. Every man may not struggle with homosexuality, or pornography, or adultery, but be assured that every man struggles with something. Too often we have double standards for grace. For some, sin becomes anything for which we are not personally tempted!

> But every man is tempted, when he is drawn away of his own lust, and enticed. Then when lust hath conceived, it bringeth forth sin: and sin, when it is finished, bringeth forth death.
>
> JAMES 1:14–15 (KJV)

In reality, even great men struggle, wise men struggle, and yes, even spiritual men struggle at some point in some areas in their lives. Each man has "his own lust," as James puts it. It makes him need God, grace, and friends to support him as he wrestles with everything from lust to laziness. Homosexuality is just one more thing on a list of many the Church must become more effective at dealing with, and we must provide a better atmosphere so that men and women who have this particular struggle can fight and prevail.

However, let's get back to David and Jonathan. They model a deep love for each other without the relationship being laced with these other complications. You don't have to be an expert on the culture of that time to appreciate the intensity of their connection in this forging of their covenant of friendship. One man literally strips himself in front of the other and gives him not only his garments but his weapons as well. And let's not forget that Jonathan is a royal, namely a prince, the son of the king, and he's meeting the man who has been named heir to the throne—a distinction that is rightfully Jonathan's. It wouldn't have been unexpected for the young prince to feel resentment at the legendary giant killer, David, who has been anointed as Saul's replacement instead of him. Instead, there seems to be a chemistry, an instant attraction of kindred souls.

Maybe we shouldn't be so surprised at how well Jonathan and David connect considering how similar the dynamics of their stories and home lives really are. Their fathers are both "absent" from their sons' lives. Both Saul and Jesse are consumed by other endeavors, and in the process largely ignore their sons. Only on the surface are Jonathan and David's backgrounds so divergent. At the core, both boys have had the struggle of growing up without a father. Ironically enough, this covenant would be sorely tested by Jonathan's father and his rage and jealousy against David. But each time, Jonathan chooses to protect his friend and honor the soul covenant they forged, even when it means deceiving his own father (1 Samuel 20). Jonathan and David's relationship fulfilled both of them. David, the triumphant warrior, a man of courage and compassion, gave a committed friendship. Jonathan, the royal heir, gave his weapons and disarmed himself. Their bonding filled a deep void in Jonathan's life and provided David with an ally who would be closer to him than the mothers of his children.

NAKED AND UNASHAMED

Consider the awkwardness most of us felt when changing in the locker room when we were teenagers in gym class, the embarrassment of baring yourself in front of your peers mingled with your curiosity about how your developing body compared to theirs. Or even the odd moment as adults when you're changing in the locker room in front of a friend or someone you know—what will they think of you standing there naked before them with nothing to hide behind?

Naked before his friend with his assets and liabilities fully exposed, Jonathan likely wondered what each of us wonders—how would his friend respond? From the baring of bellies to the displaying of birthmarks, real friendship eventually requires an open, unveiled view of who the other really is—a transparency that is critical if a comfortable relationship is to be attained. The reason we are wary of being exposed in front of other people often centers around our intense need to

> *Don't be afraid to express your need of friendship with another man.*

pretend in their presence. But what you really need is a friend with whom you have developed such trust that you can let it all hang out, so to speak. Otherwise the relationship is just one more responsibility that requires you to put on a mask, suit up in your armor, or wear a disguise for acceptance and approval. Simply stated, these relationships, with their stringent requirements, are too much work with too little reward for those men who have no time for the games.

Please allow me a sidebar here: I have heard a popular phrase often in church, and I guess I, myself, have followed suit and said it a time or two. That phrase is "My wife is my best friend." But the truth is, she is not my best friend. She is my wife, the apple of my eye, the recipient of my love. Don't get me wrong. I think that a man and his wife enjoy a special and unique bond that God has ordained. But so much of a marriage relationship is based on the complementary differences between a man and a woman. And while there is a special, deep, and unique bond of friendship, to rely on your wife as your "best friend" seems unrealistic to me. There will be some aspects of your life that simply can't be fully understood from a female perspective, just as there are things in her life that you can't understand. There will be issues between the two of you that you need to discuss with someone else, not her. Venting every frustration to her can lead to saying things that you regret. Sometimes, even in the best of marriages, your frustration is with her, something she did, so how can you get objective counsel from her? Additionally, a man often needs to be able to clear his head in a conversation with someone whom he does not feel emotionally responsible for, someone he can vent to without having to rehash and explain "what he really meant" for the next five weeks!

Many men have tried so hard to make this "all for one and one for all" idea of marriages work until they have given up their own individuality. It is not healthy for a man (or a woman) to deny himself hobbies or interests he enjoys just because he married someone who doesn't enjoy what he does. There will be separate interests and needs that must be nurtured and developed apart from each other if the relationship is to stay vital and healthy. Just because I enjoy golfing doesn't mean that my wife should have to follow me to the golf course and make us both miserable. We can be fully in love and still share different interests. Don't allow the union to destroy your own sense of personhood. If you do, you will eventually resent the loss of your own identity. Marriage is meant to provide an opportunity for you to share who you are, not destroy who you are.

I have seen numerous couples come before me for counseling wondering why their marriage is crumbling when they spend so much time together. My advice for them is to give the relationship some breathing room—spending time together is certainly healthy and life-giving to a marriage, but spending every waking moment together becomes too much. Couples who work together, work out together, teach a class together at church, shop together, vacation together, and then come to counseling together wonder what they're doing wrong. While some people may enjoy all that togetherness, there are many who cannot. It can be refreshing to get some individual time so that when you come back together again you are excited by your reunion.

If you want your marriage to last over the long haul, then bring balance and the fullness of who each of you is by himself or herself to the relationship. If you're cultivating individual hobbies and interests and learning to enjoy and appreciate who you are by yourself, then you will naturally gravitate toward your spouse with a fresh appreciation of who she is and what her differences are. You will be comfortable to cultivate other friendships that meet needs that she can't meet. You may occasionally take separate vacations—she goes on a three-day shopping spree while you and the fellows go fishing for a weekend. (As long as the "boys' night out" doesn't include a trip to a strip club, you should be fine.) Some individual time keeps the relationship healthy and avoids the undue pressure of expecting each other to fulfill a role that marriage is not intended to fulfill.

Recently, I was in Fort Hood, Texas, on the army base where thousands of men and women were being deployed to fight the war in Iraq. Some were on their way back while others were being deployed. These young men had developed friendships that would last a lifetime. They loved their families, but there was a strong bond that had developed between those soldiers who had faced the same fears and were being exposed to the same threats and adversities. One man, who had recently returned from Iraq, shared with me that the desert climate and adverse conditions did not allow much privacy. He said, "We are not young or old, black and white over there, we are just Americans. From showers to shattering glass and exploding bombs, we will see it all and share it all together." I thought to myself that in some ways that is really how life is. Black or white, young or old, we are all facing similar challenges together.

Sadly, most of us don't realize this common bond we share. We divide into our social classes, become engrossed in our work worlds, and isolate ourselves, missing out on having the strength of being an army of men who are there for one another. I feel like a bugle boy blowing a trumpet calling men to gather together and unite, to give support and courage to one another. The male species is under attack, and many casualities are occurring right here under our noses. Men are being shot down by the trials and tragedies of life and left for dead emotionally, spiritually, and, occasionally, physically. You can find cover if you have someone with whom you can honestly and openly share who you are and what you are facing in your own battles and struggles at work, at home, and, most important, inside.

SECRET SHARER

So do we need to strip naked in front of our friends like Jonathan in order to grow into a covenant relationship? While this exposure might certainly expedite the trust necessary to form such a friendship, I believe for us today this story offers a more metaphoric clue of how we bond. The act of Jonathan stripping and giving David his garments and weapons certainly has cultural implications: It represents the complete trust and openness of one man entrusting his body, heart, and soul to another man. It's similar to another cultural bonding ceremony between men that you may be more familiar with: blood covenants—the

Native American tradition of cutting oneself, often on the wrist, and smearing those wrists together in an exchange of blood. Such ceremonies demonstrated that even though these men were not related by birth, from then on they would share each other's blood, their life fluid, between them.

For us today, the blood in our covenants is our secrets. By sharing our secrets, we are binding ourselves to each other. We are opening ourselves up and saying, "This is who I am. See my weaknesses, see my scars, see into my heart. I am showing you the most intimate part of my being. Please protect it, just as I will protect yours." When we share our secrets, we are entrusting our hearts to each other, vowing to support, honor, and be honest with each other.

Do you have any relationships like these in your life today? Is there another man with whom you are so vulnerable that it's comparable to being naked or sharing blood? David would tell you that you cannot have your kingdom and maintain it without finding your Jonathan. You see, Jonathan was the key that unlocked the kingdom for David. Their lifelong friendship was a source of strength and stability and helped David to deal with his new surroundings. There was nothing to hide from Jonathan because Jonathan was not a competitor sent to compete but a friend given by God to complete what David was missing on his mission to greatness. Their friendship provided a safe place for David to go and a safe place for David to grow. There were no agendas, all barriers were removed, and all secrets shared. As we think about Jonathan stripping naked before David, about them sharing their secrets with complete vulnerability, we certainly have a model to emulate for healthy male intimacy. However, we must be careful not to take off all our clothes at once. Friendship is a striptease, not a lap dance! You should not share all of your secrets at once. Let the friendship and its layers of intimacy and secret-sharing evolve naturally. And I would also caution you to never share your secrets with a man who won't share his own. This one-sided intimacy creates an unbalanced relationship with the conditions ripe for misuse.

With many men, the sharing of secrets occurs through time spent together, through shared activities and connecting over hobbies and interests held in common. So often in our culture today, men are so overwhelmed by their busyness that they never have time just to enjoy a pickup game in the neighborhood park or to make time for a regular lunch or dinner with a male friend. And perhaps they're not comfortable sharing their secrets, cutting their wrists, revealing what's going on in their inner worlds. For that would put them at risk of being vulnerable, of being perceived as weak, as less than the "got it together" façade that they work so hard to project so much of the time.

Perhaps that's why there's such a boom in the counseling industry. Some men realize their need and will schedule in their weekly appointment with their therapist but can't make time to have lunch with a buddy or attend a concert with a friend on the weekend. So we pay someone to keep our secrets for us, someone to listen and care, to advise and counsel. But because of their role and the ethics of the profession, the professional counselor is not free to be transparent and totally open with you, nor should he be. I talk to many men who have tried counseling but get frustrated because, as one man put it, "I'm paying someone to be my friend—what's wrong with me?" To this man, it was just another sign that he had locked himself up and couldn't find his way out.

Many men wait until there's a crisis before they're even willing to go to a counselor and share secrets: when their wives demand it because the marriage is on life support; when the man's secrets start to take on an addicted life of their own and it tears at the seams of his life; when his mistress threatens to expose him; when he contracts a sexually transmitted disease from the prostitute on the last business trip; when he can't quit gambling online and now there's no mortgage payment this month. Then a man in desperation will go to a counselor and tell his secrets, when it's often too late and the consequences of his secrets have him by the throat up against the wall.

Please don't misunderstand me in my observation about counseling, for it serves such a vital role in the healing, educating, and assisting of many hurting men who are struggling through life's storms. In fact, I consulted several counselors and therapists for information on writing this book and solicited the input of my friend and colleague Dr. Tim Clinton, president of the American Association of Christian Counselors. There's even a list of counseling resources for men listed at the end of this chapter, and I encourage you to make use of it and get the help you need in whatever areas you may need. However, having said all this, I also harbor the belief that if men were willing to risk and covenant together and honor their bonds, then the need for counseling would largely become obsolete.

FINDING YOUR JONATHAN

Once men fully recognize the extent of their need and longing for a Jonathan in their lives, they wonder how to go about finding such a special brother. Just as there's no right way or 1-2-3 method for finding your spouse, I would maintain that finding your covenant friendships are often a matter of timing, chemistry, and God's goodness in your life. I encourage men to be attuned to looking for ways of relating to other men whom they might tend to overlook at first. Too often we seem to believe that we will only find our soul brother in another man with the same demographic profile as our own, but that's often the furthest thing from the truth. Those relationships are often boring or sabotaged by the grenades of petty jealousy and overfamiliarity. Often, men in the same profession may find it hard to be vulnerable because they feel competitive or jealous with one another. They may be guarded and proprietary because they think you're after their job or knowledge or personal niche in your shared career field.

You should look to build lifelong friendships with men whom you encounter who may be very different from yourself. Learn to appreciate the differences and allow them to enrich your time together. Some of the strongest relationships are between people who are quite different. But true covenant can overcome the differences and use them as the means to bring people closer. We see an example of this type of relationship in the Bible in the story of Ruth and Naomi. These women were related by marriage, but this did not ensure that they would be friends, and in fact, it might have even worked against it. (We all know the cliché about how badly women and their mothers-in-law get along.) This, placed on top of their age differences and their cultural and ethnic differences—Ruth was a Moabite while Naomi was Jewish—might have created formidable barriers in many relationships. However, they cared for each other in a way that transcended these barriers, remaining open to the possibility of learning from and enjoying each other's uniqueness.

> *Everyone needs to share his secrets. Find a friend who is loyal, transparent, and trustworthy to share yours.*

My covenant friendships are not just with African American pastors but also with white lawyers and Hispanic musicians and Jewish doctors. I would miss so much enjoyment and the discovery of the fullness of other men's experiences if I limited myself to only relating to men similar to myself. We mustn't limit chemistry in a male friendship to only other men like ourselves. Instead, we must consider our pursuit of male friendships like our stock portfolio. We must diversify. Similarly, just as investing in the stock market comes with some risk, so too does seeking friendship. You are exposing yourself, presenting your true inner being with nothing to hide behind. As I said earlier, your friendship should be nurtured and developed, and you should reveal yourself gradually. Treat your male friendships like entering a pool for a swim. You shouldn't just dive in; you should test the waters gradually. First, you wade down into the water ankle deep and test the temperature. If the water is too cold or too hot, it may not be the right pool at that time. But assuming there's some compatibility with the water, you get used to its temperature and then you step into it deeper and go farther out.

When they're testing the waters with each other, men tend to talk around their issues at first. They talk about the externals of their lives—their jobs, their spouses, their kids, their hobbies and favorite sports. It's more general than personal. But then they begin testing each other to see how the other man might respond to issues that hit closer to home. They begin searching for signs that their secrets might be safe with this man, that he can handle them without needing to fix them or police them or dismiss them.

I recall how a member of my congregation began testing the waters with me. We were involved on a missions committee together, and this man inquired about providing relief for AIDS victims in Africa, certainly a most worthy endeavor that stirred everyone's compassion. However, weeks later the man came to me in private and revealed that his wife was suffering from AIDS. It seems that she was HIV positive when he married her, and over time she developed full-blown AIDS. It was an emotional time for both of them, but they were afraid to tell anyone because of the stigma still lingering over the disease, mostly due to public misinformation and misperceptions. With tears in his eyes, this gentleman shared his love for his wife and his desire to see her through her illness regardless of what others would think. I was honored by his trust and was glad to find ways that the church and some other trusted members could minister to him and his family. But he was wise to get a feel for how I would respond to the issue in general—out there as a matter of public policy—before he revealed to me in private this most personal issue for him and his wife.

There are a couple of other cautions I would like to share with you as you proceed to find and maintain Jonathan and David–type friendships. First, while you may have one "best" friend who gets you like no one else, the reality is that you need several friends, a network of relationships that you're cultivating and enjoying at different levels. One may be more of a mentoring relationship, which we'll explore in more detail in the next chapter, another might be someone who shares your passion for fishing, another is a boyhood friend from your hometown, and yet another is a brother you discovered as you ministered together in your church. This can keep you from placing too much pressure on any one individual and expecting him to meet all your friendship needs.

Second, men today often complain about being too busy to maintain their friendships, let alone cultivate them at a deeper level. However, most of the men I know who live balanced lives find time to remain in regular contact with a handful of men whom they call true friends. Whether it's touching base on the phone once a week, having a regular time to work out together, or planning a long weekend at the beach for the next year, there's something they're sharing and building together over time. They're willing to make sacrifices and give gifts of time, of resources, of little things that they know the other will enjoy—a joke, an article from the sports page or business section, an anecdote about what you did with your kids last weekend. Take the time to invest in your brother's life just as you hope he will knit his life and heart to yours.

Finally, as you plunge into the pool and begin swimming with fellow seekers, I recommend that you keep the following in mind:

FIVE STEPS FOR SWIMMING INTO THE POOL
OF MALE FRIENDSHIPS

1. Begin slowly—test the waters before diving into the deep end.

2. Cultivate reciprocity—exchange secrets on both sides.
3. Enjoy the differences—seek out men who are distinct from you.
4. Strip gradually—become vulnerable and loyal over time.
5. Rely on each other—honor your commitment to each other.

LEAN DURING HARD TIMES

There's a rich texture to a man's life when he's in a healthy friendship with another man. Not only does he feel like there's someone who knows and enjoys him, someone who can handle his secrets, but he also feels needed and appreciated for doing the same things for his friend. The simple camaraderie and pleasure of each other's company, of sharing experiences together, of commiserating on issues that weigh similarly in each of their lives—these strands of support form a web of strength and ongoing security that empower a man to take risks he might never take on his own.

When men are willing to form and honor a covenant with another male friend, there's a support system that develops, a guardrail for each other along the treacherous curves and icy shoulders of life's road. When they have this kind of intimate friendship with other men, they know that they are not so alone. They don't have to feel like they are the only ones who feel, think, and act in certain ways—for the truth of the matter is that all of us are more alike than different, even as we are more unique than identical. We long to belong just as much as we long to be recognized for how special and distinct we are from other men. We want another man to see something in us that perhaps no one else is able to see—the passion we have for particular hobbies or interests, the unique

INCREASING YOUR RANGE OF MOTION—FOR HIM

Describe a time when you had a male best friend. What qualities did you enjoy the most? What was the hardest part of maintaining the friendship?

What are you looking for in a friendship with another man? What are you not looking for?

What keeps you from growing closer, in healthy ways, with your male friends?

INCREASING YOUR RANGE OF MOTION—FOR HER

How would you describe the male friends in your man's life?

What do you like most about his friends? What troubles you the most about them?

How do his friendships compare with your friendships with other women?

How often do you encourage him to have a "boys' night out"?

way we have of thinking or solving problems, the personal brand of craziness that is all our own expressed in our sense of humor and the way we look at life.

Then, when we get depressed or feel defeated, we have someone to lean on, someone to call when we feel alone and untouchable deep in the center of our soul. Someone to confide in when our marriage is leaking and we're tired of bailing the same emotional waters out of the ship. A brother to share in the struggles and the triumphs and the mundane experiences that comprise the journey of our lives. Do you have someone you can call at two in the morning when you can't sleep and you don't want to wake your wife because you aren't even sure what's wrong? Do you have a friend who would be willing to come and pick you up if you were in a jam and felt too ashamed to call your family? Do you have someone you trust with knowing both the best and worst things about you? I believe we long for those kinds of relationships with a solid center that will not wilt or fold when the harsh realities of life press in upon us.

Out of all the risks I will challenge you to take in this book, perhaps no other is as essential to your growth and well-being as finding a Jonathan with whom you can covenant and grow together. If you have already found this kind of brother in your life, I encourage you to let him know how much you value and appreciate his friendship. And if you are just beginning to look for him, then I ask that you be patient and look for opportunities to plant seeds of friendship with other men, open to the fresh shoots of deeper acquaintance that may take root there. Pray and ask our Father's blessing on the male relationships you have in your life. Don't be afraid to risk your secrets when the time is right and learn to express your needs with each other. His prayers and well wishes will be a source of great strength to you as you go and grow in life. The power of a brother is a mighty gift—cultivate and cherish it!

COUNSELING RESOURCES

American Association of Christian Counselors
434-525-9470
www.aacc.net

National Mental Health Association

1-800-969-NMHA

www.nmha.org

American Psychiatric Association

202-682-6000

www.psych.org

American Psychological Association

1-800-964-2000

www.apa.org

Promise Keepers

303-964-7600

www.promisekeepers.org

EIGHT

REAL MEN NEED
REAL FRIENDS

Without close friendships, men lose perspective on what is simply part of being a man at various stages of our lives.
—ROBERT PASICK, *Awakening from the Deep Sleep*

When I was growing up, I knew a boy named Freddy. His parents, like mine, were hard workers and busy most of the time. The difference was I had a brother and a sister, siblings who consumed much of my time and gave me some sense of friendship and relationship, while my friend, an only child, was often left home while his parents went about the arduous task of providing for the family. Later in life, I learned that it is critical to a child's well-being to have an opportunity to interact with others his age in order to develop critical skills for living that are not taught in school: communication, conflict resolution, forgiveness, and the inner ability to determine when we have estranged those we seek to charm. For sure, my brothers and sisters gave me plenty of opportunities to learn about conflict resolution and forgiveness. But Freddy really didn't have the chance to explore these situations and develop these very necessary life skills.

To compensate for his loneliness, Freddy developed a propensity to delve deeper and deeper into the imaginative land of children—the land of make-believe. In other words, he started to become a big storyteller. He would make up events that never happened, exciting adventures that were filled with mayhem and mystery. His tales became longer and more bizarre as he continued to turn to his creativity to fill his lonely void. Now I am sure that had his parents known that his problems were rooted in loneliness, they might have handled things differently, but often when people don't understand our struggles, they add to our pain with their constant preaching and badgering. There are some problems that are only exacerbated by nagging voices and shrieking loved ones who attempt to cure what they haven't tried to understand. The more they yelled at Freddy for making up his magical adventures, the wilder his stories became.

Freddy could usually be found playing over on the back side of the hill near the creek between the rocks. He'd be laughing and talking and playing chase, which was a common game us kids played. The only thing that was disturbing about Freddy was that he was down there playing by himself! I cannot tell you how ridiculous he looked, making motions and calling toward a tree or laughing at the river with an invisible person he had named and later described as his best friend.

Now don't worry, for, as most children do, Freddy eventually grew out of his imaginary playmate. But his make-believe friend caused his parents a considerable amount of grief. At first, they were just annoyed by his outrageous stories and odd behavior, but soon they started to worry that there was indeed something wrong with their son. Could he be crazy? they wondered.

Much like John Nash, Jr., the character in the film *A Beautiful Mind,* Freddy's invisible relationships could have indicated the onset of schizophrenia, which is accompanied by an inability to differentiate between the real and the imagined. While the exact causes of schizophrenia are unknown, it has been linked to hereditary factors, chemical imbalances in the brain, and traumas during birth or early childhood. In this disease, the brain chemicals do not function properly, thereby impeding the sufferer's ability to process the sensory data around him and interpret it accurately. For instance, someone suffering from schizophrenia might not be able to differentiate between a science fiction movie and real life, and may very well believe aliens have invaded Earth.

If this was what Freddy battled as he related to his imaginary friend, then he would not have been able to leave behind this make-believe without medical attention and clinical treatment. But Freddy was just a lonely, imaginative little boy, afraid to reach out to those of us he might have played with at the time. In his case, love prevailed and time healed. He went on to be a productive part of the community with no trace of his bout with acute loneliness and his self-prescribed solution of non-existent companions.

REAL IMAGINARY FRIENDS

I mention Freddy to you because I later realized that he had his imaginary friend to replace something that I really wanted to be to him. But he was too afraid to reach out to someone and resolved his natural fear of being hurt or betrayed by creating a controllable friend through his imagination. However, although developing attachments to real, live people carries with it some risk, a make-believe playmate can never replace the benefits authentic connections provide. While his imaginary friend might have eliminated the fear and risk of rejection, it could not provide the genuine interaction, true acceptance, and spontaneity of the real thing.

But in some ways I think Freddy was wiser than I originally gave him credit for; he got his imaginary friends out of his system early. Oh, but the rest of us, we wait until we're older, busier, and more seasoned, and then we start playing with friends who are not really there. Yes, that is right, my friend, admit it. Most men presently cultivate what Freddy got rid of when he was a child. Our friends may not be invisible, but they are facsimiles of friendship nonetheless. We don't form a complete connection to others; we relate only on the surface. We have a propensity toward developing pseudo-friends to avoid the tough task of learning and investing in real relationships, and particularly relationships with other men. Why risk being misunderstood, hurt, or disappointed?

Other men have no male friends at all. You might say to yourself, "I don't really need friends anyway. I have a wife for intimacy, a career to provide challenge, and a family to give me a sense of destiny and purpose." You are right, except most great men will tell you that these things, while very rewarding, often expend energy rather than contribute to our lives. Our wives, careers, and families require things from us: our care, our strength, our performance. A man needs to have a friend with whom he can unload his inner thoughts, gain perspective, and cross-pollinate and interact, someone he doesn't pay like an employee, doesn't need to support emotionally like a wife, and doesn't need correction or tending like his child. This is a friendship where there is no dependency, no power dynamics, just mutual respect and understanding.

But many men are afraid of forming authentic male friendships, and instead of letting themselves be emotionally vulnerable, they tend to find friend-replacements. These friend-replacements are often areas in which we can safely invest our strength without the risk of rejection, the admission of vulnerability, or the potential for a transparent gaze into our inner self and soul. I know you are saying that you don't have them, but I beg to differ with you. Many men have made their work an imaginary friend. We make our career a replacement for the voids we have and foolishly try to get personal fulfillment from public institutions. This is not an effective solution, but so many of us persist in cultivating this imaginary relationship with our job.

Maybe you are one of those people who comes to work early and stays late, a person who brings coffee from home for the company coffee pot, paints the building with your own paint, and passes out flyers on your own time. Now any of these behaviors might also describe someone who is conscientious and loyal. But watch out that in an attempt to become employee of the month, you don't find yourself becoming one of those compulsive type-A people who tries to get more from work than what work is designed to give. People who invest too much of

> Be careful not to let your job take the place of authentic friendships—money, position, or power can't sustain your soul.

themselves in their job are actually having a deep and all-inclusive relationship with an imaginary friend. These men are devastated when something goes wrong at work. They are not just financially challenged by a profit loss; they become emotionally ruined because they were having a human relationship with an imaginary friend, and they suddenly realize that companies are not people and can't offer the soul support and emotional sustenance that only real friends can give.

Ministers too often have relationships with their churches that hide under the guise of spirituality but are actually imaginary friendships. Under closer observation, the endless zeal, crowded appointments, and constant need to remain drowned in responsibility aren't a result of the call of God but the fear of life and avoidance of confronting relationships with wives, children, and friends. These men can hide for years in work and win great admiration from all of us, while secretly remaining frustrated by the fact that they are trying to get blood from a turnip. They want to make a friend out of a mission. They are heartbroken when people leave the church. They feel betrayed by any disagreement with parishioners. They are often controlling of congregations, adding more and more programs to replace intimacy. They are as guilty of the imaginary, fictitious work of make-believe as was my childhood friend Freddy.

If you are going to stop the madness and end your compulsive friend-replacement, then you should stop here and identify your imaginary friend. Name it for what it is and let's exorcise this ghostly delusion while you still have enough life left to change a habit before it becomes any more of an addiction than it already is. Turn off that cell phone at the dinner table—stop putting people on hold in front of you while you engage with people who are not there. It is time for you to build a relationship that allows real people to know you, understand you, and make a connection with you. I hear you saying, "The man is right. That is where I am and I can see it. That is what I do to avoid the risk of rejection and the hassles of being misunderstood. But now that I see it, where do I begin to correct it?" I am glad you asked.

PYRAMID POWER

As you try to develop a blueprint for healthy relationships that will decrease the risk and rejection, I direct you to listen to what Jesus says in the gospel of John when he tells His disciples, "No longer do I call you servants, for a servant knows not what his master is doing; but I have called you friends, for all things that I heard from My Father I have made known to you" (John 15:15). In this simple yet profound statement, Jesus differentiates between those who are friends and those who are not; there are things His friends know that others do not. There are distinct levels of intimacy that characterize different types of relationships. You must be prudent about who you open yourself up to. You should also realize that there are different types of friendships, and some are closer and more trusting than others. I liken it to a pyramid of friendship. At the pinnacle are those whom you are most intimate with. As you move down the pyramid, the numbers increase, but the intensity is not as great. I find that each tier has access to different levels of information. Your life, your strengths and weaknesses, your fears, triumphs, and tragedies are the commerce that describes your net worth. Everyone shouldn't have all your files, but someone needs to know who you are and where you are at all times in your walk and life. Even if they can't help you, their company alongside you eases misery and irrigates the soul.

If we were to chart Jesus' relationship with those men he allowed to have a close relationship with him, we would see John at the apex of the pyramid. Now, I realize that Jesus' primary relationship with all twelve disciples was one of mentoring and development. Still, I believe his layered style of relationships will give us some guidance for our own relationships with men. His relationship with John was special. John remained unmartyred and was defended by Christ when questioned about his lack of martyrdom. He was called "the one whom Jesus loved." John was "the one"—Jesus' main man, His best friend.

We are better off when we can identify the one who stands head and shoulders above the rest. He may be flawed, but he is clearly the one who sits at the table with an ability to be loyal and loving, who feeds your inner need for camaraderie in a way that others don't. For Jesus, it was John. For David, it was Jonathan. Who is it for you?

Now if John was "the one," then Peter and James made up the second tier of the pyramid. John, Peter, and James were Jesus' "core" group. These men were His inner circle. They were the ones who knew what Jesus needed, who interacted with Him, and impacted His life. Their friendship with Jesus was like Aaron and Hur's relationship with Moses in the Old Testament. They were not men who stayed at the bottom of the mountain. These men were called to the Mount of Transfiguration, saw who Jesus really was, and remained loyal to the end. Friends at this level are the guys whom we invite to our Garden of Gethsemane to pray for us as we face the crosses of life—marriage, ministry, and all the nuances of being a man of God in a world of temptations.

On the next level of Jesus' friendship pyramid were the Nine other disciples. Now, I am not suggesting that you go find nine guys for the next level. Your "level nine" may only have five board members. But I am pointing more to how Jesus layered His relationships with men in categories to suggest that you diminish your risk when you limit your levels and layer your access. Some people are in your life because they stimulate you intellectually. These are men who engage you in stimulating conversations and speak effectively about things for which you're passionate, whether it's chemistry or world affairs. These friends provide you with shop talk and intellectual exchange. They stimulate your creativity and enhance your effectiveness by giving you fresh ideas and creative dialogue. Perhaps others at this level have no understanding of you intellectually, but they get you in other ways. One man is a great golfer, and he motivates you on the golf course. There may be a friend who is a great partner in a workout room. The friends at this level help fulfill distinct areas of your life.

The fourth level of Jesus' pyramid are the Seventy. "The Lord appointed seventy others also, and sent them two by two before His face into every city and place where He Himself was about to go" (Luke 10:1). These are persons with whom you have a good working relationship but who do not know you and should not know you personally. Jesus related to them only through the delegation of duties and the dissemination of responsibilities. Yes, He laid hands on them. He even commissioned them, but He didn't engage with them on deeper levels. I have seen great men destroyed over and over by making friends of those with whom they should remain professional. No weaknesses shown on this level, no resting with them, no weeping with them: Jesus kept His relationship with them clearly defined. These guys can't handle you crying in the garden in a moment of frustration in your career, not enjoying your marriage, or dealing with an embarrassing problem with your son. They need only know that you can tread on serpents.

Finally, the fifth level is represented by the Five Thousand whom

Jesus fed. The vast majority of people in your life are there for the feeding and not for the friendship. They are with you for what they can get from you. While that may sound crass, it is true. However, what makes you able to cope with their incessant appetite is the fact that you have a few folks on higher levels who contribute to you, irrigate you, and make it possible for you to have enough deposits to withstand the constant withdrawals that the vast majority of people will make from you throughout life.

There certainly have been many times in my life when I was parched by responsibilities, overwhelmed by circumstances, and my creativity thwarted by frustration. And I was able to withstand these moments because, as busy as I was, I made time to irrigate my life with some relaxing down time with friends, who renewed me and released me. They renewed me because they offered me fresh perspectives, and they released me because they were people whom I didn't have to impress or perform for, people to whom I could admit that I didn't have all the answers at all times to everything.

I call this kind of friendship a positive extramarital relationship, as opposed to the all-too-often demonstrated negative one. However, you don't have to be married to have one. And if you are married, it doesn't mean that you don't need one. Of course, friendship does not replace the deep and rich intimacy that comes from marriage, but I think it helps to protect that relationship. My relationships with close friends become an elixir to my life, my wife, and my sanity.

I often tell women that they should not be jealous of their man's friendships. These women, mothers, wives, and sisters must realize that the need for a friend is not an indication that their relationship with their man is defective or dysfunctional. They need to understand that an occasional boys' night out, golfing trip, camping trip, or afternoon out washing the car with the other guys doesn't mean that Daddy isn't coming home to stay. Yes, ladies, he will be back, and, in fact, he will be back stronger if he can go outside and play. Allowing those we love to experience the fulfillment that only male friendship can provide makes it possible for them to stay with you over the long haul, instead of them feeling like they have to break away to meet a simple need for their growth as an individual. His need of a friend isn't a sign for you to load up the camping gear and jump in the truck! Let the brother go so he can grow. Give him a chance to be all he can be. He will be back, and if he doesn't come back, he probably wasn't going to stay anyway. Marriage shouldn't mean incarceration, and a wife is not a warden.

> *Ladies, don't stifle your man's friendships. These relationships keep him strong, sane, and strengthen your marriage.*

I also tell women that your husband can be a great man, but don't make him be your girlfriend. I love my wife, but I don't want to know the latest trends in women's fashion, what color nail polish is popular this season, or which cleanser takes off makeup in a flash. Similarly, there are some subjects that are of little interest to my wife but are significant to me. This is not to say that we should not share our passions with our spouse, but there are some matters that you are better off discussing with those who find them equally fascinating. Women need girlfriends and men need male friends with whom they can discuss a myriad of subjects. For instance, I have several friends who are pastors and run ministries of their own. These friends make it possible for me to come home without having to vent every frustration about work. It is often burdensome for me to cast all my cares on my wife. But I can share my work problems with my pastor friends because they face similar circumstances and share some of the same concerns.

Like the multiple streams in the Garden of Eden, it is important that you have more than one stream of relationship to build you and strengthen you. These extra relationships irrigate the masculine soul and eradicate the weeds of stress, thus making your life more fruitful.

Men with similar interests can fortify each other, giving us sufficient fuel to nourish our marriage and the other areas of our life.

CONTACT BY CONTRACT

Now I know you may be saying this is too much work. But before you run off into the world with your invisible playmate and say you cannot handle close relationships, just wait a minute. You may still fear forming friendships, but remember, you may be vulnerable but you are not unprotected. There is a light at the top of the pyramid. That is God Himself. The place that He holds in your life gives you the strength to love others. He is your defense against rejection, your wisdom, and your ultimate resource. Tap into Him, but know that even He said that relationship with Him alone wasn't enough. It was God who said that it was not good for man to be alone. This He said of a man who had a job, a place to stay, and a close relationship with his Creator. There are levels of need and levels of supply. You can't get from God what you should get from friends. You can't get from your friends what you must get from your wife. Each relationship has levels, needs, rules, and terms of engagement.

In fact, I think that the true secret to success for relationships centers around a good understanding of what the terms and expectations may be for each relationship. Even if you have to amend them later, it's so vital to have a mutual comprehension of the boundaries, borders, and benefits of each relationship that you enter into. The Scripture asks, "Can two walk together unless they are agreed?" (Amos 3:3) and emphasizes this need for each party to be in accord with the terms of the relationship.

There must be an action plan for your friendships; you must delineate the terms of your covenant. You wouldn't buy a house or a car or a new washing machine without having some kind of document informing you of the terms of the relationship between buyer and seller. Why should you enter into a friendship without knowing the expectations and obligations that it entails? It's not that you can anticipate every action and reaction that may occur and try to make the friendship conform to a preconceived pattern. Friendship is not a chess match with calculated moves and countermoves. But because there are so many unforeseen, natural occurrences and incidents in a real friendship, you need something to fall back on when tensions develop and dynamics shift. You need to know how you'll handle it when he doesn't return your call for three days. Is that his typical m.o. because he's on the road and you shouldn't be alarmed, or is he sending you a not-so-subtle message about your relationship? Maybe he prefers emailing over talking on the phone. Perhaps he needs more time to process his feelings and to resolve a conflict than you do. Will the two of you try to get your families together and see if they hit it off as well? What if your wives don't particularly like each other? Will you part ways then or just keep it as a friendship between the two of you?

When I shared this information and these questions with one friend, he responded, "Bishop, that sounds like more work than my marriage. Why all the rules? Why can't I just let whatever happens, happen?" I understand his concern, and let me reiterate that I'm not encouraging you to prescribe and direct the course of your friendship as if it were a staged production. But there's no getting around it; relationships of all kinds require effort. There is no such thing as a free ride. That is why you don't have the capacity to "take up" with everybody. Real relationships cost something in terms of time, thoughtfulness, and openness. Even in your marriage there should be deliberate communication that explores and explains the territory of your relationship before you reach the critical junctures. Ideally, good premarital counseling provides these tools for navigation and negotiation so that when the two of you get stranded in the wilderness of unanticipated conflicts and tumultuous circumstances, you have compass points to stabilize your direction. You need a North Star to guide you when the darkness shrouds your vision.

Friendships should have the same kinds of tools at your disposal. Once it's clear that the two of you are connecting and that both of you want to pursue an ongoing commitment of friendship, then gradually start talking about how each of you wants to operate. Allow for growth and change as the friendship naturally evolves over time. Decide how often you'd like to get together, whether or not you want to have the freedom to rely on spontaneity in the midst of each other's busy schedules or whether you want to schedule lunch together once a week. Maybe you both want to start a new hobby together, join a winter league basketball team at the Y together, or commit to sharing a ministry project at your church.

From my experience, men like to know the rules of engagement, to know what to expect and how to relate. Is it okay if I call you anytime I need to? Can I call up and shoot the breeze when I'm bored and lonely or only call if there's an imminent crisis? Can I just drop by and help myself to what's in your refrigerator? What level of intimacy are we talking about here, what level of the pyramid? Will we keep it business-related or move beyond to a deeper personal realm? These questions must be addressed, my brothers, if we are to establish a worthy foundation for substantial exchanges in which both parties are to grow and flourish. Otherwise, the tenuous bonds begin to wither and crumble at the first disappointment or uncertainty about where things stand between you. The climate of friendship must be nurtured and nourished by clear communication and an understanding of the shared goals.

This understanding must include permission to confront and to challenge, to say the hard things that must be said from time to time. If you only have a cheerleader in your friend, then you will not be forced to face the flaws in your own character that need addressing. One of the greatest gifts in any true covenant friendship is that you have someone who won't let you get away with dodging constructive criticism or avoiding needed improvements.

I have a very good friend who is in the same line of work as I am. Though people have often tried to pit one against the other, we have never allowed it to happen. Both he and I have a fairly good amount of testosterone and maybe a dash of ego too. However, we know how to control that competitive edge and not allow it to destroy our friendship. Instead, we build each other up by offering advice and constructive criticism. We may not always like to hear what the other has to say, but we both trust that the counsel is based on experience and knowledge, and we always have each other's best interest at heart.

Take a moment and count the men in your life who have the authority and platform, the courage and strength to say hard things to you because they care for you and your growth. These are essential if you are to become the full man living a balanced life that God has created you to be.

TEAM BUILDING

As you begin assessing the relationships presently in your network, and wondering where each one may belong, I encourage you to do two things. First, I think it's helpful to begin diagramming your own pyramid of friends in order to gain a sense of perspective. And you don't have to have all the levels filled or evaluated. Leave room for growth as you glimpse an overview of where you are at this present time. But after finishing this chapter, I challenge you to sketch out your own pyramid and jot down the names of your relationships at each level. You can categorize or generalize the Five Thousand in the bottom layer who feed off of your contributions. Then jot down those who come to mind in the realm of the Seventy. Then the Nine who are closer and more of insiders to your private endeavors and goals. Then the pair near the top. Then the one.

Depending on where you are in life, there may be some empty slots at the top of your pyramid. Or perhaps you already have a best friend and a couple of homeys that you hang with. Then give thanks, my brother, and think about how you can pour into and receive from these men who are so instrumental in your life. But for most of us, I'm guessing that there's still room at the top and a certain amount of uncertainty regarding who should be the one, as well as the other couple of close confidants. In fact, many men often ask me at ministry conferences and in private counseling, "What should I look for in a best friend? What's most important in this covenant friendship?"

While numerous characteristics and dynamics factor in to who you want to be your Jonathan, I believe it's helpful to keep one primary trait in mind. Like the chemistry in your marriage, the relational dynamic between you and your soul brother should be one of a complementary nature. This doesn't mean you're complete opposites, but it does mean that you appreciate the differences even as you share like-minded areas of interest or lifestyle. You should each be able to understand where the other one is coming from in order to appreciate the distinctions between you. Most important of all, you must know what the other one needs in the friendship and be able to supply it naturally and in a way that feels comfortable and enjoyable. Your needs should mesh with what your friend enjoys giving. And what you enjoy giving to him should intersect with what he needs in the relationship. If there's not this sense of reciprocal gratification, then the friendship becomes rooted in obligation and degenerates into one more drain in each of your lives. Keep this in mind when considering whom you want to be "the one."

Perhaps your friend tends to be melancholy and battles with his mood swings and pessimistic outlook. Unless you are a comedic type person who enjoys cheering up your friend and can roll with the punches of his up-and-down nature, then it may be hard to forge a brotherhood of the soul between you. Or maybe you know that you can't handle having one more thing scheduled in your appointment calendar and you long for spontaneity and the liberation of dropping your briefcase, taking off your suit jacket, loosening your tie, and joining the pickup game around the court in the park. After days or maybe weeks of not communicating because of your busy schedule, you want the freedom to pickup the phone, dial your friend, and tell him you're picking him up in a half hour. Obviously, if he's as busy and his schedule as regimented as yours, then this may not work. He must be a flexible, easygoing person in order to enjoy your gift of spontaneity. It's important to know the similar areas that you share as well as the areas that allow you to surprise and enjoy each other.

When a candidate runs for the highest office in the nation, he chooses someone whose strength will complement his limitations and thereby create a sense of wholeness through their collaborative covenant for leadership. While many people remember how great a leader JFK was, they might not know that he was greatly enhanced by his vice president, Lyndon Johnson, and others on his staff, such as his brother Robert Kennedy, who served as Attorney General. And what would Nelson Mandela be without the support of South African Vice President Thabo Mbeki? This teamwork is what made athletes like Joe Montana and Jerry Rice sizzle on the football field. I dare say that Michael Jordan was made better on the court by his associate Scottie Pippen. In the same way that Time and Warner merged for the betterment of both institutions, friendships are life mergers for the enhancement of both parties. There is no question that my life is made fuller by my friends and confidants. Many times I would have collapsed at hard junctures in my life if it hadn't been for someone in the wings saying, "Man, I know you can make it through this—just don't give up!" From encouragement to just allowing me to have an "off duty" moment, I was able to stand the glare of the light by the shade of a friend.

You cover and complement each other in this way. One of you may rely more on strategy while the other is more seat-of-the-pants. One's the comedian with the funny lines, and the other's the straight man setting him up. Perhaps one of you may be more outgoing, more aggressive, more of a natural leader who takes charge. The other one of you may be more thoughtful, more introspective, more indecisive, more inclined to loyally support those whom you trust.

In short, relationship needs must be based on compatibility. My best friend and I are totally different, but he needs me for who I am and I need him for what he brings to the relationship. I think that is what makes the friendship work. While I will admit it took me a while to accept the fact that he doesn't always respond like I would to any given situation, I learned to understand him and allow him to be different from me without trying to evangelize him into being like me. The most amazing thing was that learning how to be a better friend helped me to be a better husband and increased my skills at understanding and communication. Warning: When there is an emotional attachment, there may be a few bumps along the way! He and I had a few knock-down-drag-outs in getting to that place of comfort with each other.

As you think through your pyramid and the kind of friend you want at the top, don't be afraid to sever present relationships that aren't working. You need not make a lengthy explanation or justification, depending on the level and depth of it, but you must commit to clearing out the fake friends in your life and cultivating the ones who can take root and provide your soul nourishment by what you receive as well as give. Making a soul friend takes time, and this is all the more reason why you don't have time to waste on superficial relationships that are dead-ending and draining.

So clear a new path for yourself and those men with whom you

INCREASING YOUR RANGE OF MOTION——FOR HIM

Who do you wish were your Jonathan? What are you doing to cultivate this relationship?

Who is in your inner circle of closest friends? Do you need to add to or subtract from this group?

Write out a list of associates who are in your group of Nine. How would these men describe their relationship to you?

Which of your friends are your peers and truly challenge and supplement you rather than just benefit from you? Which friends belong higher on your pyramid and which ones belong among the Seventy?

INCREASING YOUR RANGE OF MOTION——FOR HER

Does your man have a best friend? If so, how does this friendship improve the quality of his relationship with you? If not, how do you think this type of friendship could benefit the both of you?

Who is in the inner circle of your husband's life? Who does he need to move farther down the pyramid? Who does he need to risk more with?

What do you value most about your man's friends?

would like to relate to in lifelong bonds of friendship. Don't be afraid to take risks, to acknowledge and name what you're truly looking for in a brother, and to seek him out. This relationship is every bit as important as your marriage, your relationship with your children, and with yourself. If you are to grow and flourish, then you need a brother on the journey at your shoulder. Let your heart awaken to this natural desire and take the steps to make it happen. As you see your pyramid fill and solidify, you'll experience a renewed sense of what it means to love others and be loved, to know your purpose and pursue it, and to be at peace with yourself.

Finally, my brother, remember that real men are not intimidated by each other. They compliment without competing, they support without superceding, and when they arrive at the place of their predestined dreams, they are connected, joined at the hip, and anchored by the covenant that was established through the trials of life. This is "the one," the inner circle and the family who knows *you*, not just your stats or degrees or accomplishments.

You need a strong brother whose eyes are dancing with pride and admiration when you succeed, a confidant who knows your weaknesses but keeps them private. He is as happy to see you win as he is to see himself be victorious. If he has shared your sorrows and has known you through them, then it is only right that he share your successes. Go ahead, love somebody unselfishly and unconditionally. They may just love you back! Jesus taught men this by saying, "By this shall all men know that you are my disciples, that you have loved one another."

Part Five

A MAN'S
RELATIONSHIP
WITH HIS WOMAN

"If Americans can be divorced for incompatibility of temper I cannot conceive why they are not all divorced. I have known many happy marriages, but never a compatible one."
—G. K. CHESTERTON

"The unblemished ideal exists only in happily-ever-after fairy tales. Ruth likes to say, if two people agree on everything, one of them is unnecessary. The sooner we accept that as a fact of life, the better we will be able to adjust to each other and enjoy togetherness. Happily incompatible people is a good adjustment."
—BILLY GRAHAM

- *In 2000, there were over 21 million divorces in the United States.*
- *People between the ages of twenty-five and thirty-nine make up 60 percent of all divorces.*
- *More than half of all new marriages will end in divorce. This includes couples who are Christian and crosses most demographic and economic categories.*

NINE

———◆———

BALANCING THE POWER
OF LOVE

The cure for love is marriage, and the cure for marriage is love again.
—UNKNOWN

I don't know what it is about the evening air that so profoundly affects the emotions of the soul. The weeping in the night that David mentions in the Psalms reflects the intensity of our feelings bubbling up over the brim of our hard day's work. As darkness descends, we do away with all pretense and have time to meditate and reflect on the day that has passed. Nighttime often makes people more honest about their needs as well. Loneliness, ignored all day, camouflaged in business clothing, is now stripped naked and clamors for some kind of connection. Something about the night intensifies the struggles we have and forces us to take off our masks and face who we really are inside. In the night, men who are distinguished and well-groomed, professional and staid, surf the Net like wild predators, suggesting things in the anonymity of the Internet that they would never mention when morning light breaks through their window panes. Like vampires seeking the blood of new victims, these desperate creatures feel a longing in their souls that can only be satiated by human connection, no matter how aloof or indiscreet.

Marriage also changes flavor at night. Men, and women too, expose themselves in a way that they would never dare do during the day. People who were busy all day find solace and comfort in each other's arms, moving into each other's presence in some special rhythm attained when you experience what I call "sleeping chemistry." I am not talking about sex. No, this special nocturnal dynamic occurs through the dance of the sleepers who express themselves by cuddling and snuggling throughout the night. To me there is nothing as intimate as purely sleeping with someone. Please allow me to repeat that I don't mean the activity of sex; obviously, that is intimate, but sleeping, tossing, turning, rolling over, and snuggling often express and meet our needs in a deeper, more loving way. Sadly, love loses some of its language and reduces its vocabulary when couples only join together for sex. Once finished, they divide and never touch, speak of it, or savor who they are outside of this five-minute—oops, sorry fellows, I mean forty-five-minute—passionate embrace. Perhaps if I illustrate this desire as I experienced it recently during my own dark night of the soul, it will clarify this notion of sleep intimacy for you.

It was late into the night when I awoke. I'm not sure of the time, but my heart was beating like a conga drum. Was it a bad dream that had awakened me? I yawned and stretched the length of the bed and decided to roll over into the warm, soft flesh of my wife, who I knew was lying next to me. I moved gradually, not wanting to wake her; I simply wanted to absorb her warmth and touch. My unconscious plan was to nestle myself in her side and fall back to sleep, content in her embrace. However, my plan was foiled as I realized that my wife had somehow become intertwined in the sheets. I was able to touch her, but the sheet was somehow lodged between us. Yes, we were together, but the real joy of flesh against flesh was arrested by what might have been one of those computerized blocks that simply reads "ACCESS DENIED!" in big red letters.

As I emitted a quiet sigh, I became a bit annoyed. This 100 percent cotton, super-thread-count sheet was thin as paper but tough as a female warden. I knew that if I pulled and untangled and twisted the sheet away, I'd wake up Serita and appear like some pervert trying to take advantage of a sleeping woman when all I really wanted was the comfort that comes from sleeping with someone whose inner warmth is a sedative for the soul. I mean, can't a brother get a little hug?

My wife lay sleeping peacefully, unaware that there was a slight barrier between us, oblivious to my decision both to turn toward her and then to turn away. She slept through it all and never knew my thoughts in the middle of that night. Since we were not as connected as I would have liked for us to have been, I rolled back over to the east and left her facing west. She never once suspected nor realized that the dark enticed me, my need of her compelled me, and my love for her invited me. She might never know that a man shows himself more in the dark than he will in the day. She might never know that I reached for her in a way that words will not describe. And she was oblivious to the fact that something for which neither of us was fully responsible had isolated us. A little thin sheet had crept between us, and as is often the case, it was the little things that constrained me. All I knew was that we failed to connect, and without that connection, marriage is one long and exhausting night. It left me with insomnia in my soul!

I realized the next morning that a sheet is not really a major problem in a marriage, but it serves as a metaphor for so many more barriers that threaten to disconnect the intimacy we crave in our relationship with our spouse. I think it is important to note that often it is the little things that destroy a relationship. Most people end up in divorce court trying to figure out how they got there. It isn't always the big issues that assassinate love and deny the connection that we all seek. Instead, it is often the little things that come between us, and no one is really sure how these obstructions, these sheets, got so tangled up and we ended up partitioned and not at all as together as we used to be. So often we grope out in the dark anguish of our aloneness, hoping to connect with our companion, seeking company for the soul only to be blocked by crossed communication, misappropriated anger, or the essential but oh-so-mundane matters of day-to-day living when you have a home to up-keep, a business to run, and a family to tend to. Too often our relationship is severely strained, and as hard as we try to connect, something or another, or we ourselves, keeps us from touching when we need it most.

Although there are numerous sheets of separation that will cling to each of you and seek to divide your relationship over time, perhaps the three most potent are power, money, and sex, what I like to call marriage's PMS. Just as a woman's monthly cycle can produce extreme discomfort, agitation, and irritability, so too can this other PMS cramp the healthy function of the marriage relationship.

Too often I fear that these three topics are not being addressed by the Church, or if they are, they are diluted and sanitized. In our churches, power in the marriage is often handled by mishandling a few key Scripture verses about submission and female roles. Rarely is there an equal emphasis on the male role and the husband's submission to his wife. When finances are brought up, it's all very pious—give to the Church, pay your bills on time, and be frugal even as you delight in what the Lord has provided. There's usually not a discussion about the power of debt to suck the life out of a couple's mismatched money goals, about one partner's workaholism and greed, about another partner's shopping addiction and inability to budget. And sexuality, well, in marriage that's supposed to take care of itself, right? All those troubles and temptations from when you were both single have suddenly evaporated. As we all know, this is not the case, my friend.

So as we investigate the dynamics between a man and his woman, I'd like us to use these three topics as stepping stones to navigate this most crucial relationship. And the first one to tackle as we peel back the sheets and nudge you over toward a closer connection with your wife is finding a balance in the power of love and a power in the balance of love.

LOVE TRIANGLE

So often I hear couples talk about how in most relationships there's one partner who needs the other partner more, and this person is the one who sacrifices their power to keep the other one happy. Obviously, this promotes an unhealthy, unbalanced, lopsided relationship that will only foster bitterness, resentment, and unbridled distrust between man and wife. I believe that in order to strike a balance regarding the power in a relationship, each person must recognize the variety of his or her needs as well as the needs of their partner. It's not just one need but the complex layers of need—each of you has different needs that the other can touch like no one else. It is vital that you look to your relationship as a banquet to feed both of you; one cannot gorge him- or herself while the other goes hungry.

But at times, our appetite for love becomes so ravenous that we lose sight of nourishing the other half of our dinner party. I believe that one of the reasons we fail to notice our spouse's needs is because sometimes we fail to notice who our spouse is. What am I talking about? Well, it is so easy to stop seeing the person you said "I do" to and only see the roles that she fills—the housekeeper, the mother, the chef, the temptress, and the one who keeps your appointments straight and your life running in order. What happened to the woman you fell in love with? Remember her sense of humor, her insight, how her smile made your heart melt? When was the last time you really looked at her? Stared into her eyes to see her heart? All too often, we get caught up in life and become so busy that we just pass each other by without really seeing who it is we're living with.

When a man sees his wife more as a mother than a lover, intimacy may be sacrificed. It is important for both him and his wife to remain as sensual and affectionate as possible. Even though mounting responsibilities come with the addition of children, both partners should want to love and live as they did before the demands of life restricted the connection and got tangled between them. If he sees her more as a roommate, a service giver, a mother, or a church woman rather than a wife, it may make him feel alone and lacking in fulfillment. Women must remember that they are not just mothers, choir members, or evangelists. She may be an office manager at work, but when she is alone with her husband, a wise woman should be able to shed the restrictions of who she is publicly and reconnect with him on the basis of who she is personally and who he is to her.

Some men fail to see or perceive their wives because they only see the image they have of her—images created by our past sexual and relational experiences that now impact our current expectations. Most men bring multiple previous experiences into their marriage. Your mind is like a sponge, and it has been soaked full of experiences that become the point of reference by which you define what you are expecting from the love you now have with her. These incidents may have occurred in previous marriages, past lives before Christ, or weak moments of lustful indulgence. They may be scenes you saw in a movie or a shot from a magazine. Or they may be in the form of messages we received from our parents or friends about what a wife should be. These expectations can be positive or negative, but either way, they are dangerous to the joint mission you should have with her. Your marriage is far too personal and private to still be picking up unwanted frequencies from past impulses, memories, and persons who should no longer have an influence on you.

We sometimes try to force all of the images we have of women onto the woman we're with now. But in order to come to a whole relationship, a balanced and strong union, we must exorcise these expectations and embrace the person who shares our bed. Friend, you do not have the power to make her anything but what she is. So when we begin to talk about power, let's start with having the power to remove all the sheets that you put in the way of your true intimate desire to bond with this woman. I know you want me to discuss all those sheets that she places in the way—perhaps her infatuation with the children, or maybe it's her insatiable need to climb the corporate ladder—that leaves you feeling ignored and underappreciated. Or maybe it's her connection with her mother that is so strong that you think you really married both of them. These issues deserve to be discussed, but I won't do them now. Instead, let's talk about all that you, my brother, bring in between the two of you that blocks the warmth of a loving relationship.

THERE'S SOMEONE THERE, BUT NO ONE IS HOME

Adam, where art thou? That is the question God asked the first man, and it remains the question of interest today. You know, most of us come home physically but not mentally and emotionally. Too often, many of us find it easier to disconnect and only appear to be present. We are not really engaged with our wife and family. We send a body double who looks like us, a stunt man, who makes the moves we should be making, while we remain detached for various reasons. Many men find it hard to remain attached emotionally. It costs us so much to continue to pour into what seems like an endless abyss of insecurity in our wives. We weary of reassuring her while secretly needing a bit of reassuring ourselves. It's too frightening to bare our souls, afraid we might get hit with a barrage of accusations, demands, or reprimands when we're at our most vulnerable. So eventually, we just stop participating emotionally. Oh, we still show up for work, punch the time clock, make love, take out the trash, and discuss the checking account, but it's like we're watching ourselves on TV, not really connecting with our own lives.

Sometimes this disconnect happens because you have been beaten down verbally and are tired of the constant "we need to talk." Or you've made a mistake in your past for which forgiveness has been denied so long that you have ceased to seek it and have become an inmate to a marriage that exists only to claim tax deductions, group discounts on travel, and a little convenient sex, but not much more. Your marriage has become a mere shadow of the promise it once offered. Sometimes you wonder if it is even worth continuing on.

> *Both partners in a marriage have needs; feed each other well and you'll both be satisfied.*

But you have the power within yourself to overcome the icy environment that you occasionally fantasize about leaving. You can bring your marriage back to the splendor it once was. You can have a relationship that is mutually fulfilling and love-giving. You just have to work a little at it. Men, repeat after me: I will not give up or give in and allow myself to be defeated until I have done everything I can to see God's grace materialize in my house. Amen.

Now let me tell you about Danny. A strong, resourceful black man, Danny is a hard-working person. He is quiet and young and vibrant. His work in the sawmills isn't glamorous, but he works hard and is fairly well compensated. He is a thirty-something, somewhat muscular guy who has rough hands and a tender heart that he works feverishly hard to hide from his brothers, who drink machismo Kool-Aid for lunch.

Danny is a Christian, loves the Lord, and has a nice family including five children and a bright wife, who is also a born-again believer. She works hard, is well compensated, more educated than Danny, and can be a bit driven and ambitious. Danny came to me because he and Ellen were having trouble connecting emotionally. She has a scarred childhood and works hard to hide her brokenness by being an overachiever at work. Sadly, she is an underachiever at home. She doesn't take care of the house, makes love only when she feels it is needed, seldom is playful, and borders on being a hypochondriac. Still, Danny loves her. He realizes that he has his own issues, has made some mistakes along the way, and is trying to make the marriage productive.

At the time I started counseling him, she was controlling him. She is more verbal and has a temper like a tornado locked in a grocery store, and he usually lapses into stony silence. What Ellen didn't realize is that outtalking a man doesn't equate to changing him. Ellen was a warden type because her mother before her was a verbal police officer handing out tickets to anyone who broke a rule. This was Ellen's idea of love. She loved Danny and did not want to lose him, but she was gradually pushing him away into a brooding, unhappy silence. The sad part of all this is that she had no idea what pain she was causing her husband.

While Ellen has an in-your-face personality and looks to confront the issues, Danny tends to retreat, opting to stay out with the boys instead of going home to face Ellen's wrath. In fact, he has been spending more time at the gym and less time at home. There were tears in his eyes when he told me, "Bishop, I can never be the husband Ellen wants me to be, so why should I bother trying?"

I began speaking to Danny about the power of speaking up. Oddly, many men will speak up and even fight other men when attacked, but they become sullen when they are underappreciated, unhappy, or otherwise attacked by the female in their lives. It's as if they carried over their childhood lesson of being seen and not heard. But they are grown now and need to verbalize their needs. Silence is not golden in a relationship.

If you do not learn to speak up, when you finally do speak you will either do it as you are storming out the door or, worse still, by raging into a temper tantrum, a manifestation of the child in you acting out of frustration because you aren't able to get control of life and love.

But you do have the power to change things, sir, and I am going to share with you the advice I gave Danny—a brief action plan of what you can do to add more value into your life at home. Keep reading.

Silence of the Lambs. Many of you probably recall the chilling film from a number of years ago in which the young woman detective is searching for a serial killer. She recalled hearing the lambs bleating in the area where she was raised as a child, and while at the time she longed for them to stop, now their silence signals tragedy, the permanent silence that comes with loss. If you are to add value to your relationship with your wife, then you must learn to communicate effectively and honestly. There are numerous books, conferences, and videos on the differences in the ways men and women use language—from Mars and Venus to love languages and everything in between. While these are beneficial and insightful, communication basically comes down to the willingness of both parties to maintain an ongoing conversation. This exchange must include expression of needs and desires, room for difficult emotions such as anger or frustration, and an attitude of loving compromise. Men, if you retreat into silence, then you're going to lose your voice and slaughter your marriage. Speak up, even if it means writing your wife a letter or sending her an email to kick off the conversation.

Exercise the power to change. Change in a relationship is not only essential but inevitable. Whether you like it or not, your wife, your marriage, and you yourself are all in a constant state of flux. The trick is being deliberate in the directions you want to change in. You must learn to grow together or else your hearts will find outside interests and passions to pursue and you'll lose sight of each other. Think about the kind of relationship you want to have and consider what action, decision, or conversation you could have today that would move you in this direction.

Change your priorities. Many men say that their wives and families are important to them, but that's not always what their actions reveal. If you are sincere in wanting to improve your marriage and be a better husband, then I encourage you to look at your calendar for this month or even this week. When I was in school, certain teachers would tell us that we needed to be spending at least two hours on homework for every hour of being in class. Well, our priorities for home are the same way, I believe. For every outside obligation or commitment or indulgence, is there comparable time and deliberate attention given to spending time with your wife or children? Many men go to the gym religiously but never have a regular date or time away with their wives. They assume the relationship will always be there, by default, until one day she's gone. Make your priorities match your commitments.

Acknowledge you're a work in progress. This seems so simple and obvious, but I can't tell you how many men walk around so uptight because they feel like everyone, especially their wives, expects them to be perfect and have their lives all together. Usually God provides ample reminders of our frailty, fragility, and fault lines on any given day to keep us humble. Instead of fueling our inferiority and insecurity, we must remain accepting of ourselves as His work in progress. I encourage you to keep track of your changes and areas of growth as well as targets and goals for who and where you'd like to be. Remind your spouse that you know she is a work in progress as well by not expecting perfection from her. Show grace and embrace the grace that is given.

POWER TO COMMIT

Quiet as we keep it, men want love as much as women. However, it is often difficult for some men to commit to relationships and all the responsibility that is involved in "being there" for someone else. These men often do well with the initiation but have difficulty following through with the weight of the sustained relationships.

You might think I'm just talking about a man who is trying to figure out why he has not been able to successfully make the commitment though he is deeply attracted to a woman whom he loves. But I'm also talking to married men. "Why would he talk about the power to commit to married men? If we're married, haven't we already committed?" Nope, not necessarily. You see, I have encountered many men who have exchanged the nuptial vows, jumped the broom, and walked through a shower of rice on their way to the intoxicating honeymoon but have failed to make a commitment. They are legally, spiritually, and physically married. It is the emotional marriage that doesn't seem to take place for them. They are AWOL emotionally and send mixed signals that confuse women and destroy families. These men are not mean-spirited and can be quite loving at times. They can offer affection and support when they deem it appropriate—Valentine's Day, birthdays, anniversaries—but when faced with day-to-day expectations and the hard work of building equity between them and their wives, they fall into a quicksand of excuses and become disgruntled, or disappear like Houdini, surfacing occasionally but never attaining prolonged, sustained commitment. They run their marriage like it was an affair, a great date, or a cruise that has no destination. They are a woman's worst nightmare, either disappointing her or hurting her.

The Bible says, "For this cause shall a man leave his mother and father and take unto him a wife" (Genesis 2:24). He has done all of that without too much trouble. But after the honeymoon is over and the process of building intimacy and strength in the fabric of the relationship begins, he falters with the second half of the Scripture. It says, "And they shall cleave together and become one flesh." This part seems to be difficult for him. He fails miserably and doesn't seem to be able to find a good reason to justify his fear, his phobia of commitment. Steven Carter and Julia Sokol say in their book *Getting to Commitment* that these persons, whether male or female, "typically don't let these ties develop naturally. More often than not, they are more connected to their fantasies than they are to another real living human being." Perhaps the Psalmist David, who is obviously a deeply spiritual man, a great leader, still has trouble connecting emotionally with a woman most of his life for this reason. He has a series of failed attempts though he has much to offer, is obviously extremely sexual, enters into multiple affairs, is sensitive in many ways, and is successful and, according to Scripture, quite attractive. David does well with friendships with men, specifically with Jonathan. Perhaps it is because the friendship doesn't have the deeper responsibility of being a brook for someone else's need, sexually, emotionally, and spiritually. David is relieved by Jonathan's love but still seems to have difficulty making that richer, more significant relationship with his wife, or I should say wives. I suspect that Jonathan was safe for him and he didn't feel as vulnerable. "Your love to me was wonderful, surpassing the love of women" (2 Samuel 1:26).

Most men who are commitment-phobic appeal to women like a movie promotional. They are exciting, and the brief sound bite that women see from them is riveting and gripping. It is when she buys into the commercial and takes on the movie that she realizes the trailer was better than the film itself. He is simply not there. Like a bad movie, all the components of a good movie are present, but something is missing, even if she can't initially put her finger on what it is. She feels guilty for not being happy. She is confused because all the ingredients are there for romance and bliss. "Why doesn't this work?" she wonders. Sadly, she has often invested much of her time and strength before she can figure out that, much like a bad movie, his advertisement is better than the product purchased. When it comes to establishing a loving relationship, he is all thumbs, and the love falls to the floor and both of them are disappointed. Not just her, but him too. He is painfully aware that he can't do it—he wants to, but he just can't seem to "go there" when it comes to love. These men are emotionally impotent and need Viagra for the heart. He simply finds it too difficult to remain as connected as he starts and wilts under the pressure of a normal love life.

Love is much like Black Gospel music. In gospel music the singer sings a line and the choir responds. The lyrics are accomplished through a call-and-response session. In relationships, it is difficult when one of you is making the call and the other is not responding. She often is giving the call, and he finds it almost impossible to make the appropriate response. In fact, her open, unbridled love often spooks him and leaves him intimidated inside. He hears her calling, but he has pushed the Do Not Disturb button. Ultimately, in spite of her anxiety and willingness to ignore the obvious, she soon realizes that she is in the relationship alone. His lights may be on, but he is not at home.

Fellows, I find that the easy part is connecting physically. Sex often is a torrent of deep, rich, satisfying experiences for many of us. The honeymoon is what so many of us do well. It's the followup that kills many men. It has been said that the devil is in the details. If that is so, then there is a legion of devils in a marriage. You see, it is after the thrill

> *You can't just go through the motions. . . . You need to express your emotions.*

subsides that real relationship skills are tested. The "next level" of love has to go beyond the courtship into the investment and rewards, the losses and returns that make marriage a lifelong process. Many men have trouble investing and not seeing immediate gain, or they only give partially, never fully investing. These men may be great givers; they come bearing what is easiest for them to give. Often they provide incredibly well, but when questioned about love, they show receipts of their purchases in lieu of investment of time and tenderness. This man is a cash register jammed full of one-hundred-dollar excuses, but, unfortunately, he has no nurturing, no affection, and in essence no groceries on his shelves. They give presents as a way of offering peace for their obvious inability to attach personally and emotionally.

If this sounds like who you are, then it is time for you to take that first deep and abiding look within and ask God for the grace to confront your be-at-home phobia and for patience with yourself and with others. Showing your scars and talking honestly about them with your wife may be the second step, but the first one is confessing to God. God has not given you the spirit of fear. There is no doubt that your fear is not from Him, although something catalyzed the fear in you. What was it? And how are you going to overcome this thief that is robbing you of the great and deep satisfaction that comes from a heart that has made a positive connection and can find peace and security at home?

If what I have described doesn't at all sound like you but may explain why your wife seems so aloof to you though initially she was passionate and vibrant, then maybe you should have a talk. Men are not the only ones who find it difficult to maintain the power of emotional commitment. Carter and Sokol also say, in their book *He's Scared, She's Scared*, "In our personal lives, too often we find ourselves creating distance between ourselves and our partners. We construct extraordinary barriers and create complicated situations so that we will never be truly vulnerable. To commit ourselves to the act of loving means that we are committing ourselves to a potentially risky situation in which our tender heart might be hurt." Fears about commitment are common to both sexes. This isn't just a male problem. I only handle it as such because this is a book about men. Still, I have seen countless men whose hearts are aching from being involved with a woman who suffers from what Carter and Sokol call "commitmentphobia."

Thank God that no matter who is showing the symptoms, there is a cure. But God can't heal what neither of you will confront. Confront it and let God begin to open you up and heal you from the thief that is robbing you of the love you so badly need and are so unable to receive. Move that sheet and cuddle up closer to make the connection.

POWER PACK

As you proceed in exercising your ability to improve your relationship, the first thing you must keep in mind is that you have the power. God created you with the power. Power is mentioned in Scripture both as authority and as force. All of us have it as believers. Many men have been so repressed by circumstances, liabilities, and adversities that they lack confidence in their ability to make a difference. Since most of us have not been born to be rulers, we tend to abuse power when given us because it is unfamiliar and foreign. I believe that God is a God who empowers us, and being a believer gives me an authority that is significant. Being a man means that I also have authority, God-given authority, in my house and in the world around me. He created us with innate power that enables us to rule and to reign in positions of strength and significance.

Several years ago I developed a conference called ManPower. These Christian-oriented, gender-specific meetings were designed to encourage men to appreciate who they were created to be in Christ. When we are not emasculated by sin and social systems that deteriorate our impact, we can easily become men of influence and affluence who still possess a sense of spirituality. Our focus began with the grassroots emphasis of empowering men who may not fully recognize that their ability supercedes their adversity as they grow to become giants for God. I cannot tell you how desperately we need to see men in our community who have the facts, the force, and the discipline to exercise the dominion that God gave us. Too often the man with the dominion has a hidden agenda and something to prove that hinders his ability to lead and to serve.

This is no small task, as many men have only defined power in terms of sexuality, money, or career. These things without God are merely images of success but may not give the real power that transforms the desperate need many men experience to find significance in life, particularly as he grows older. David really needed to find his own significance, and his struggle shows in his inability to master personal relationships. One cannot have an enriched marriage when it is funded by an emotionally and spiritually bankrupt man.

Paul says that he can do all things through Christ who strengthens him. Now that is power. The "all things" kind of power is more than just "church things." He said *all* things. Simply, that means that if it is a thing, you can do it. If it is a mountain, you can move it. If it is a wall, you can scale it. Filled with force and girded with capabilities, you are without question the man for the job.

The challenge is in advising men that they have the power, and then training them not to abuse that power in their personal relationships. You see, power without temperance leads to tyranny and abuse. Some women have recoiled from the message of the man being the head of the house because they see headship as abusive to them. This is not true. If a man knows who he is and *whose* he is, then his strength is a complement to his wife and not a liability. When a married man knows he has the power, he must then grapple with sharing this power with the one he loves while maintaining his masculinity. This brings me to the importance of mutual submission.

We must remember that power is shared between man and wife. This is the missing link in the submission message. The Scriptures are clear that the man is the head of the house. Power comes from God (the powers that be are ordained by Him), and He shares His power with man in creation and in the development of the family. The Word states clearly that the man is the head. It does not say, however, that he is superior to women. This order is to give structure in marriage, not the dominance of one gender over the other. Think of men working as soldiers in service. They are all created equal, but each one has different rank and assignments. This is not done to degrade but to give some semblance of order. The same is true in our marriage. The man is clearly the head, but as a friend of mine so aptly says, "If we're the head, then the woman is the neck! How can the head turn effectively without an agreement with the neck?"

You see, the marriage relationship is a dance between two lovers, with a variety of positions, exchanges, and movements within the commitment of a lifetime partnership. The key to navigating the many dances that life requires is hearing the same rhythm, being in harmony so that a syncopated synchronization flows out of your partnership. Whether it's buying a house and allowing the one who is more gifted in business dealings to lead the negotiation process, handling the kids and working out a strategy for relating to them together, or navigating between the sheets, the key is to share the same rhythm. The relationship doesn't work when you're each hearing a different rhythm, out of step, clumsily maneuvering around each other, over each other's feet, and running into each other. When you're not operating at the same tempo, then your dance of harmony becomes an awkward blast of noise.

LOVE'S LABOR LOST

To keep the melody flowing sweetly and your steps in sync in a marriage, the partners must divide up the responsibilities so that neither one has to feel like they must do everything. While the work is still sweat-inducing, brain-taxing, and muscle-tiring, its burden is lost when love divides it. Allowing each partner to excel in his or her area of expertise and natural inclination makes for a closer dance of delighting in and needing each other. This is especially important for men to embrace, since we often feel cultural pressure to be competent in all areas. So, brother, let go and turn that woman loose at what she does well. If your wife handles money better than you, then be grateful and let her handle the finances. If she's more confrontational, or a better negotiator, or enjoys home repair, then give thanks and allow her giftedness to benefit your partnership. You must delegate chores and tasks according to individual strengths and abilities to ensure that you're not duplicating efforts. Just as in the bedroom, the man doesn't have to be on top. There's freedom of movement and enjoyment in trying different positions so that you are both mutually satisfied. As you might realize, posture doesn't necessarily control power. It doesn't make you any less of a man to say to her, "You are on top of this situation better than I would be. I really need your expertise about it. On the other hand, when it comes to another situation, I promise that I'll be on top of that one."

Sadly, we often allow ego to abort the joint mission we have together because we are insistent on doing things we don't do well. Working together is critical, admitting that each of you has strengths and weaknesses, so that you can divvy up the responsibilities and create an incredible teamwork.

What can she count on you to do effectively? I find that in any relationship, a man has to know what he brings to the table in order to feel like he is an asset and not just an ornament. Hopefully, women reading this will help men who may not be as grounded as they would like to be by pointing out to him things that you think he does well. Many men have never had anyone who believed in them enough to tell them what they do well. Pointing out his power is important, especially when a woman has her own strengths. Maybe his power isn't in the size of his paycheck. Maybe you love him for the size of his heart. Maybe his power isn't in his ability to handle finances, but he is great at handling the kids. Whatever it is, a man is greatly benefited by a woman who can point out his power. I know that when my wife says that I do something well, it heightens my desire to do it. Too often women spend more time criticizing than they do encouraging. It is sad that some do not recognize the power of encouragement to the masculine soul. "The wise woman builds her house, but the foolish pulls it down with her hands" (Proverbs 14:1). A good woman is highly effective at pointing out strengths. This woman is a treasure to a man and serves as an incredible asset.

The same woman who is a relentless encourager of her son may not be nearly as committed to encouraging her husband. I think many women overlook that the first relationship a man generally has with a woman is with a mother. She is encouraging, comforting, and supportive. Many men still look for those attributes in a wife. Sadly, our society applauds these attributes in a mother but frowns on them in a wife. Realistically, all of us are continuing our lives with the opposite sex from a conversation that began with our parents and continues in one form or another in our marriage. Women, you have tremendous power in your tongue. Your words can make or break us as we open up and share with you in relationship.

Many men hate coming home because they have become convinced (often by the one who wants them to come home) that he doesn't do marriage well. A psychologist friend of mine often tells women that the behavior you reward is the behavior he will repeat. Simply stated, men gravitate to what they believe they do well.

Still, that doesn't mean that we men should run away from the challenge at home and toward the convenience of some extramarital affair if we're not being praised at home. When a man seeks affection from sources outside his marriage, what he's really doing is turning toward someone who applauds him. If you go there just to be applauded, then you will make many trips to these women who serve as nothing more than a great hotel or vacation site. But no matter how luxurious the hotel, it is still not your home. Too often that is what happens to men. We run to the sound of the clapping. We experience a great vacation in a quick relationship that only lasts a few months or years with someone new, rather than fixing the problems at home. We try to spend the rest of our lives living in hotels, but they were not designed for prolonged stays.

Or we give up. We just quit. It is easy for us to walk away. But if you want to stay, you have to learn how to encourage yourself if you are not blessed with a woman who knows how. What do you do when you need encouragement and you're not getting it at home like you should? Before you go out and get some surrogate encouragement from some illicit source, you may have to do what David did in a dark place in his own life. The Bible says that David "encouraged himself in the Lord."

So many women base their responses to their husband and their understanding of the dynamics of the relationship on what they observed from their own parents' marriage. For many African-American women, in our matriarchal culture, they view the way their mothers dominated their fathers and consequently vow to be more flexible, more responsive, and often more dependent on a man. In other households, where the mothers were controlled and dominated by their husbands, their daughters grow up and want to make sure that they are not run over like their mommas.

The key, of course, involves breaking out of this dominant-or-doormat mentality and seeing the many layers of interdependence that must be allowed to develop in a healthy marriage. Each must depend upon the other in mutual trust. When this is the case, submission virtually becomes a non-issue because both husband and wife serve and love each other with a devotion that is selfless and generous. This trust is so important. We see this reinforced in Proverbs 31:

> Who can find a virtuous wife?
> For her worth is far above rubies.
> The heart of her husband safely trusts her;
> So he will have no lack of gain.
> (vv. 10–11)

Can the man trust his wife enough to give up his macho façade and allow her to see his weaknesses, to view the chinks in his armor, the dings in his sword, and still respect and love him? David couldn't help but expose his dents and dings of character to Bathsheba, and she couldn't keep from noticing that the king whom she loved was capable of great deceit and hypocrisy. As they're forced to rely on each other through the shared scandal of their affair and commingled grief of losing their child, there's a new level of trust forged, an emotional vulnerability that cannot come cheaply or quickly.

PULL BACK THE SHEETS

Growing up, I observed my own parents' marriage as tempestuous and volatile at times, with undercurrents of tension that could erupt into verbal abuse and powerful resentments. As a result, I questioned whether or not I would ever be willing to subject myself to the risk of a similar dynamic by marrying. I loved children and longed for a partner and a family but didn't want the chronic tension and underlying animosity that often permeated the relationship between my mother and father. I didn't want to duplicate my parents' mistakes and shortcomings. So when I met my wife and committed myself in marriage to her, it was an incredibly emotional experience for me.

At the time I knew she was a wonderful gift from God and that I loved her. However, I was naive about what it meant to begin this new adventure of leaving my parents and cleaving to her. The Scripture says, "Therefore a man shall leave his father and mother and be joined to his wife, and they shall become one flesh" (Genesis 2:24). At first I thought this verse was just about sex, about the physical joining of the two bodies to become one flesh. However, gradually it dawned on me that this act of cleaving to my wife takes a lifetime and that it involves all dimensions of our relationship, not just the physical. Leaving your mother and father may mean not allowing your issues with their relationship to infiltrate your new life. Leaving and cleaving are critical to the union's success. Some men never resolve the struggle they had with their parents, and the wife pays the price for something that his mother or father did or didn't do.

> When a woman empowers her man, it helps him embody more of who he truly is.

It's the same kind of realization I had the morning after the fiasco with the sheet of separation coming between me and my wife and my desire for the simple intimacy of sleeping alongside each other's body. In both instances, I appreciated the truth of how often it's the little things that separate us. A sheet is thin and seems relatively insubstantial, yet it was enough to keep us apart and separate me from the closeness I wanted with my wife. We must not allow these little things to get in the way of intimacy. Men, be creative in finding ways to make time away from the kids and the household routines. Surprise her with a vacation or long weekend where it's just the two of you with no cell phones, no kids' requests, no floors waiting to be mopped or tables needing to be dusted. Pull back the sheets that are necessary but that nonetheless can hinder your intimacy.

INCREASING YOUR RANGE OF MOTION—FOR HIM

Which of the three issues of PMS—power, money, or sex—troubles you the most in your marriage?

How do your past relationships affect the way you relate to your wife? What issues from the past do you need to face so that you can move forward in the present?

What priorities need to change in order to improve your marriage? How do you need to change the way you spend your time?

What sheets need to be pulled back in order for the two of you to grow closer?

INCREASING YOUR RANGE OF MOTION—FOR HER

What do you see as the greatest obstacle to intimacy in your marriage?

What do you wish was different in the way you two communicate?

What do you wish you could change in yourself about the way you respond to your husband?

What do you believe will make your marriage stronger?

In light of this, the second thing that occurred to me the next morning was why didn't I simply unpeel the sheet and slide up next to my wife? I was afraid of being misunderstood or misperceived, or misappropriated. Sometimes men who will fight through anything in their career give up too easily on their personal life. It might be worth ripping through a sheet to reach the prize on the other side of the obstruction. Although I am not suggesting that you rip your sheets literally, I am saying that you have to work at getting through the little things that can come between you and your spouse. I had allowed something that was supposed to cover us both to come between us. Men, let's be real for a moment. Often we do not move the little things out of the way that we could to facilitate closeness with our wife. If there was a problem at work, then we would stay late to find a way to work it out. Yet many times we do not show the same tenacity at home that we do to build our career. I have challenged myself to be sure that I have lit a candle before I scream at the darkness. I know that there are challenges even in the best relationships, obstacles that require you taking the lead and moving them out of the way. I believe that we often wait for the woman to resolve issues at home while we resolve issues at work. But relationships require everyone working for the betterment of what we have together.

So often the shared responsibilities become one-sided and get in the way of true intimacy. If you don't want to imbalance the relationship, then you must find the rhythm of your needs and learn to dance and lead and, yes, every now and then even a strong man needs to be able to follow a woman's lead. Otherwise, you'll be left on the dance floor alone, tripping and stumbling to catch up with a partner who's no longer in your arms. My brother, don't let this happen—stop lying there sulking, stop threatening to go somewhere else, just pull back the sheets!

TEN

MONEY: FOR RICHER OR POORER

The problem with money is that it makes you do things you don't want to do.
—FROM THE MOVIE *Wall Street*

I often counsel and minister to many professional athletes and high-profile people. Many of these celebrities have prenuptial agreements to assess what's his and what's hers and how things should be distributed in the relationship, particularly if the marriage does not succeed. I'm sometimes surprised by the level of specific legal language used to detail and protect particular properties, automobiles, business ventures, and other status symbols. I think that if the two individuals put half as much effort into making their marriage work as their attorneys invested in their prenup, then the contract would be superfluous.

While I understand why such contracts may be necessary to protect one's assets, I find no template for such an agreement in Scripture. Indeed, I believe that such contracts may undermine the fundamental notion of a marriage as a partnership, a 50-50, 100-percent-from-both-parties relationship, where both assets and liabilities are all shared equally by the individuals. For richer or poorer, in sickness and in health, in good times and in bad times. This is the ultimate nuptial agreement, the vows exchanged at the time the commitment is honored before God and man. The couple agrees to share all parts of their lives together, yielding each other's individual interests, desires, hopes, fears, and dreams to the new entity of their union as they leave and cleave. It's an investment that requires maximum capital in order to yield a return larger than either partner is capable of producing by himself or herself. So much money is spent on the wedding, but the real expense comes afterward.

This partnership includes sharing both the debts incurred as well as the rewards of financial attainment, bearing together the sacrifices of success as well as the security and pleasure it can bring. In short, the checkbook now has two names on it! With few exceptions, most couples have at least one joint account that allows them both to deposit and withdraw funds. Many of the problems emerge when one does more depositing and the other does more withdrawing. But the dynamics of finances and managing the household, perhaps even sharing a business together, run much deeper than simply who works, who spends, and who signs the checks.

Consider this for a moment: Would you agree to form a corporation with another individual without a financial plan? Then why do so many men enter into marriage without ever discussing the fine points of financial freedom and frustration? For marriage is a covenant, ordained by God to reflect the relationship between Christ and the Church, including the resources shared between them. Handling money has the potential to unite a couple in closer harmony as they share their labor and enjoy a larger harvest than what one could accomplish alone. However, the love of money also has great power to undermine their intimacy as it draws them into separate pursuits and individual expenditures. Based upon what I continue to see firsthand and what I read in established studies, financial distress remains one of the greatest impediments in a marriage relationship and is often the leading cause of divorce. Let's examine some of the economic indicators that often divide a man and wife and see how they can be overcome.

JOINT ACCOUNTING

A handsome couple in their early thirties recently entered my office, each one looking a bit downcast and embarrassed. Obviously, I knew their marriage was in distress from the dynamic between them. You could tell something was going down just by the very different demeanor that each one possessed. Here was this strong, chiseled young man with his jaw clenched and his head bowed like he was about to receive his sentencing for a guilty verdict in a courtroom. His bride, on the other hand, might have been his polished, pedigreed, and pedicured attorney, a petite, focused young lady with impeccable grooming, a tight-lipped smile, and dead-set eyes. They each shook my hand, hers more forceful than his grip I might add, before sitting together on a sofa across from me.

Racing through my mind were the possible reasons they might possess such expressions in light of scheduling this meeting in the first place. As I made small talk about our church service the day before, about my own family and theirs, I tried to put them at ease even as I anticipated an extramarital affair coming to light, an addiction to pornography, or an emotional attachment to the workplace. Soon our chitchat took a serious turn, and Jackie confirmed my suspicions by saying, "Tyler has a problem." I nodded in understanding, encouraging either or both of them to continue. An awkward silence ensued as I searched to find the young man's eyes, but before he could speak up, his wife continued: "He has a problem with my job. He doesn't like the fact that I just got promoted for the third time in two years and that I now make more than twice what he makes."

As we tried to remove the shrapnel from the wounds that each party took in this marital skirmish, I was saddened but not surprised that such a positive and encouraging improvement in the workplace could cause such a negative and toxic effect in the homeplace. And Jackie and Tyler are not alone by any stretch of the imagination. I encounter dozens of couples with similar issues and read about many, many more. In fact, a recent *Newsweek* cover story focused on the plight of successful black women, ladies who are educated and achieving strides in the corporate world that their mothers never dreamed of. How could such wonderful news carry an edge that wounds their personal lives? The article goes on to focus on the widening gender gap between African American women and men, citing statistics that show 24 percent of black American women have risen to the professional management tier, while their black male counterparts have only increased 17 percent at this corporate level. These savvy sisters are also earning more than their male counterparts as well as other women, shattering the so-called glass ceiling with the agility and finesse of a jeweler cutting new facets into the face of a beautiful diamond.

And I certainly applaud these women with a standing ovation of commendation for their hard work, their bright minds, and innovative insight. However, whenever I sit before a couple like Jackie and Tyler, I realize that there is a downside, that such success doesn't come without a price, and that despite Jackie's opening statement, it's bigger than just "Tyler's problem." So many personal and financial dynamics intersect and often conflict with one another, becoming a labyrinth of frustration, jealousy, and competition between two partners who should be functioning as a team.

Certainly I'm not advocating that women should give up their jobs just because their man has a problem with her success. And I'm not suggesting that as a man with a successful wife that you should feel intimidated, inferior, or invalidated by her achievements. However, the financial realm in and of itself is already a hot button of conflict for most couples, so that when a new dynamic is introduced, the perilous path of financial health and unity suddenly becomes a minefield. In an abbreviated manner, here are the issues that I discussed with Jackie and Tyler in order to find a healthy balance between her success, Tyler's self-esteem, and the strength of their marriage.

FENCING LESSONS

One of the first crucial areas that we discussed involves what I call "fencing lessons." No, it's not about each one of them taking up a sword and brandishing it about like swashbucklers; it's all about knowing how to place fences around their jobs in order to keep the wild animals of workaholism, ubiquitous cell phone calls, and late-night reports from trampling the tender garden of their relationship. In a prior generation, it was typically the man who was career-driven, obsessed with promotion, committed to going the extra mile for his company. He would work late, travel frequently, and trust that his wife knew that he was sacrificing time out of the home in order to be an effective provider. While hard work does entail overtime and occasional seasons of sacrifice, too often this becomes the standard mode of operation.

> *Don't let your commitment to work impose on your commitment to each other.*

Now men are getting a taste of what it's like when their wives face the same kinds of demands on time, energy, and resources, which forces her to divide herself between the office and home. Based on the many couples, especially those in their twenties and thirties, who share this area of concern with me, I find that too often they schedule in every slot on their Palm Pilot calendars without making an appointment for the most important relationship in their lives. When I question these couples' scheduling strategy, they smile at me as if I'm old-fashioned, as if making a date with your spouse went out with bell-bottom pants and leisure suits. But I often point out that however twenty-first century, postmodern, Generation X or Y they may be, time is still time, a limited resource moving forward with or without our intentional use of it. I'm afraid these young, independent, educated professionals often feel that since their marriage is a partnership of strong, talented individuals, they will naturally thrive or at least survive.

But I'm here to tell you that if you don't contain your work life and segregate it from your home life, then your career will consume the marriage like a campfire blazing outside of its circle of rocks and roaring into a life-threatening forest fire. To both the husband and the wife, I say leave your cell phone off at crucial times when you are together—at the dinner table, before bedtime, when the kids are away—and you have the chance for some conversation and physical intimacy. Commit to not working overtime unless it will have a tangible positive impact on your relationship. In other words, if you can both make the sacrifice of being apart while one or both of you works, but your sacrifice will allow you to take a two-week vacation alone together next year, then it may be well worth it. But when overtime becomes a lifestyle habit, a way of detaching from the home, the kids, the problems that can't be solved with a spread sheet and a quarterly audit, then the marriage suffers. Especially during times of stress and important deadlines, I believe it's essential that you also budget in some down time, some rest and reward time for when the project is completed and the two of you can celebrate together.

Just as I've heard from most couples like Jackie and Tyler, you're likely saying to yourself, "But Bishop Jakes, you don't understand. In my

field, if I don't put in sixty hours a week, if I don't take those extra training classes, if I don't make the sales trip to Orlando, if I don't finish this
report by Monday . . ." On and on the litany goes that anyone who's ever
worked can recite. Yes, my friend, I hear you and I understand the demands you are facing. However, I must ask you to pause for a reality
check of the severest variety. Ask yourself this before you agree to the
next infringement of work on your homelife: "Is this project, deadline,
business trip (whatever the case may be) worth losing my marriage over?
Am I willing to be alone and CEO before forty, or do I want to find another route to success that enables my marriage to remain my priority?"
You see, it isn't who makes the most money that causes the marriage to
falter; it is the failure to attend to the critical need that each of us has to
feel like we are significant to the other's life. A man needs to know that
his presence is important to her and gives her something that she cannot get from the work place. Without that preferential treatment, he
shrinks into what I saw sitting across from me at the office that day! I realize this seems extreme, a kind of either/or ultimatum that forces you
to choose between two major components of your life that are not mutually exclusive. But they are not equals, and when you slide into thinking that they can sit side by side on the balance beam, then your work
will become the four-hundred-pound hippopotamus sinking the seesaw
and leaving your spouse suspended in mid-air on the other side.

Maybe you feel as I do. As a man, I have always prided myself on
being a good provider. My father taught me a strong work ethic for
which I am grateful today. However, I have to tell you that like my father, I sometimes get carried away. Always giving *things* instead of *me*,
gradually I learned that while money is important—and I'm going to
share some suggestions later in this chapter that may help you make better use of your money—providing for the family isn't just about decimal points in the checkbook. They need time with you, which in many

ways requires a larger provision of the resources of your heart and soul. I had to learn that sometimes it was essential to slow down a minute and give them quality time with me. If not, my actions devalue me as a contributor and overinflate finances instead.

Most women don't marry the money; they want the man. It is critical that you come to realize that you are more valuable than your resources. I admit that I'm forever struggling to get the mix right. If I am home and available, it often means that I'm not maximizing myself financially. There are constant demands, such as casting issues for the play that may be touring, contracts to be reviewed for a music artist, a real estate venture going awry, not to mention funerals, weddings, and my ministry needs, which are vitally important, a call that I have from God. So it seems that everybody wants something from me. God wants more of my time in prayer and study. The companies I have demand more and more of me as they grow. And my family still needs to know that they are not the last thing on my list. I could be gone twenty-four hours every day and still not finish all that I have to do. Do you feel that way too? But I have to remember that if I am gone all the time, my relationships suffer and business becomes the glue that holds us together. Romance dissipates, and all we start talking about is who has to be paid and who isn't performing well. That's talk for the boardroom, not the bedroom!

Your marriage can turn into a business arrangement without some time invested into it. You see, to the man who is the primary breadwinner, there are so many things that can consume him and leave him stretched too thin. All I can tell you is that you must constantly seek God for that proper mix of time away and time invested. Your time spent with your wife and family is a great investment, and when you don't spend the time, you're saying that what you have is more important than who you are. My friend, believe me—the giver is always better than the gift. And the second thing I would like to say is that there are ways to make your money work for you instead of you always going out to work for it.

MASTER BLUEPRINT

I'm consistently amazed at couples who come before me with financial strains on their marriage but who do not have a plan implemented for how the business of their household will operate. Often each partner feels vindicated for spending over what they're earning because they're both working hard and exhausted by the toll of commuting, carpooling, cooking, cleaning, and raising kids. He wants to reward himself with new Bose speakers and a flat-screen TV for their home entertainment center—the cherry wood console that still hasn't been paid off from the splurge of last Christmas. She wants to buy a new dishwasher, one that doesn't sound like a crescendo of white-water rapids bursting through the kitchen and drowning out all sound and attempts at conversation. Neither wants to compromise, neither wants to delegate, each assumes the other will handle the bills and cover their slack, and the result is more debt, more frustrated resentment of each other, and more shame over what feels like economic failure but which is actually lack of eco-communications.

> You need to communicate and enumerate your income and your expenses—then make a financial plan you both agree on.

No matter how long you've been married, no matter where you may be in your relationship, if you haven't come up with a master blueprint for how you're going to make, spend, and save money in your household, then I exhort you to do this as soon as humanly possible. Make an appointment with each other and remove as many distractions as possible. Release each other from past anger, disappointment, shame, and regret over poor spending habits and lost opportunities. Pray together for the Lord to bless your discussion and provide you with a clear vision for the house you want to build together from the blueprint you are drawing. This creates the team work that I think is essential for cooperation in the house. You must communicate the vision. How can you be frustrated about a vision that you have not shared sufficiently? Sharing is not bickering, complaining, and arguing. You need a constructive strategy that enables you to be helpmates to each other.

> Then the LORD answered me and said:
> "Write the vision
> And make it plain on tablets,
> That he may run who reads it.
> For the vision is yet for an appointed time;
> But at the end it will speak, and it will not lie.
> Though it tarries, wait for it;
> Because it will surely come,
> It will not tarry."
> (HABAKKUK 2:2–3)

Spend several hours going over what's coming in, what's going out, and how it's traveling toward your goals. Delegate according to giftedness if possible. Perhaps she will handle all of the annual bills—insurance, income tax, club memberships and dues—while he manages each month's bills and invoices. If neither of you handles money particularly well, then investigate hiring an accountant, who can help you balance your income with a strategy to pay off debt, share the responsibilities, and plan toward attaining the goals and toys you will both enjoy. Often there are free or minimal-cost debt counselors who can be employed temporarily to help you consolidate your expenses and gradually devise a plan to help you get financially free. There is absolutely nothing wrong with crying out for help. You may resent paying someone to help you do what other couples may be able to do for themselves, but better that you pay an expert for an area of need than to continue suffering the hemorrhage of debt and regret. You will recoup the expense of paying an accountant as you see and taste the benefits of financial stability.

Don't leave God out of the process. Financial freedom is a divine promise. You need His intervention, and one of the ways you ensure that is through your tithes and offerings. The Bible teaches this both in the Old and New Testaments.

"Yet from the days of your fathers
You have gone away from My ordinances,
And have not kept them.
Return to Me, and I will return to you,"
Says the LORD of hosts. "But you said,
'In what way shall we return?'
"Will a man rob God?
Yet you have robbed Me!
But you say, 'In what way have we robbed You?'
In tithes and offerings.
You are cursed with a curse,
For you have robbed Me,
Even this whole nation.
Bring all the tithes into the storehouse,
That there may be food in My house,
And try Me now in this,"
Says the LORD of hosts,
"If I will not open for you the windows of heaven
And pour out for you such blessing
That there will not be room enough to receive it.
"And I will rebuke the devourer for your sakes,
So that he will not destroy the fruit of your ground,
Nor shall the vine fail to bear fruit for you in the field,"
Says the LORD of hosts;
"And all nations will call you blessed,

For you will be a delightful land,"
Says the LORD of hosts.
(MALACHAI 3:7–12)

Regarding your blueprint, I certainly don't want to add any guilt or compound whatever feelings you may have regarding money by bringing up giving and tithing. But I often see couples who disagree on whether to give (she wants to, he doesn't, or vice versa), how much to give (she'll give 15 percent, he'll give 5), and when to give (he wants to plan on it every month, she will wait until the end-of-the-year bonus comes in). But brother, may I be honest with you? A tithe is 10 percent. This is what the word means. Generally, I encourage couples to find some ministry, some mission, some way to make a sacrificial gift to their church, but it is better when it is done in agreement. There is a great deal of power gained in giving when there is an agreement between the two of you. As a man, when you line up with Scripture and offer up the tithe as the priest in your home, God honors that in a special way. It wasn't Sarah who took the lead in giving. It was Abraham who offered up tithes of all they had. If you have been the one who has been out of alignment about this, fix it now. Stop asking God to bless an area where you refuse to obey His Word for your life.

STICK TO THE PLAN

So look at all areas of your financial house, each room of the blueprint: your transportation and automobiles in the garage; your appliances and conveniences in the kitchen; your children's expenditures and future needs, including their college education; your rooms for storing up the grain for a time of famine or emergency; your window with an inspiring view of the future goals you wish to attain. Make a plan and work your plan in small steps as necessary, giving each of you feasible home-work until your next meeting.

This may seem common sense and something so many of you are al-ready practicing in your home. However, for too many couples it re-mains an ideal, a good idea in theory that never gets executed, even as resentment grows faster than the interest rate on your overdue credit card bill. And as new opportunities occur—for advancement, for ca-reer change, for entrepreneurial endeavors—make sure that you are of one accord as to how to proceed. When you reach an impasse, then con-sult a handful of your most trusted friends who can be objective enough to help you make the right decision, even as they commit to pray for your wisdom and discernment. For instance, when she's offered a job in Cleveland but it means he has to begin all over again in his field, then you may have to find a compromise or a way to transform individual goals into joint goals. Otherwise, the job becomes an illicit partner tempting your spouse away from you and toward a solitary life of career accomplishments. It's a temptation we must constantly be on guard against. Frequent communication and vigilance of your blueprint will safeguard against making selfish decisions that are one-dimensional and not double-sided.

You should also feel the freedom to change the goals and alter the blueprint as you both grow and change into different people. Just as your honeymoon cottage had to be expanded to allow for a nursery and children's rooms before it evolved into a rec center for teenagers and was then transformed into an empty nest for the two of you again, so too must your financial house plan change. Some seasons require different financial goals before others can become part of the house. You will want to get a handle on maintaining a budget and paying off debt before you take a huge risk for a new endeavor and quit your day job. So keep it up-to-date.

I cannot tell you how unwise it is to max out all your credit cards and allow your financial promiscuity to be an investment vehicle for some-one else. What do I mean by that? I'm glad you asked. Many credit card companies are getting 22 percent on your debt, compounded annually. This is more return than Wall Street is getting currently. Anyone will loan you money at this rate. They are making huge returns off your debt, and just making the minimal payment required is helping them make more and more. Here are some steps you can take to assess where you are with debt:

1. Get your credit report.
2. Dispute anything that is not accurate.
3. Consolidate debt by refinancing your house, which generally gives you a much lower interest rate on an equity loan.
4. Make payments above the required amount, as it is applied directly to the principle.
5. Retain the credit card but restrict its use for emergencies and car rentals.
6. Always inquire about the interest rate and not just how much the payments are.
7. Use cash payments when possible and keep track of where you spend it.
8. Checks are good for record keeping.

Now let's talk investments. The Bible says that the wealth of the un-just is laid up for the just. Well, if the just are coming into wealth, do you have a plan for that wealth accumulation?

If you invest in the stock market, then you know that each day an-alysts prepare a report from Wall Street with that day's activities, over-all Dow Jones index, and trends for the market. They then advise their clients on a strategy based on that new data. Similarly, stay abreast of your home financial index, if not on a daily or weekly basis, then certainly on a monthly and quarterly basis. Learn to make changes as necessary, as sudden expenses emerge—and they always will as long as transmissions go out, pipes burst, and refrigerators break down—and you need to shift and reallocate funds. If you remain flexible and focused, your blueprint will serve you well throughout all seasons of life, including successful ones.

Which brings us to another area of concern. Often couples come to me who have "made it," at least in terms of achieving a level of financial freedom that surpasses their goals and often their dreams. It's as if they've won the Monopoly game and now don't know what to do with themselves because they can afford clothes from Dior instead of J.C. Penney's, a new Mercedes instead of an old Taurus. I advise them to revise the plan and find new goals, new investments, and new ways of giving back to others. Again, they must learn to grow with their success, and to grow together. Also, it is critical that they put in place a financial portfolio that enables them to maximize all the many deductions and allowances that help against double taxation.

I am the fifth-generation descendant from a slave. All of my ancestors from slavery forward were entrepreneurs. I have learned the blessing of investing in real estate. I strongly believe that the promise of Abraham is still good today. Everywhere your feet trod, God says, I will give you land. Land is a good investment if it is well thought out. Some of my real estate investments have done well for us. I've also invested in my interests. Record labels and touring plays have all been outlets for my entrepreneurial interests. I bet you have some interests too, talents that you may not be fully utilizing. It is my prayer that new visions will emerge as you consider what you can do to move your family into the field of their dreams. As I said earlier, share those dreams with your wife so that both of you can merge your efforts to team up on the dream. It doesn't have to be equal income to be equal sacrifice, you know. Unity is critical to financial well-being and wealth accumulation. My wife and I want to leave our children better off than our parents were able to do for us, to send them to a university that we couldn't afford to attend, and to facilitate other dreams that I'm sure you have as well. In the midst of working feverishly on these goals, I also realize that leaving them money without wisdom is like leaving them gasoline without a car. Let them hear you making financial plans—not arguments now, but plans. You may have heard it said that it is not what we leave to them that is as important as what we leave in them.

My children know that I continue to value and rely on my wife's perspective on business and financial decisions. At least once a year, usually more often, we take a long weekend away together and make one of those days a strategy session that includes a "State of the Jakes" address. You know how the president delivers a visionary speech to Congress each January that outlines his economic and domestic policy for the country in the coming year? So do I outline where we are as a family, what's on the horizon, and where we should anticipate going in the next season. I open the meeting up for comments from all of us, assessing and looking for problems that may be creeping in but of which I am not aware. My wife has priorities and concerns that need to be considered. Sometimes the children do too. This forum helps them really think about the business of living and not just joy ride through childhood without investing creative thought and living with purpose. It's proved to be an invaluable time for us to align ourselves with each other, with the common goals we outlined many years ago but that need changing or revising and, most important, with the goals that our Lord has placed before us. This improves our ability to communicate with one another, a necessity in all areas of our relationship, and facilitates an openness from which we continue to grow, long after our meeting time has ended.

Indeed, we often draw wisdom by keeping the parable of the talents clearly in mind. I believe it's an important piece of vital truth that applies to all areas of our lives.

> But his master replied, "Wicked man! Lazy slave! Since you knew I would demand your profit, you should at least have put my money into the bank so I could have some interest.
> Take the money from this man and give it to the man with the $10,000.
> For the man who uses well what he is given shall be given more, and he shall have abundance. But from the man who is unfaithful, even what little responsibility he has shall be taken from him."
> (MATTHEW 25:26–29, TLB)

DIVERSIFY YOUR PORTFOLIO

As couples seek to handle money wisely, to plant shrewdly, and to harvest abundantly, I encourage you to diversify your portfolio. By this I mean that you should both be willing to look at your goals, gifts, and gainful opportunities and find creative ways to step outside of the traditional methods of running your household. As I talk to couples about the ways they handle money, I'm convinced that so much of what we spend money on has nothing to do with what we really desire and enjoy but rather with so much of what we feel as external pressure to conform. While there's certainly a place for "fake it till you make it"—that is, for paying attention to your appearance, your mannerisms, your etiquette to match with those at the level to which you aspire—there's also much to be said for throwing off the trendy garment of consumerism for its own sake.

My hope is that you can be confident enough in your own tastes, preferences, and goals to place your resources on those bull's-eyes rather than the targets of your peers, the people you see on MTV, or the Joneses next door. So many couples put themselves at jeopardy to purchase a new SUV, TIVO, and the latest designs from Gucci and Louis Vuitton, when they would rather be outside hiking with their kids, driving a ten-year-old Jeep, and living out of debt so that they could start their own business from

> *Never mind what the Joneses are doing—they don't pay your bills!*

home. And if one partner is committed to a different lifestyle than the other, then of course this only compounds the stress fracture into a broken bone in the body of their marriage. As one brother once told me, "I struggle with an affluent wifestyle!" You must find a way to balance the work and the rewards, the sacrifices and satisfactions, the compromises and capitalism of your two-person company.

Once you've identified your shared goals and found a way to align your hands along life's keyboard for the duet you've agreed to perform together, then you are ready to diversify your portfolio by learning to think outside the traditional box. Perhaps your dream is to start your own company together in five years. So that means that you will each accept the most lucrative job possible at present, save as much money as you can during those years, and then be prepared for one of you to stop working and start the business. Or maybe it means that she works her higher-paying job for now while he's primarily responsible for child-care and homecare until the kids are in school and then he finishes the book he wants to write. Perhaps there are entrepreneurial opportunities on the side that can maximize your income without taking you away from the home. The key is to think creatively and not feel inclined to get stuck in the dual-income, whopping mortgage, expensive-is-better lifestyle that so many couples become mired in like quicksand. Diversify your portfolio so that there are numerous investments returning life-long dividends for you, your wife, and your family.

RESPECT TO REAP

A friend of mine who is a financial advisor assisted me in preparing the following action points to help you respect your money so that you can reap the benefits. Here are the top things to think about with respect to your money:

1. **Insure the big financial risks in your family.** Most young families do need life insurance, primarily to pay a mortgage and create some ability for the family to live without the income of the deceased spouse, and possibly to pay for some college costs for children. The one more often overlooked is disability income insurance. This replaces your income when you are disabled. Disability is not only more common than death but is often a bigger financial crisis because expenses may go up (health care, medical costs, rehabilitation) and income may go down simultaneously. For a single-income family, this is a huge risk.

2. **For many families, consumer debt is a plague.** It is high cost, often for goods whose importance or value diminish quickly (a stereo, that new wardrobe, or car). Thus, the "high" goes away, but the payments don't. The payments mortgage your future—they suck up your raises, your bonuses, and your ability to buy things tomorrow. What ever happened to that old idea of "if you can't pay for it, you don't need it"? While there are exceptions to this rule, for most people the exceptions have become the rule. Get on a plan to reduce consumer debt as much as possible or eliminate it altogether.

3. **Find as many places as possible to save for a rainy day.**
First, use any vehicle that provides tax advantages, like a
company-sponsored 401(k). A plan like this brings not only
tax advantages but in many cases the company matches
your contributions. If you don't have one, use an IRA and
fund it as often as you can—even if it's in small monthly
increments. In savings, time is your greatest ally. Starting a
savings plan ten years earlier, even with smaller amounts,
makes a huge difference in how much you accumulate for
whatever your goals may be.

4. **Turn off the TV when financial "experts" come on.**
Financial experts who appear on television are often talking
about very short-term trends and trading (not investment)
ideas, and rarely talk about the only thing that works well
for most people—a long-term strategy of saving a little and
investing consistently. It's boring, it doesn't make good TV
or newspaper articles, but for most people, it works.

5. **Talk to your children about money.** I'm always amazed
how often children know next to nothing about money.
The schools certainly don't teach it, so if parents don't, who
will? There are websites that offer teaching tools for parents,
but the best way may be to talk to your kids—teach them
how checking accounts work, how valuable a credit rating
is, how you budget your money (even if it's something you
have trouble with), what insurance is for. If you need to
learn more yourself, what a great thing to do with your
children. Many community colleges offer personal finance
courses—try one of them.

6. **If someone is trying to "sell" you a financial product
or service, follow the money trail to make sure the
recommendations made to you are best for you.** The

first thing to ask someone selling financial products or services is how they get paid. If they can't or won't tell you, end the discussion. It is *not* a coincidence that insurance agents tend to make recommendations that end with you buying insurance, or that a stock broker (one who makes no money without selling a product) will recommend stocks. There's nothing inherently wrong with selling financial products for commissions, except that for too long the buyers have not been willing to ask the question "how do you get paid?" and demand a full and complete answer. As a buyer, once you know the answer, consider how these incentives impact your evaluation of your financial advisor's recommendations.

7. **Think about the unthinkable.** Dying. Most of us won't spend much time thinking about this. The result is that too often, when an unexpected death occurs, no one knows what the survivors have left, no one knows where the wills are (or if they have been done), whom to contact, and so on. In the worst cases, a traditional marriage means that a surviving spouse has never been involved in the family's finances and does not know what to do, whom to turn to, or what the family's assets are. This is the last thing a grieving family needs to deal with during a time that is already extraordinarily stressful. A periodic discussion of these issues goes a long way, even if it is only to talk about where things are or who the family relies on in the event that something does happen to one spouse or the other.

Perhaps some of the things I have shared are just repetitions of basics that may seem elementary to you. For others, the concepts may seem premature and too advanced. But ponder these words in your

INCREASING YOUR RANGE OF MOTION——FOR HIM

What is your greatest concern about money in your relationship?

How does your philosophy of finance differ from your wife's?

Describe the way the two of you communicate about money. How can you change the negative feelings and fears into a more open and honest form of communication?

What is your master blueprint for you and your family's finances?

What keeps you from pursuing a more balanced budget?

What action steps can you take to getting out of debt and having a healthier financial future?

INCREASING YOUR RANGE OF MOTION——FOR HER

Describe the dynamics between the two of you concerning money. What issues come up again and again?

How does your philosophy of spending and saving compare to his?

How much debt do the two of you share? How does your awareness of it affect your relationship?

What gifts do you possess regarding money and finances? What gifts does he possess? Are you currently allowing each other the freedom to apply those gifts in the right areas?

What is your vision of where the two of you will be financially in ten years? What is your contribution to getting there?

heart and understand that while it is true that we all need money to live and that often money does fuel our dreams and pursuits of those dreams, money is not an indicator of your success or the health of your marriage. Don't allow yourself to get caught up in the vanity of needing toys and trinkets to know your worth or the value of a loving relationship with your wife. Don't allow your ego to get in the way of her success if it's working in all the other areas.

Money is a wonderful resource that can provide innumerable opportunities to build a life together. If gained correctly, it can be an asset in sending your children to schools, financing your dreams, and securing yourself against unexpected calamities, afflictions, and emergencies. But you must remember that you are your greatest asset. Don't seek the wealth and lose yourself. Don't seek things and stop seeking God. Don't sacrifice your spouse and your family to attain that which rusts and burns and gets eaten by moths. You needn't be wealthy to enjoy the intimacy of time spent together, of sharing and fulfilling common goals, and of living and giving within your means. Continue pressing onward toward mastery of this fiscal resource that so often hinders us when it should be helping us. Commit to renewed communication about your finances, create or re-create your financial blueprint, and be prepared for God to bless your marriage.

ELEVEN

━━━⟨⟩━━━

SEXUAL HARMONY WITH THE ONE YOU LOVE

It is not how much we do but how much love we put in the doing. It is not how much we give but how much love we put in the giving.
—Mother Teresa

Of the three issues that have the most profound effect on relationships—Power, Money, and Sex—I'd bet the one we're focusing on now is the one that grabs your attention the most. And it's not that I believe you're some pervert, flipping through the pages frantically just looking for juicy details to stimulate your supercharged imagination. No, I say that this topic arrests our attention for two reasons. First, our sexuality is part and parcel of who we are as men and women. We are created in the image of God, but He gifted us with distinct sexuality. "So God created man in His own image; in the image of God He created him; male and female He created them" (Genesis 1:27).

Sexual identity, sexual feelings, and the desire for sexual activity are woven into the fabric of our being, a strong, brightly colored cord holding so many other threads together. So it becomes next to impossible to talk about the closest of human relationships between a man and a woman without acknowledging that sexuality plays a major part in the equation. Sex has the potential to be the most intimate, most pleasurable connection between two human beings, but there is also a flip side: Sex can create a painful chasm between a man and a woman. It can be a sword that severs the heart and takes two lovers and turns them into strangers. I'm not talking about the kind of problems that Viagra or a new negligee can resolve. Sometimes problems in the bedroom are more complex and run much deeper. As you know, and as we'll explore momentarily, our sexual relationship with our spouse often becomes the playing field where all other areas of our relationship either contribute to our closeness or deter the intimacy that the gift of sex is intended to promote.

The second reason that sex remains such a vital area of concern for men today involves our culture and the rampant, blatant, wriggle-it-in-your-face mentality of the media. You can't channel surf up and down the remote without encountering steamy soap-opera lovers heaving and breathing, commercials with cleavage displayed more than the product for sale, and sit-coms with couples promoting perversity with laughter and innuendo. I even read about a cable news channel where all of the anchors and reporters take off all their clothes as they read the news in the nude. What's the world coming to!

CORPORATE COPULATION

Our contemporary society has sold us love in sound bites. We receive messages about what love should be from magazines, commercials, and movies. The denizens of Hollywood, although unable to control their own love lives, have been greatly responsible for influencing our own. From Richard Burton and Elizabeth Taylor all the way to Halle Berry and Billy Bob Thornton, we have witnessed hot scenes of intense, all-encompassing, limb-entangling love relationships. We see them in passion, in love, and in laughter, and we crave to duplicate the same dance of desire in our own lives.

Much like a pornographic production, the scenes are simulated to enhance the reaction of the viewer. What happened in a few minutes on-screen is the result of many takes shot over and over and then edited to make you think that these people are actually bionic as he holds her pinned to the wall and suspended in air for twenty-five minutes. Despite the fact that Hollywood love scenes are not realistic, these interactions become the standard of what we think love and marriage ought to be. Caught up in the intensity of the film, we forget that these scenes are choreographed, the lines rehearsed. All mistakes and passionless fumbles have been edited out. Big-screen love scenes are unreal fantasies designed to titillate and to up box office sales. But we should not attempt to re-create this movie magic. They should put a warning label on films with these scenes: Do not try this at home—it doesn't work!

Hollywood love isn't real—not the steamy, smoldering hot bedroom or the tender, warm-fuzzy interactions of Ozzie-and-Harriet types on the daily television shows. I am no prude, my friend, and I'm as grateful as you are for the rich, sensual gift of sexuality that God has given us. But the pervasive use of sexuality as a controlled and packaged commodity in the media escapes the honest reality of human intimacy. In short, relationships are hard work, you get tired of many positions that life puts you in, and there are no marriages that do not have bloopers and retakes, apologies, and repentance.

You must also realize that although sex is such a potent force, it cannot be what binds the couple to each other. When you're in the springtime of your relationship, the physical attraction and instinctive chemistry between you and your woman can be so strong. And depending on your maturity and past experiences—and more important, what you've learned from them—the passionate exchange of bodily fluids can often obscure the real magnetic power of a loving relationship.

In the early stages of your coupling, the gentle caresses and ecstatic release within each other's arms appear to be all you need. But seasons change, my friend. The springtime evolves into summer. The blazing sun of career and children and aging parents fades into autumn when your own body changes as does hers. What will sustain you by the time the cold winter winds of life whip through your doorway?

Too many men learn late in life that no matter how powerful sex may be in their lives, no matter how driven, how aroused, how intense their need for sex, it cannot take the place of love. For if you haven't experienced the power of your woman's listening ear, her nurturing touch on your tight-as-knots back, the power of her expressive eyes across a stranger-crowded room, then it's tempting to think that sex should come first. But we don't spend all of our lives in bed, despite what Hugh Hefner and Larry Flynt might have us believe.

So between these two powerful forces at work in your life—your inescapable sexual self and the inundation of sexual images and messages in the media—I believe the reality of two bodies connecting in the marriage bed becomes more challenging than ever. You know the power of sexual connection provides an intense physical and emotional bonding like no other. But you're also battling the many subtle and not-so-subtle expectations that flicker behind your eyelids in fleeting images from billboards, magazines, and plasma TV screens. You want to believe that your manhood is not dependent on size, shape, acrobatic ability, or endurance. Yet, from my observation, the media and our culture is now treating men and their bodies much as women and their forms have been treated for so long: as objects, commodities to be assessed on muscle tone, rugged appearance, and porn-star proportions. Just as women can't live up to the air-brushed breasts and curvaceous hips of their media counterparts, men can't compare with the computer-generated, six-packed gym rats in the Abercrombie & Fitch catalogue.

So what's a brother to do? In helping couples, especially men, deal with sexuality, I'm afraid that often the Church has stuck its head in the sand, an ostrich on the beach of beautiful, well-toned, oily bodies in bikinis and Speedos. But we must realize that this is society's baggage and bondage, their secrets and uncertainties, not the Creator's. For it's clear right from the beginning of the world that God intends for human sexuality to provide a physical, emotional, and psychological experience for unity.

Eve is taken from Adam and there begins the lifelong attempt to reconnect. Sex is the celebration of that original oneness from which two were divided from the whole and given permission to come back and visit their original construction through the awesome ritual of copulation. This delightful, stimulating experience is denied the unmarried in Scriptures but is totally encouraged for the married. It is through

> *Sex is a natural, wonderful gift from God to be cherished by a man and his wife.*

this glorious worshipful joining that God invites a man and his wife to partake in the awesome act of creation; with Him, bride and groom collaborate to give life to our children and legacy to our existence.

What an amazing gift intercourse is. It is only natural that we crave it, enjoy it, and celebrate it. Sex is a life force. No wonder the body explodes in ecstasy when we couple. But it is more than body meeting body. Good sex, divinely ordained sex, is a blissful soul union. Sex makes a man feel loved. (On the other side of the bed, women need love to have sex, but for now I'm focusing on the male perspective.) For a man, being sexual brings him center stage with his emotions. Sex provides an outlet for him to confront his emotions and express them to his wife in the most private of settings. He learns that it's okay for him to feel, to share, to be intimate—both outside of bed as well as in the passion of physically loving his wife. This is why the casual encounter or one-night stand deceives us with a kind of false intimacy, a pleasurable distortion of the accumulative emotional vulnerability that occurs with the same partner in the marriage bed. It's like a starving man desperately turning to fast food for a well-balanced diet instead of the freshly prepared, home-cooked meal. The quick-and-easy, deep-fried, sweet-tasting morsels will satisfy initially but will only clog the arteries and undermine the intake of real nutrients that the body and soul so desperately crave.

SEX IN THE CITY

If extramarital sex doesn't truly satisfy, then you may be wondering why so many men turn to it for consolation. I believe that many men are attracted to affairs not because they aren't having sex at home but because they are bored with themselves, with what they're pouring their life's energies into, and with what's required of them in their relationship with their wife. I know you are saying they probably do it because their wives aren't responsive sexually or are prudish or unduly religious about something that is as God-ordained as communion or baptism. I know you may be saying that sex is important to a marriage, and you are right. However, all men don't cheat because of something his wife isn't doing. Many men enter into affairs hooked on the sensation of excitement, needy for an ego boost, looking for validation as they wonder, "Do I still have *it*?" This is why men in midlife may be especially vulnerable as they face the large questions about who they are, where they're going, and what they'll leave behind. You begin to question all the aspects of your life and wonder how you ever made it this far. You feel overwhelmed and wonder why your wife isn't fulfilling you as she once did. Often your emotional needs have changed and she doesn't understand that you are not who you were ten years ago. The truth is, you don't understand it either! Your emotions are awakening, in some ways your passions are emerging. In other ways your physical needs and capabilities are changing as your testosterone level shifts. The questions swarm at you, particularly when you're alone or when you slow down enough to allow their sting to penetrate.

Having an affair is an easy diversion. You can get caught up in the illicit passion of secrecy, the stolen moments staged around the sexual act just like the films we were discussing earlier. The woman adores you and provides you with that ego boost and energy blast that camouflage the raging need for soul comfort that gnaws at your heart. She doesn't know what kind of father you are to your children, how you leave the cap off the toothpaste, or how you forget to pay the cable bill each month. She doesn't know about your inner fear of being dependent on a woman, about your grief over the loss of your parent to Alzheimer's, or about how you like your favorite meal prepared. She only sees you in the role of the married man who sneaks her away to clandestine passion in hotel rooms, the powerful sexual animal of her fantasies in the afternoons. And you see her as the object of your desire, a woman who's stepped through the screen of your own fantasy films, detached from the reality of gaining weight after childbirth, driving carpool to soccer games, and experiencing early onset menopause.

I can't help but wonder if this is how David got himself into trouble with his wandering eye as he strolled upon the palace roof and surveyed the lives going on around him one fine spring night.

> In the spring, at the time when kings go off to war, David sent Joab out with the king's men and the whole Israelite army. They destroyed the Ammonites and besieged Rabbah. But David remained in Jerusalem.
> One evening David got up from his bed and walked around on the roof of the palace. From the roof he saw a woman bathing. The woman was very beautiful, and David sent someone to find out about her. The man said, "Isn't this Bathsheba, the daughter of Eliam and the wife of Uriah the Hittite?"

Then David sent messengers to get her. She came to him, and he slept with
her. (She had purified herself from her uncleanness.) Then she went
back home.

The woman conceived and sent word to David, saying, "I am pregnant."
(2 SAMUEL 11:1-5)

It seems noteworthy to me that David has remained behind in the
city while his peers and commanders are off waging battles in the wilderness. David, the mighty king, with his ten thousands slain, who rose
from the shepherd boy with the slingshot who brought down Goliath
to the fierce warrior defending and advancing Israel against marauding
tribes, didn't go to fight. I wonder if he's bored and looking for a challenge, looking for something—or someone—to touch his soul and give
his life meaning. So often this is what men really long for when they go
looking for sex. We blame it on testosterone and our physiology, but so
often what we want in a quick sexual encounter is not the release of
pent-up physical pressure but the filling of our souls. Someone who notices us and admires us, who accepts us and enjoys us for who we are.

David notices Bathsheba, inquires about her, and remains undaunted
when he finds out she is a married woman. He is the king after all, and
I doubt that he was surprised to end up in bed with her after he sent messengers to fetch her to the palace. So many men, particularly in midlife,
become like David and isolate themselves from their peers and then go
looking for fulfillment in a woman they barely know, someone beautiful merely glimpsed from afar. And as we find with the rest of David and
Bathsheba's story, the consequences eventually catch up with these men.
The offspring of this union precipitates David's panic, his willingness to
deceive and deny, to place an innocent man's life on the front lines of battle. When this baby dies in childbirth, it serves as such a powerful reminder of the stillborn dreams that men face when they get in too deep
with an illicit attempt to fulfill themselves.

My friends, I exhort you not to go looking for your life's fulfillment by becoming a voyeur of life and living vicariously between the sheets with a woman who is not your wife. Recognize your temptation for what it is and trace its source to the dissatisfaction in your soul. Turn to your God for strength and sustenance, realizing that sexual fidelity is foremost faithfulness to your Lord, not just to your wife. If the only reason you are faithful is because of your wife's beauty, her love of you, and her finesse as a lover, then eventually you will be compelled to look elsewhere when her looks fade, she's upset with you, or she's unable to perform physically because of illness or injury. You will then justify your adulterous liaison based on her shortcomings and inadequacies. I'm afraid this is what many men are already doing, and even if they're not having an affair with the office receptionist, then their affair is with money, pornography, or alcohol.

No, our foremost weapon against sexual temptation is our trust in God's goodness, including His gift of a wife. This is the powerful realization that David faces once he has come to terms with the gravity of his transgression:

Against You, You only, have I sinned,
And done this evil in Your sight,
That You may be found just when You speak,
And blameless when You judge.

Create in me a clean heart, O God,
And renew a steadfast spirit within me.
Do not cast me away from Your presence,
And do not take Your Holy Spirit from me.
(PSALM 51:4, 10–11)

If you're battling an addiction to fantasy and illicit affairs or struggling with pornography, strip clubs, or prostitutes, or improprieties of any kind, then I encourage you to face the impact of your failures and realize that this is not about sex but about the swirling tumult of emotions cascading from your heart down into the recesses of your soul. You must see beyond the sexual desire, excitement, and guilt of your situation and look to your Creator for His forgiveness, loving-kindness, and mercy. He's a gracious God and more than willing to run down the path to welcome you, His son, home. Don't grovel at the pig trough of debauchery and lascivious living when there's a banquet He's prepared for you at home.

A note to my sisters here: You must realize that sex is important to a man. Rationing out sex to him in the same way you give a dog a bone if he sits up or rolls over may have dire consequences. Sex is not a reward, but a joyous union of man and wife in which both partners can find intimacy and fulfillment. Remember, you are the only fountain in the house for him. Be sure you are flowing with creative, loving sensuality that is inviting and attractive to him. Sex is not a duty or a reward; it is a part of your ministry to him and to yourself. Don't allow your indifference toward sex to nullify my efforts to assist him in finding love at home!

SEXUAL HEALING

Some years ago Marvin Gaye had a hit with a song in which he sang about sexual healing. I'm sure many men played that song while bed springs creaked and car seats bucked wildly. Mr. Gaye's melodious voice, strong lyrics, and dynamic band paved the way for both affairs and marital bliss. But the truth of the matter is his song suggested that indulgence brings healing to the feelings with which most of us struggle. But I am sad to report that sexual promiscuity and lustful indulgence doesn't really bring about any type of healing. In fact, it may even complicate things as we add more and more faces and images to the surface before us throughout the day, fighting for placement in the screen of our minds. This mental overload often creates frustration in godly marriages, as we long for the images on the screen while we lie down with the woman God gave us. These images, if not cast down, become idols for the sexual altars of the masculine soul.

I have seen countless men, Christians and non-Christians, who struggle with sexual addictions or, at the very least, temptations. I have heard people tell them, "Just pray, brother. God is going to strengthen you." Some have begged God to take it away from them. But sexual passions are not the problem; they are a gift from God to be appreciated. But what you don't want is to be controlled by the passions. I believe that control for a man begins within, and what we must strive for is mastery over our own struggles. This is not an event, my friend, but a process. Few of us can report that we have mastered this as if it were a foe that is vanquished, never to return. Instead, sexual temptations come on a man at different times, for different reasons, and in varying degrees. Don't be surprised or discouraged when your illicit feelings creep up on you. I know it's difficult. It's like Pharaoh, who let the Israelites go and then tried to recapture them. What a tragic time it is to see Pharaoh after you have left his house and said you were free, and yet here he comes again.

Still, by God's grace, you can prevail. I want to encourage the brother who has fallen into the mire and mayhem of sexual cravings. I understand your pain. I am a man with passions, just like you. Please don't think for one moment that I am somehow exempt from the struggle. I, like all men, am with you in the struggle. Many of you have had

Sexual temptations are all around us, but the love of God can shield us.

pasts that seemingly do not want to submit to your decision to walk with Christ. Some have had issues born from abuse, prison, childhood trauma, and more. Some have tried to get the feelings of validation through multiple affairs. Sadly, these women may say all the right things initially, but eventually the rhetoric fades and the demands, complaints, and betrayals emerge. Many of you know what it is like to be a good man trapped in a bad situation. But don't give up. When you fall back to your perverted ways, look to God for redemption. I've learned that pigs lay in the mud and that sheep cry to get out of it. Maybe it is the same sin and the same issue, but when you are really a child of God, there should be an uncomfortability with sin that makes you cry out to God for His cleansing and grace. God's way is still the best way. Sometimes a man has to ask God to help him want for his life what God has ordained for him without crossing the line into wanting more than what he should need. That's right. Call out, "Lord, help me with me! I have a problem that only You can fix." These conversations with God strengthen you in the weak places that we all have. I believe that unbelief is at the root of sin. We have trouble believing that God's way will fill the void in our lives. You know what? It may take some work, but ultimately, God knows how to get you to the right place without taking a wrong turn. Trust Him. It is the first step to heeding His counsel for you.

Sexual sins lead to embarrassment, shame, and disgrace. My prayer is that you will not have to travel down the road that many men travel only to find out that it is a dead-end street. Turn around. That is what repentance is. Just acknowledge that you don't want to go farther down a dead-end street and then change directions. One thing David was good at was admitting his sins and asking God for help. Don't stop talking to God about the parts of your life that are in contradiction. Silence isn't golden when it comes to sin. Here is a prayer that you can use to bring up the issue with God and seek His grace for your renewed strength and victory. You might not need the prayer right now. You may be on the mountain. But sooner or later, you may find this prayer to be a blessing to you. Save it.

Lord, thank you for being touched by my infirmity without condoning my
sins. I come to You to discuss the things that I know You see that may
be displeasing to You. I hate the fact that my conduct is painful to You.
And I am sorry to be a disappointment to You in any way.

God, help me to change the part of me that threatens to destroy all that
is good in me. Give me the grace to stop reckless behavior that enslaves
me to passions that I am not proud of. Lord, I thank You for mercy, forgiveness, and, most of all, change. Change me into the man You want
me to be and give me the patience to accept the process that leads to
my recovery. I will no longer look down at any man who struggles, as
I now understand his pain and ask You to heal both him and me as we
seek to be more like You. In Jesus' name. Amen.

WELCOMING THE WARRIOR

One of the most difficult things for men to do is to remain committed
to coming home—physically, sexually, and emotionally. The man who
really wants to come home may have to pray from time to time to find
rest for his soul and healing from his addiction. But it definitely helps
when there is a woman who knows what to do to ease the trip back
when a prodigal man is trying to return.

Many ladies often ask me what they can do to improve intimate re-
lations in their marriage, as if there's some secret to male satisfaction that
I've newly discovered. Or they ask me what they can do to safeguard
their marriage against the predators of adultery, addiction, and emotional infidelity that plague so many couples in our country. While there
is no single, simple answer to this set of well-intended questions, I often
come back to reminding ladies of how important it is to welcome their
warriors home, to applaud their man's return from his workaday world,
whether he's a firefighter out saving lives or an accountant operating out

of a home office in the basement. As the seasons of a man's life shift, I believe this receptivity on the part of his wife is crucial to the health of their relationship, both in and out of the bedroom.

Another thing women should remember is that as men go through various ages, their sexuality changes along with the rest of them. During each of the various stages, men need to feel like they possess virility and masculine potency. At certain times, this potency may come from his accomplishments, his toned and muscular body, or his charisma and personality. Overall, though, this virility needs to reside in him, in who he is, and in what he can offer simply by walking through the front door. For regardless of how a man is defining himself and connecting it to his sexuality, he wants to feel like a warrior returning from the battle when he comes home.

There are some things a man can only get from a woman who makes him know his power and strength in her life. A welcoming committee of bassinets and unpaid bills, broken washing machines, and PTA meetings might not be the best greeting for him. Sometimes he just needs his lover—not the mother of his children, not the keeper of the household, not even his partner. Sometimes he just wants to come home to his woman, his bride, his wife. Yes, sometimes he needs you—his strength and his source of comfort. Be there for him and greet him when he comes through the door.

Here are some tips to help you welcome your man home:

Greet him at the door. Stop what you're doing and let him see your love for him in your eyes, your smile, and your embrace. When Saul and David returned from battling the Philistines, the women danced in the streets before them, jubilant and exultant in their ceremonial sensuality. They sang, "Saul has killed his thousands and David his ten thousands!" and rejoiced in celebrating the victory of their present king and his successor. While this reflects Jewish custom, it also taps into the core of a man's need to feel welcomed, celebrated, and attended to when he returns from fighting the battles that he encounters on a given day, whether they be a Philistine giant slain or a big project completed at the office. Whether he's a plumber or a pilot, when he comes home he longs to be recognized for the efforts he's putting forth, regardless of their scope or size. If there's no response, no recognition when he comes home, then soon he won't want to come home and he will seek applause before another audience where he is appreciated and esteemed.

Speak words of love and welcome. Men find self-esteem in what they do; women find it in knowing they are loved by those most important to them. Women have the ability to render their men impotent, not necessarily physically but verbally and emotionally by the way they respond to their husbands' accomplishments. If wives are so wrapped up in the house, the kids, and planning what's for dinner, then they will begin to miss their husband's arrival, and he will sense this and soon feel that it makes little difference whether he's there or not. We want to believe there's a place to rest our head, to be welcomed for who we are and not what we do, to be embraced no matter what the circumstances. This touches our soul and arouses our loins, perpetuating our desire to reciprocate this kind of unconditional love and fight for her protection and well-being all over again the following day. This isn't sexist chivalry but simply the reality of the way a man is wired.

Initiate lovemaking. As I stated earlier, sex makes a man feel loved. For you to initiate lovemaking shows your man that he is desired and admired. Your overtures tell him that you want to be intimate with him, that you crave the closeness as much as he does. This makes him feel secure in his masculinity, in himself, and in the relationship. It gives him comfort to know you want him and thus he can be naked and not ashamed as you come together in the sacred space of your marital bed, as well as in your interactions outside of the bedroom. Just reaching out to him in the darkness will make him feel safe, loved, and welcomed at home. Touch him, talk to him. It does to him the same thing it does to a baby. It soothes his masculine soul and will be sure to get a real reaction and an attitude of gratitude!

SEASONS OF LOVE

In the Tony Award–winning musical *Rent,* there's a song that captures the essence of this provocative Broadway drama. "Seasons of Love" is the signature song of this show, a passionate anthem to living one's life fully engaged with each single day of the three hundred sixty-five that comprise one full year. I believe this advice resounds and resonates just as accurately in the dimension of our sexuality. We must allow ourselves to experience the fullness of our sexuality, and our wife's sexuality, in all dimensions of our lives, 24/7, and not just in those moments of passionate bliss in making love.

You're likely well aware that sex changes as we go through the ages and stages of our life. For young men, sex is more about the physical and the erotic. It's all about penetration and the exchange of bodily fluids. But as a man matures and begins to grow older and wiser, he realizes that there's much more to sexual closeness than acrobatic positions, g-strings, and jockstraps. Sex is about soul connection. And it doesn't begin in the bedroom but in the living room, in the daylight hours. Sexual soul connection occurs when you look into each other's eyes across a room, when you find a seductive email waiting for you from her at the office, when you give her a call just to let her know she's inside your thoughts.

As you change, don't be afraid to evolve and grow, to try new ways of pleasing each other and keeping the soul connection strong. Take sensual baths together, wrestle outside in the frosty cold air and have a snowball fight, slow-dance in the kitchen when a sultry love song comes on the radio. I love to come up behind my wife in the kitchen when she's cooking and hold her and kiss her neck and then back away, leaving both of us wanting more time alone later.

So many men view the changes in our sexual life as a decline that is an inevitable part of aging, but it doesn't have to be this way. Yes, there may be more ramp-up time, more desire for touching and holding instead of climaxing, more time to hold each other, but this may be even more enjoyable than what you experienced as a young man. Ironically, by the time a man realizes his need for affection and touch, his woman—who has been longing for this all along—has resigned herself to a quick encounter and wants to get on to other things. I encourage you not to allow this to happen. Slow down and enjoy the physical sensuality of your woman's presence no matter where the two of you may be in life stages or emotional ages. Men need to be touched just as much as women.

It takes a lifetime to make a marriage. I compare the lifelong dance of marriage to what we used to do when we would go out to the disco back in the seventies (if you can't remember the styles, then thank the Lord for His mercy!). In the disco, in order to be a good dancer, you had to know when to change dances and dancing styles as the music changed. One song and we're

> *There is so much more to sex than what happens between the sheets.*

all gyrating around and doing "The Bump," the next minute the melody has changed and it's a slow dance. Before you can say *Saturday Night Fever*, the song changes again and it's time to do the hustle. I hope you can understand what I'm trying to convey here with my analogy. You and your partner must be able to feel each other and know when life's music changes so that you can adapt to the next dance and stay in sync with each other. This is true in the way that you love each other physically and sexually as well.

INCREASING YOUR RANGE OF MOTION——FOR HIM

What are you doing to combat the many temptations with which our culture surrounds us?

What secrets are you carrying about your sexuality? Find someone whom you can trust to unburden yourself to and ask them to pray for you.

Why is it so difficult to talk to your wife about this struggle? What can you do to allow her to help you in the battle?

What can you do to enhance your romantic interactions with your wife?

INCREASING YOUR RANGE OF MOTION——FOR HER

How can you help him battle the temptations of pornography and secret fantasies?

How worried are you about infidelity? If you've battled infidelity before, where are you with it now? Do you trust him? Will you ever?

How welcome do you make your man feel when he returns home?

What can you initiate that will increase the sensual love the two of you share?

After power, money, and sex, what remains in the relationship is often the incredibly resilient underlying strength of a tender, vulnerable friendship. I see this in shopping malls where an older couple walks for the exercise, holding hands and enjoying each other's company, a look of contentment and completeness on each face. They have lived to enjoy the give-and-take wrangling of the power plays and strength struggles, they have discovered the joy of their sexuality in ways that far transcend whatever may or may not be happening between them in the bedroom, and they have communicated similar goals and means of attaining those goals financially. They've arrived at a different level of marriage, a different season, one that may seem far removed from where we are at present but from which we can learn nonetheless.

My brother, I encourage you to do what is necessary to reach this stage of a mature relationship. Don't allow the obstacles of PMS or other relational snares to entrap you and prohibit the kind of intimacy and rich ambrosia of loving connection that God concocted in marriage. Give Him thanks for the woman He has provided in your life or the one He may send in His timing if you are presently single. Recommit yourself to discover the secret of joyful, soulful, and holy sex!

Part Six

A MAN'S RELATIONSHIP WITH HIS CHILDREN

———❦———

*"I cannot think of any need in childhood as strong as
the need for a father's protection."*
—SIGMUND FREUD

*"The father who does not teach his son his duties is equally
guilty with the son who neglects them."*
—CONFUCIUS

"Example is not the main thing in influencing others, it is the only thing."
—ALBERT SCHWEITZER

"It doesn't matter who my father was; it matters who I remember he was."
—ANNE SEXTON

———❦———

TWELVE

FATHER OF YOUR FUTURE

Acting is just a way of making a living; the family is life.
—Denzel Washington

The other day, as I was shaving, I noticed that my eight-year-old son was there watching intently as I razored away my now-graying stubble. I was concerned that he might try to shave too soon. Maybe I was worried because I remember myself attempting to shave what was at best peach fuzz on my skin when I was his age. In fact, I actually damaged my skin trying to get to manhood too quickly. So I was well aware of what an eager boy might do some evening if left to his own devices. I shaved and talked, trying not to allow him to see where I keep my razor. But knowing how rambunctious a boy his age can be, I suspect that my attempts were a little futile as he likely noticed more than I counted on.

But that doesn't mean I still won't try to shield him from the mistakes I made from growing up too fast. Oh, I don't mean just the shaving part. This is just a good visual metaphor for a deeper problem with our young people today. They simply grow up too fast. They are overexposed to too much sex and sizzle before they are able to manage it emotionally and spiritually. They pressure themselves to become grownups long before it's time for them to put away childish things. What can we do to stop our sons from shaving too fast? How can we keep our daughters from stepping into high heels and seductive apparel too soon?

These questions reverberated inside my mind as I shaved my face and glanced down at my son, watching as he imitated my every move. He stood in front of the mirror with his legs slightly apart, looking a little like he was a cowboy with leather chaps on. It was clear that he was trying to look as masculine and macho as possible, quite a feat for an eight-year-old young man. Still, he was adamant about making a good impression. He wanted me to know he was a man in the making. He really was too. But the concern is not to rush the making of the man. Many men have rushed to what appeared to signal manhood without being ready to handle the responsibility and privileges that come with being a man.

My mother tried to convey this insight to me since I was quite precocious as a child. She said, "Don't be in such a hurry to grow up. Growing up isn't all it's cracked up to be." Her profound wisdom fell on deaf ears as all I could hear was the liberty bell of freedom ringing up ahead of me in adulthood. I heard her but I didn't listen and was later shocked to encounter the liabilities and responsibilities associated with my development.

I am listening now, but it is too late. Like many others, I mourn the loss of innocence taken too soon and not savored long enough. I missed my own childhood much like I missed the early childhood of my older sons. My life raced by me in a blur. I was thrown into adult responsibilities at an early age, and there was no time or space left for childishness. I had places to go and feats to accomplish. I had something to prove, but now, in retrospect, I wonder to whom I was proving it. Like my son Dexter tracing his fingers across his face as though he were shaving, I realize I had the right stroke but at the wrong time.

It's funny, though. Through my son I get a taste of the childhood I didn't get, and through me he gets a taste of the manhood that lies before him. Both of us enjoy the visit. When my older sons were growing up, I was too busy trying to make a mark, feed the family, and pastor the church to notice the way they whizzed by me and grew up like weeds, almost while I wasn't looking. My, how time goes by too quickly. You blink and they have hair on their chest and a date for the prom. Where did their childhood go? I guess it went where mine did. It seems that real childhood today is a luxury of the privileged few. Most of us have answered the call to duty as if it's a warrant for our arrest. It apprehends us, captivates our youth, and mesmerizes us, keeping us from enjoying the one brief season of real wonder in our lives. Maybe a midlife crisis is just a desperate man's attempt to regain Paradise Lost and enjoy it before he's in Paradise Final!

DADDY DAYS

Like my son wanting to shave too soon in an attempt to leapfrog into manhood, many young men jump into fatherhood as a sign of their virility and arrival into the world of their own fathers. But there are equal numbers of grown men who are not emotionally equipped to embrace the demands and to savor the joys of fatherhood. Just because you can produce sperm, share it with a woman, and conceive a baby doesn't mean you have what it takes to be a father.

Conversely, there are many men who have never conceived a biological child but who have fathered dozens. Perhaps you are a single man reading this and haven't embarked on this part of the journey yet, or perhaps you and your wife are unable to conceive your own family. You still have incredible potential to mentor and to father children with whom you come in contact—at your church, a local community center, Big Brothers, or a school nearby your home. You must realize that a father's gifts are needed now more than ever and that if you're willing to love a child, then biology need not be a barrier.

And it won't be easy even though it will be vastly rewarding in ways you never imagined. For a man's relationship with his children adds yet another set of variables to the complexity of his life and the seasons of his soul. Daddy days with our children remind us of the passing of time, of our own childhoods that have now vanished before our eyes except for the flickering images played across the screen of memory. When a man fathers a child, he is forced to contend with so many emotional and spiritual issues that he might be able to ignore the rest of the time.

One primary conflict that emerges is the struggle between embracing the many tender feelings that come with having a child and protecting oneself from such incredible vulnerability. Many men have learned to hide their emotions—notice that I didn't say control them, for we can never control how we feel but only how we respond to those feelings. Pretending to control our emotions is part of being tough and macho in our culture, but it's also a convenient way to hide and not allow others to know they have the power to hurt you. This area of defense, of course, comes under attack when a man falls in love and proceeds into a marriage relationship with his woman. But the tenderness, the desire to protect and to provide for another, that a man feels for his child can catch him off guard. There's no back-and-forth dance like there is with his wife. No, the arrow from his child flies swift, direct, and sharp into his heart. I have seen many of the toughest-appearing, most rough-and-ready men you could imagine reduced to a moist puddle of tears when the topic of their children arises. Inmates with tattoos, scars, scowls, and bulging biceps unlock the bars around their hearts when you ask about their children. I've seen it in their eyes many times. Aloof, professional types, with their three-piece English suits and intimidating stares, can turn into the friendly neighbor next door when you ask about their kids.

Men must realize and accept the enormous power that our children have over us. In many ways, I believe this power can be even stronger than the bond between man and wife, because divorce and infidelity can sever a marriage, but the ties between parent and child last our entire lifetime. I'm afraid, however, that when many men recognize their feelings for their children, and the incredible need that their children have for their daddy, they become overwhelmed by fears of inadequacy, inferiority, and impotence. A friend of mine told me, "I feel like my kids are so needy. And I'm not sure I have what it takes to meet all their needs. It feels like I'm just going to be sucked up and consumed into this black hole of them needing me too much."

SECRET RECIPE

I believe we often feel this way—that we don't have what our children need from us—because we never got what we needed from our fathers. But fatherhood is not a secret recipe passed down from generation to generation like the formula for Grandpa's barbeque sauce. You don't have to have had a great childhood with perfect parents to be a good father to your children. If that were true, then none of us would be qualified, for all of our parents—even the best ones—failed us in some ways. No, the key to being a good father to your children emerges in the staggering simplicity of taking care of yourself, being authentic with your children, and spending exorbitant amounts of quality time with them. Let's examine each of these briefly.

Good fathers live balanced lives and know how to take good care of themselves. So much of this book covers this topic and its myriad facets that I won't go into a lot of detail at this juncture. However, please keep in mind that if you're not living a balanced life, not making time for yourself, not finding alone time with your spouse, then what you give your children will be an exhausted, frustrated Dad who comes home by default, not by deliberation. Jesus makes it abundantly clear that we are to love others as we love ourselves. He said, " 'And you shall love the LORD your God with all your heart, with all your soul, with all your mind, and with all your strength.' This is the first commandment. And the second, like it, is this: 'You shall love your neighbor as yourself.' There is no other commandment greater than these" (Mark 12:30–31).

As we've discussed before, this doesn't mean some kind of self-indulgent, all-about-me kind of love, but it does mean a healthy sense of setting boundaries and taking care of your own needs because you realize that only then can you take good care of others. The flight attendant on the plane always makes a point of saying that in the event of an emergency, when the oxygen masks drop down, you must secure your own mask first before helping children or others in need.

As you know from your own experiences, we learn so much about life and how to be a man by observing our father. Much like my son watching me to learn how to shave, we mimic and imitate those actions and patterns we see in our parents, even if they are unhealthy and dysfunctional. All the more reason that we must live deliberately and change unhealthy habits that we may have picked up from our parents or from our own weaknesses. Just because our father was a workaholic who was sometimes in the home but never present doesn't mean that we must follow suit. Just because our parents missed our ballgames, forgot our recitals, and ignored our accomplishments doesn't mean that we can't give our own children so much more.

Live a balanced life, my friend. Use this book and other resources—your friends, your church, your dreams—to overcome areas of burden that threaten to capsize your he-motions journey. The best example you can give your children is to show them what it looks like to take diligent care of your own needs without becoming self-absorbed. Let them know that there are times when you need to be alone, times when you need to be alone with their mother, times when you need

> *Break the past sins of your father by loving your children in the present.*

to exercise. But also let them see the effects of this caretaking time when you come back and have more energy and presence to devote to them. If they see you taking marvelous care of yourself but you're never there for them, then your care-filled preparation is not fueling your commitment to your children.

Good fathers reveal their authentic selves to their children. Our children see the best and worst of us, and for most of us men, it's just another frightening fact that justifies guarding our hearts against them. They know when we come home late, they see us walk around exhausted and overwhelmed (hopefully, not too often!), they scrutinize our interactions with our wives, and they watch our eating habits. While I certainly don't advocate making your child your confidant or best friend, I do think that you should allow yourself to be real with your kids. Allow them to see you express emotions—so important for both sons and daughters to observe in their fathers.

Some of the most tender moments with my children occurred when I was grieving the death of my mother, their grandmother, to whom they were very close as well. I'll never forget my daughter coming to me and not saying a word, but simply looking into the pooled tears about to burst from my eyes shortly. She gave me a hug and kissed my cheek and simply sat beside me in silence for a few minutes before moving on.

My oldest sons came by the house often to check on me . . . watching me, whispering to their mother, "How is Daddy doing?" You don't have to act like Superman to be a hero to your kids. . . . Just be real!

While it's important to allow our kids to see us grieve, diffuse stress, and express anger appropriately, it's also important for them to see us celebrate, to enjoy simple events at home with them, and to be silly at times. One of my fondest memories of my parents is seeing my father, weary from his second job and probably beginning to suffer the then-undiagnosed pains of his kidney disease, jump up and grab my mother when his favorite song came on the radio. My mother was preparing our evening meal and in no mood for foolishness at first. She swatted him away and tried to get back to peeling her potatoes, but he persisted with a silly grin on his face and a twinkle in his eye and pulled her back toward him. My mother could not deny his contagious, spontaneous joy and began to two-step with him there in the evening shadows of our linoleum kitchen floor. This allowed me to see them as real people, a man and his wife in love with life and each other, untouched, at least for a few moments, by raising kids, paying bills, and worrying about tomorrow. I was amazed to see them dance. I was raised in that generation when most parents didn't show affection in front of their children. They thought intimacy was too private. But seeing them dance made me so happy! It was from them that I learned about love.

I also think about the way David danced before the Lord upon his return to Jerusalem after securing the Ark of the Covenant. "Then David danced before the Lord with all his might; and David was wearing a linen ephod" (2 Samuel 6:14). Basically, the king was out in the street dancing in his underwear! His wife Michal, Saul's daughter you'll recall, harshly criticized her husband for disrobing and whirling about with such abandonment and disregard for royal propriety. But David makes it clear that his exuberant dance was honoring to God, a pure, unfettered response to God's goodness and presence in his life through the return of the Ark and all that God had brought him through. This provides a powerful example for us to allow our children to witness our passion, particularly in worshipping and celebrating God's faithfulness to us. While I encourage you to spare your children the sight of your weaknesses that we know Noah displayed to his sons, your restraint and appropriate boundaries should not inhibit your spontaneity, creativity, and celebration of God's goodness.

Good fathers spend exorbitant amounts of quality time with their children. For many men reading this now, I suspect that this might be the hardest suggestion to practice. Not because you don't want to be with your kids, but because you leave your time with them to be a filler, something that happens by default when you're not working, not ministering to others, not helping your wife around the house, not recharging yourself with alone time. I recall one man who had recently divorced his wife and moved out of the home he had shared with her and their three children. He was a self-admitted Type-A chronic workaholic, always traveling to make the next big deal, typically talking on his cell phone and multitasking even when he was having down time with his family. He told me that now that he was divorced and shared joint custody of the children with his wife he was a better father because he was forced into scheduling his time with them. His wife certainly resented the fact that he had always been too busy for the kids when the two of them were married but that now that they were divorced he was spending deliberate time with the kids.

Another gentleman told me about his high-profile career in the telecommunications industry and how his work constantly kept him from spending quality time with his two daughters. Then he developed multiple sclerosis and was forced to cut back his sixty-hour work weeks and overplanned weekends. He soon had to give up his career and allow his wife to support the family while he stayed home and battled his disease. The surprising upside of his debilitation, he told me with tears in his eyes, was that he got to be home when his girls came back from school, he got to help them with their homework when his body permitted, and he was able to enjoy watching movies, taking walks, and playing Monopoly and checkers with them. He had to lose his physical health in order to increase his paternal health.

My friend, don't wait until divorce, disease, or some other crisis compels you to spend more focused times with your children. Make them a part of your schedule right now. Take them with you on trips when possible, and accompany them on their outings to the mall, to the ballgame, to school events. You may find yourself doing some things that are not your first choice of leisure activities—laser tag with overzealous ten-year-olds, chick flicks with your teen daughters—but your presence there beside your child who does enjoy them will be worth more than any investment can yield—the lifelong appreciation of your children.

By the way, a man who doesn't spend time with his daughter is setting her up for confusion about men—who they are and how they operate. A man who doesn't love his daughter openly and unashamedly creates an insatiable thirst for male love in her that is dangerous. Don't leave parenting her totally up to her mother. Having a great mother does not negate the fact that she needs you too!

A FATHER'S FAILURE

Another area that so many men seem to struggle with as they parent is their sense of failing their children and not knowing how to change the course of the relationship. After a divorce, or after a reformed workaholic finds time for his children, or after an alcoholic becomes sober, he often discovers that his kids no longer trust or even respect him. Some men are then tempted to allow their guilt and shame to outweigh their child's ongoing need for them, and their need for their children as well. Please listen, my friend, and let me assure you that it's never too late to love and father your child, no matter how much damage may have gone down the drainage ditch of your lives over the years. They may have rebelled and run away or resorted to drug use or theft or deception in their attempts to discover themselves and their way to a meaningful life. While their relationship with you will be a factor in their rebellion, don't assume that you are solely to blame. The best fathers have prodigal children, who often must experiment with the harsh realities of life before appreciating what they have in their parents and family.

Or perhaps you were the one running away and have abandoned your children, either by leaving them behind physically or by deserting them emotionally, walling off your heart from them by staying busy and unavailable. In either case, I encourage you to take the initiative with your children and find some way to reach out to them. If there are issues between you, don't try to make some Hallmark moment happen; just be real with them, and give them reason to begin trusting you and loving you again. Show up and stay there in their lives.

Certainly no one knew more about failing his children than David—the king of Israel, husband to many wives, and father to many offspring. At least a dozen of David's children are named, and we don't know how many others existed in the shadow of their famous father. And among David's children who are named, so much rivalry and rebellion exists within their relationship to one another and to their father that it makes any contemporary soap opera look like a child's puppet show by comparison. The two most momentous incidents within David's family involve an incestuous rape and an attempted civil war, linked by the involvement of David's son Absalom in both ordeals.

Indeed, it seems quite ironic to me that Absalom's name means "peaceful," but that his life and relationship with his dad was anything but. Son of David's wife Maacah (2 Samuel 3:3) from the royal family of Geshur in nearby Aram, Absalom first emerges as the consoler, defender, and ultimately the avenger of his sister Tamar, who was tricked and raped by their half-brother Amnon. While there are enough dynamic dysfunctions to keep a team of modern family therapists working overtime in this situation, what seems key to me is David's absence from this entire sordid affair. Amnon plays

> *A father's love is an essential nutrient in a daughter's development and a son's growth. Don't play hard to get with your own children.*

sick and asks his father to send in Tamar so that she can bring him food and tend to his illness. David complies, apparently not knowing his son well enough to even imagine Amnon's true motive and obvious infatuation with his half-sister.

David's absence, however, becomes most conspicuous after the crime is committed. After Amnon rapes Tamar and turns her away, she does not go to their father and report the crime and seek solace. What father would not want to comfort his baby girl after such an insidious violation? He, the most powerful man in the kingdom, perhaps in the known world at that time, who should have been in charge of covering his family with a veil of protection, had failed his daughter. So instead of her father, Tamar turns to her blood brother Absalom, and he takes her in and vows to kill her incestuous rapist, their half-brother Amnon. David is nowhere on the scene. While we can argue that Tamar and Absalom don't give David a chance to exact revenge and punish Amnon, it seems striking that they don't even consider it. Could it be that they were used to their father's preoccupation with his other wives, children, and battles of his kingdom?

David finally gets involved after Absalom cons his father into sending Amnon to Absalom's house, where of course he's killed by his rage-filled brother. Now David finally gets upset and worried and perhaps appreciates the enormous gravity of the depravity of his sons for the first time. And I can't help but believe that surely the link between these two treacherous events reminded David of his own notorious moral failure—his affair with Bathsheba and the murder of her husband, Uriah the Hittite, another situation where an immoral sexual union erupted into violence. Did David wonder if his sons were so inclined to repeat the pattern of his mistakes because they were woven from the same fabric as their father?

So often it seems that our children do struggle in many of the same areas as their fathers. I've wondered before if perhaps this is the reason that the Old Testament Scriptures reveal that the consequences of a father's sins shall be reaped onto his seed for many generations:

> For I, the LORD your God, am a jealous God, visiting the iniquity of the fathers upon the children to the third and fourth generations of those who hate Me, but showing mercy to thousands, to those who love Me and keep My commandments.
> (EXODUS 20:5—6)

When I notice my son watching me shave and pretending to do the same so that he can someday wield the razor, I realize that too often we forget the enormous impact we have on our children from day to day. No matter how they may perform in school or on their report cards, our children are the most conscientious learners we will ever have the privilege of teaching. They are dry sponges just waiting to be filled, and they will absorb and carry with them what they hear us say and observe us doing for most of their lives.

BRIDGING THE GAP
THROUGH PRAYER

Dear God,

I wish I could pass to my children only my good qualities and none of my weaknesses. But I fear that a man cannot separate those traits he wants to pass on from those he does not. I now realize that many times as my older sons and daughters were growing up, some of the mischief they got into was a reflection of my own issues. Sadly, there was no way to divide the best part of me from the worst part of me. I couldn't control which parts of me I passed on to them. Lord, since I can't control the flow of human frailty, please help them with the outcome of the human experience as you have helped me all of these years.

Amen

Perhaps it's no wonder then that David's son Absalom reveals not only his father's penchant for violence and vengeance but his political ambition as well. For out of the animosity between father and son over the raping of Tamar, the two men end up vying for the kingdom that David has worked so hard to establish. This plot for political turmoil seems to originate when Absalom flees to his uncle's home in Geshur and waits for his father's wrath to cool down. By manipulating his uncle Joab, Absalom finally returns to Jerusalem and attempts to regain David's forgiveness and good graces. At first, however, the mighty King David cannot swallow his pride and set aside his self-righteous concept of justice in order to forgive his son for something that echoes his own crimes. "And the king said, 'Let him return to his own house, but do not let him see my face.' So Absalom returned to his own house, but did not see the king's face" (2 Samuel 14:24). How often do we allow our pride to come between us and our ability to bless and forgive our children?

Finally, however, Joab intercedes and David relents and embraces his son at long last. "So Joab went to the king and told him. And when he had called for Absalom, he came to the king and bowed himself on his face to the ground before the king. Then the king kissed Absalom" (2 Samuel 14:33). It seems so important to me that despite the heinous crimes and offenses committed on both sides of the relationship, here was, at least at this moment, an honest attempt to forgive and move forward in their relationship. David and his son connected at least for the briefest of moments.

Too often, I'm afraid, we wait too long to forgive our children, and we wait even longer to ask their forgiveness of us. I encourage you to accept that so many of the choices you made—even good choices in pursuit of worthy goals, let alone the selfish and destructive decisions—have hurt your children and built a wall of defensiveness and indifference between you. Sometimes I believe this is especially true when our children remind us of ourselves, when we spot the same passions and proclivities in them that we know were once boiling in us or perhaps

> *Never underestimate the power you have as a father on the lives of your children.*

that still simmer below the surface. When we see them veering off life's highway in the exact same spots where we crashed and burned on the shoulder of the road, it's difficult not to want to save them even as we feel our own regrets and remorse wash over us. But realize that they are separate individuals and that while you cannot always protect or save them from life's dings and dents, you can help them refuel and repair so that they can continue on their journey.

Sadly enough, the truce between David and his son was only momentary. For Absalom became intent on replacing his father as king and began conspiring against David. The son's treason included recruiting David's top counselor, Ahithophel, and initiating a civil war within the kingdom. Once again, I wonder if despite the betrayal and turmoil his son caused, David felt a sense of kinship and compassion for his son's actions and political ambition. Like his father, Absalom is passionate, intense, thoughtful, and personally charismatic. So much like David that in many ways Absalom would seem to be a natural successor to his father's throne.

Even David himself was forced to battle his own predecessor, Saul, a man who was initially a father figure to him. And as many of us know or anticipate, there does come a time when our children succeed us, taking our place in the family business, taking on the responsibilities that we have shouldered for most of our adult lives. Eventually, we must make peace with the notion of our child replacing us in the workforce, in society, and in the family.

But this was not such a time for David and Absalom, for in the end, the son's ambition and the father's past mistakes collide in a violent fashion that costs Absalom his life. David is then forced to deal with even more grief than he imagined possible. "Then the king was deeply moved, and went up to the chamber over the gate, and wept. And as he went, he said thus: 'O my son Absalom—my son, my son Absalom—if only I had died in your place! O Absalom my son, my son!' " (2 Samuel 18:33).

Perhaps there's no greater grief that a parent feels than when he loses his child, whether that is due to death, drugs, incarceration, or the acrimonious accumulation of abandonment issues over the years. When Absalom's flowing hair catches in the branches of a large oak tree as his swift mule carries him through the forest of Ephraim, he's caught like a wild animal in a trap, suspended until his life is drained by three spears from Joab.

Despite his many failures and his vast grief, David did promote his lineage to the throne in the form of his son Solomon, his child produced with his wife Bathsheba. Solomon, of course, proved to be wiser and richer than his father and provided the bloodline of succession that leads to the heritage of the Messiah, Jesus, who is described as being of the House and Sign of David. How fascinating that David's offspring—from the woman with whom he committed adultery and for whom he murdered a man—should turn out to be his heir who provides him with a link to the Savior. You've likely heard it before, but I believe that so often our gravest mistakes and most hurtful failures create the places out of which we see God's greatest glory shine in our lives. It's not too late, my brother, to turn around from whatever wrong directions we may have chosen and allow God to heal us through our legacy. If we are willing to pour into our children with the deliberate passion that grows from the wellspring of our humility and dependence on God, then He is committed to working through our flaws and the cracks in our characters and producing new life.

A FATHER'S FIRE

We've already discussed some ways to accomplish more faithful fatherhood, but let me share a few more suggestions that might prove helpful in your interactions with your sons and daughters. I am far from a perfect father and now realize that many of the sacrifices I've made for my family and much of the time and energy I've devoted to ministry have robbed me of precious times with my kids that I can never recover. However, I also realize the ways in which I have sought to be a more present Daddy, engaging with my children's lives and simply enjoying the variety of who each of my children is becoming, a vibrant and diverse bouquet of young men and women. These are simple areas I return to again and again in my own pursuit of remaining passionately ablaze in my children's lives:

STOKING THE FIRE OF FATHERHOOD

1. **Be there.** As we've discussed and observed with David's example, it's so essential to spend not just quantity time with your kids but also as much quality time as possible.

Being there also means being emotionally present for your children, allowing them to see your own fears and insecurities at times even as they witness your delight and appreciation of them. I encourage you to look for areas where you can spend more intentional time with your children this week.

2. **Learn from them.** There's so much that our young people have to teach us—about themselves, about ourselves, and about who God is. Too often we feel like our children look to us for all the answers, when they really just want us to be honest and fair with them. If we realize that we don't always have all the answers, know all the rules, or practice what we preach, then we become open to allowing God to speak to us through our children. Such receptivity can keep us young at heart as we experience the innocence and beauty of youthful exuberance.

3. **Be their father before their friend.** Even as we learn from our kids and move toward a time when we can interact with them as adult to adult, it's vital—especially during the formative years—that we maintain boundaries and set household rules. I think it's important to give children a structured lifestyle. This includes things as simple as eight o'clock bedtimes at early ages and then moving the time back as they get older. Doing this gives them some sense that age brings freedom but not all at once, because, as you well know, freedom brings with it responsibility, and I am not always sure that we are as ready as we think we are for the responsibility. Don't try to be your child's best friend, looking to them for affirmation and validation. Be confident in who you are and seek encouragement elsewhere so that

you can be the firm and gentle father your children need foremost.

4. **Separate the baggage.** You must always remain aware that many of your responses to parenting stem from your own childhood, your own relationship with your parents, and your ability to forgive the past in order to move into the future. I knew a young man who told me that as his son approached his twelfth birthday, the man became increasingly anxious, troubled, and depressed. Shortly after the birthday party, my friend was thumbing through a photo album from his own childhood and realized that he himself had been twelve when his own father had abandoned the family and then killed himself. Watching his son approach a traumatic and vulnerable age in his own life made this man afraid for his son because it rekindled old wounds within him. My friend finally regained peace when he realized that he is a very different man from his father and that he was not about to abandon his family or give up the fight.

5. **Forgive and ask forgiveness.** Ask for your children's forgiveness when you know you've failed them or you recognize an area in which you have hurt them, either unintentionally or selfishly. Similarly, practice forgiveness with them often, showing them the grace, mercy, and love of our Heavenly Father. Keep in mind, however, that sometimes the most loving response means maintaining boundaries, enforcing consequences, and providing disciplinary reinforcement. Help your child to know what it means to take responsibility for his or her actions, primarily by your example.

INCREASING YOUR RANGE OF MOTION—FOR HIM

What legacy do you want to leave to your children? How can you make a small action each day to contribute to that legacy?

How is baggage with your own father interfering with the way you want to father your own children?

What's your greatest struggle as a father to your children? What keeps you from being more vulnerable and authentic around them?

INCREASING YOUR RANGE OF MOTION—FOR HER

How would you describe your man's involvement as a father to his children?

How much time does he spend with the children each week? How can you encourage (not guilt or pressure!) him to spend more time with them?

How can you allow his children to see more of his authentic self? What can you do to make him more comfortable in front of them?

---

6. **Offer your blessing.** Often I observe many men who are willing to spend large sums of money on presents for their children for Christmas, special birthdays, or as incentives for significant accomplishments. However, when it comes to offering words of blessing to their children during these times, it's as if the Sahara Desert suddenly blows into his throat and arthritis grips his hand so he can't utter a word or write a sentence. Words have such tremendous power, especially with our children. Whether it's saying what's in

our hearts, even if we don't know the right words or sound particularly eloquent, or jotting down a simple note saying how proud you are, I encourage you to bless your children at every opportunity.

7. **Pray for them without ceasing.** Perhaps one of the best ways we can love our children is by interceding for them with God. When my children were young, and even still with my eight-year-old, I enjoyed our bedtime ritual of reading a story and saying our prayers before the lights were turned off and they closed their weary eyes for a good night's sleep. And even though it embarrasses some of my image-conscious teenagers, I still like to pray for them in their presence, aloud. I want them to know that I hope for them and that I'm praying for their futures. And I want them to experience my faith in action, establishing a spiritual legacy that they can continue with their own children. So often we may feel powerless in our desires and attempts to shield and protect our kids, but we can always pray for them and entrust them to God's care.

Yes, my friend, it takes incredible reserves of courage, patience, perseverance, and love to be a father. But as a man who is seeking balance in his life, discovering more of who he is and where he's going, you have it in you to be available for your children and to take the most incredible risk of all with them: loving them as your Father in heaven loves you.

Part Seven

A MAN'S
RELATIONSHIP
WITH GOD

"We are in danger of forgetting that we cannot do what God does, and that God will not do what others can do."
—OSWALD CHAMBERS

"God always answers in the deeps, never in the shallows of our soul."
—UNKNOWN

- When a child leads the way in commitment to a church, 3½ percent of families follow.
- When a woman/mom leads the way in commitment to a church, 17 percent of families follow.
- But when a man/dad leads the way in commitment to a church, 93 percent of families follow.

⟞⟟⟞〰⟞⟟⟞

THIRTEEN

A MAN AFTER GOD'S OWN HEART

God prepares great men for great task by great trials.
—J. K. GRESSETT

I know a man who confided in me his most prevalent fantasy. He imagined himself running away, much like a little boy might sneak out of the house late one night with only his backpack and teddy bear. My friend says that his life overwhelms him and that he often finds himself daydreaming about disappearing from his life. Something is missing, he says. As much as he enjoys his work, he finds its demands unceasing, always urgent, and unsympathetic to his responsibilities in other areas of his life. As much as he loves his wife and children, he feels consumed by their need of his time, attention, and provision, always asking, needing, and hoping that he has more to give. As much as he cares about his church and its ministry, he knows that he's overcommitted and wearing the fabric of his faith dangerously threadbare.

"One day I'm going to wake up, shower, and get dressed for the day, but instead of taking my usual exit off the interstate toward my office, I'm going to keep going—maybe toward the airport or maybe toward the state line. Either way, I'll just drive until I want to stop and eat or take in the sights. Maybe I'll buy a plane ticket and fly to France or Alaska or New Zealand or Zimbabwe. Somewhere I've never been where I'll find what I'm looking for."

"And what makes you think you'll find it somewhere else?" I asked him. He looked at me puzzled and then became more distressed. I could tell my friend was heading toward a kind of breakdown if he didn't take some time away for himself to replenish his reservoir, so I encouraged him to schedule a vacation. "I don't do well on vacations, Bishop," he replied. "I schedule too many activities and feel pressured to have a good time. Besides, I'm still me just in a more beautiful setting." He couldn't even allow himself time off without feeling the need to be efficient with his time! But with his final statement, I realized that my friend was telling me the secret to his situation. The problem, of course, was not with the demands of his personal circumstances as much as with the storm within himself.

Instead of a vacation, I recommended that he make a spiritual retreat, a time alone in the desert of his soul to get in touch with himself and, more important, with God. "The thought frightens me to death," he told me in response, "but it sounds like a place I need to be running to rather than running away from."

SOUL FOOD

I don't think my friend's fantasy is all that unusual. Life is overwhelming, and most men don't take adequate care of themselves, as we've discussed in other chapters. However, there's a greater need that many men neglect just as much as they often neglect their bodies and personal needs: their soul-need for a relationship with God. We get so caught up in the digitalized hum of our hi-tech lives that it's difficult to hear the still, small voice of God's Spirit in us. We feed the body with high-protein diets and tone our muscles in the gym, but we never partake of soul food or exercise our spiritual muscles.

I'm convinced that if a man is going to succeed in maneuvering through the various he-motions of his life, then he must have a constant compass to provide him with a True North, the ultimate GPS that will never fail him. When we overlook our relationship with God or get caught up in worshipping false idols, such as money, work, or sex, then our soul dries out like a sponge and our spirit becomes parched. We know that something is missing, so like my friend who wanted to run away from his life, we think that if we change the circumstances that we'll be fulfilled. This is only partially true, for we can't run away from ourselves, and we can't run away from God. David was certainly aware of this truth even in the midst of his own desire to run away from his troubles:

> Where can I go from Your Spirit?
> Or where can I flee from Your presence?
> If I ascend into heaven, You are there;
> If I make my bed in hell, behold, You are there.
> (PSALM 139:7–8)

No, we cannot run from God, not forever, and certainly not for long if we want to know peace in our hearts and purpose in our steps. We must spend time alone with Him, seeking His wisdom and allowing Him to speak to us in His time. The things that we often put before Him are for us to use and enjoy within the context of His blessing and instruction. It's not that God doesn't want us to enjoy sex—He simply doesn't want its pleasure to have power over our hearts as a soulless method of gratification and escape. It's not that God cares how much money we make—He simply wants us focused on our need for Him and to be good stewards of the resources that He has entrusted to us. But too often we make our bank accounts and our next sexual conquest our gods, living from dollar sign to decimal point, from flirtation to fornication. If we are not in pursuit of the one true Living God, then our idols and addictions will leave us as dehydrated on our life's journey as drinking honey in the desert. Yes, the honey is sweet and can provide sustenance for a while, but it is not intended to provide the essential oxygen and fluid nutrition to our bodies that water can. Have you ever eaten a spoonful of honey and tasted its sweetness dissolving in your mouth? If you're like me, one of the first things you want to do after tasting honey is drink a large glass of water—its sweetness only heightens my thirst.

CRIMINAL CONFESSION

So what does God want from us? How can we drink from the cool, sweet water He offers us? How do we connect with Him on a heart-to-heart level? I believe many men are intimidated by their perception of perfection or, perhaps better expressed, by their misperception of imperfection. For God does not ask us to get our act together before we come to Him. No, He delights in meeting us where we are, running down the long, dusty road to meet His prodigal sons when they finally come home to Him. I'm convinced that too often we keep feeding the pigs at the trough, eating like one of them ourselves, rather than realizing that we don't have to come to our Father as a successful, rich, well-groomed, happily married parent of 2.5 kids in the suburbs. What keeps you from turning toward home and running to meet your daddy?

One of the most powerful sermons I ever heard as a boy was from an old revival preacher who visited our church, one of many on his circuit throughout the Southeast. A tall, thin, dignified man, he didn't possess a seminary degree or know the finer points of theological debate, but he did own an astute and thorough knowledge of God's Word and demonstrated a powerful anointing to deliver God's message to His people.

I'll never forget sitting in the front row during one of his weeknight services, mesmerized by his presence as he stood at the front of the church in his dark blue suit, crisp white shirt, and navy tie. This preacher prayed and then began his sermon with a heartfelt confession. "My brothers and sisters," he began, "I have something heavy on my heart that I must confess. I am an adulterer. I am a murderer. I am a man who doomed his child to his death." And then he paused and became choked up with emotion, moist around the eyes, and momentarily diverted from his sermon.

Well, you can imagine the silence in the sanctuary as every eye remained transfixed on this man and the incredible admission he had just delivered. The old preacher began to lose his solemn composure and broke out into a nervous sweat as he dabbed his handkerchief to his brow and tried to continue. Certainly, I'd heard rumors before from the gossipy old ladies at our church about some of the deacons and other church members who were suspected of engaging in immoral activities. However, I'm not sure any of us had ever heard such a powerful, personal confession as the one that man spoke with those three simple sentences.

This brother continued by sharing how he'd lived in an apartment building in Atlanta, where he had once been a wealthy business owner and church leader in his community. One day he was out on his balcony near the top of his building when he looked down and saw a beautiful woman sunbathing on the balcony of the apartment just across from and below his own. I remembered being engrossed by his vivid description of the sister's beauty and how he asked neighbors in his building until he learned her name. Then he arranged to "accidentally" meet her in the lobby one afternoon, and the next thing he knew, they were starting an adulterous affair. This older gentleman seemed sincerely sorry to have to share such information, and several times he mentioned his ongoing struggle with his conscience and with what he knew to be true of God's Word. However, he began to love this woman and to plot ways to steal her away from her husband, especially once she became pregnant.

Perhaps others in the congregation were starting to figure out his rhetorical purpose by now, but as a young boy of ten or so, I still believed that this man was telling his own true story. When he got to the part about being on the draft board and sending this woman's husband away to the front line of Vietnam where the man would be killed, I had to pick my jaw up off the floor. Then it began to dawn on me just about the time this old preacher stepped out of his role as a modern-day David and directed us to Samuel's account in the Scriptures. But he had delivered his sermon already, as far as I was concerned. His dramatic and larger-than-life performance as a passionate man who knew God but also knew the sensual lusts of the flesh and justifications of the will was mighty powerful.

But this old preacher was not done. As he became energized with the anointing of the Spirit and raised his voice in a passionate delivery of God's message, I was stunned by his main point. "David is referred to as a man after God's own heart," he said, "but David was so far from perfect that many of us would consider ourselves better than him if he sat across from us. To become people after our Lord's own heart does not require perfection—we would all be doomed then. No, it requires a passionate heart, an honest conscience, and the perseverance to keep seeking Him when we fail."

SOFT AT THE CORE

His words obviously stayed with me and impressed upon me a desire to be a man like David: not perfect—but passionate, forgiven, and faithful. Indeed, David was not perfect, yet he was favored by God. Recall how Scripture characterizes the contrast between David and his predecessor, Saul.

> "You acted foolishly," Samuel said. "You have not kept the command the LORD your God gave you; if you had, he would have established your kingdom over Israel for all time.
> But now your kingdom will not endure; the LORD has sought out a man after his own heart and appointed him leader of his people, because you have not kept the LORD's command."
> (1 SAMUEL 13:13–14)

On the one hand, the differences between Saul and David seem obvious. Saul is described as foolish and disobedient, while David, by implication, is said to be a man whom God has sought out because he has a heart set on God. However, when we go back to considering many of the mistakes and sinful excursions into sensual indulgence and proud resistance that we see over the course of David's life, it's tempting to wonder whether David was foolish and disobedient too.

Don't stop praying for areas in your life where you have not been a model Christian.

We don't need a jury from Court TV to make a case for his crimes being just as bad if not more consequential than Saul's. So what is the difference, then? I can't help but believe that so much of why David is described as a man of God emerges from the center of his heart.

On special occasions my wife bakes this delicious, ooey-gooey chocolate dessert. It's like a cupcake on the outside, but when you cut into it, out pours this rich, warm, hot fudge filling. You'd never know by looking that this beautiful, elegant little indulgence has such a soft filling in the middle. I believe David was the same way. In fact, one of his father's servants describes David to Nathan in this way: "I have seen a son of

Jesse the Bethlehemite, who is skillful in playing, a mighty man of valor, a man of war, prudent in speech, and a handsome person; and the Lord is with him" (1 Samuel 16:18). On the exterior, David is ruddy and good-looking, tough and rugged, a real man's man. But on the inside, he is sensitive, musically inclined, creative, poetic, and tender in his knowledge of and devotion to his God.

Similarly, I believe we are called to maintain a soft, tender core that's growing in its pursuit and reliance on God. We don't have to be a giant-slayer or a war hero to be like David. We don't have to compose poetry on a pretty hillside while sheep graze and the clouds go by. But we do have to make our relationship with God the top priority of our heart and stay fixed on Him like a heat-seeking missile homing in on its target. David knew such a desire when he wrote, "As the deer pants for the water brooks, so pants my soul for You, O God" (Psalm 42:1).

LIVING WATER

Just as we should hydrate our bodies regularly with clean drinking water, so should we take daily sips of the Living Water that Jesus offers us. "If anyone thirsts, let him come to Me and drink. He who believes in Me, as the Scripture has said, out of his heart will flow rivers of living water" (John 7:37–38).

Now ideally, a man would daily stay in touch with his spiritual needs and hold an ongoing conversation with his Creator in prayer, reading and receiving wisdom from time spent in God's Word. However, most men are energy efficient and want to be able to see some tangible rewards from their efforts. Pretty soon the disciplines of prayer and Bible study, of ministry and spiritual reflection, seem far removed from the pressures of juggling funds to pay for new braces, working overtime to finish the report, and being home in time to see your wife before she dozes off. When forced to choose between the physical demands of life and the spiritual disciplines, a man often focuses on the more urgent, in-his-face needs.

Meanwhile, other men won't even pretend to have good intentions regarding their time spent pursuing their own endeavors rather than God. Some men tell me that in part they're afraid of what will be required of them if they give themselves to God and allow Him to shape their lives as the Master Potter that He is, molding and turning our humble lump of clay into His masterpiece. I call this the "missionary syndrome," because often these men share their fear with me that if they give themselves wholeheartedly to God that He will require them to move to Siberia or South Africa and become an impoverished missionary to indigenous peoples. I usually tell these men two truths: (1) God will certainly ask us to do things that we're uncomfortable doing, acts that will require courage and sacrifice; (2) He will never send us to do a job for which He hasn't equipped us and given us a measure of peace concerning our involvement. While I can't promise you that God won't call you to be a missionary in some remote and desolate land, I can assure you that He will only ask it of you if that is who He's created you to be. I'm not sure that I have ever seen Him take a man that He's gifted as an artist, accountant, or auto mechanic and asked that man to abandon his gifts and grit out a job for the long term. Yes, there will be short-term sacrifices and inconveniences, but alongside it there will be long-term vision and peace-filled perseverance.

Like a man traveling through the intense severity of the Sahara who does not pay attention to his body's need for water, a man who does not attend to his spiritual thirst in this life will dehydrate his soul. It doesn't matter how much money you have in the bank or how far your available line of credit extends. Your wife may be an incredible woman of beauty, passion, intelligence, and compassion who loves you as much as you love her. Your career may offer a level of unique personal satisfaction and reward as you pour your talents into its lifeblood. You may serve your church and be known as a gifted teacher and wise counselor, a reliable ministry partner whom others turn to for comfort and strength. You still need God.

Forgive me if I state the obvious, but I'm continually amazed by how many successful, bright, and passionate men reach a level of burnout because something's missing in their lives only to realize that they've neglected their relationship with God. Oh, they never intend to set Him aside or ignore His presence in their lives, but they've learned to make it on their own and haven't been forced to rely on Him as their sustainer and Savior. Or they have bought into a religious compartmentalization of God as if He's just another weekly appointment, a client who needs their attention on Sunday mornings and maybe one other night during the week. But I dare say that until a man establishes his relationship with God as the foundation for the other areas and relationships in his life, he will consistently struggle with finding his true purpose, enjoying the fruit of his labor, and tasting peace that passeth understanding in this life. Until you commit yourself to knowing the God who created you, you will run the risk of being only a small fraction of a man, a benign portion of your potential, and only a decimal of your destiny.

So if you have not made that commitment to knowing Him and giving your life over to Him, I encourage you to invite Him into your life with humility. Many men have been exposed to religion, exposed to cultural Christianity, without ever having experienced the personal intensity of a burning bush encounter with God and the Son He sent as our sacrifice, Jesus. And I'm afraid there are numerous reasons why so many men are soured and scared and repulsed by what they see in many churches—the hypocrisy, the legalism, the favoritism, and self-righteousness. Too often it seems as if the Church has become big business, more reliant on psychology than salvation, and more intent on entertaining its congregation than worshipping God and serving the Body of Christ.

I don't mean to sound harsh, so forgive my brief and generalized tirade for a moment, for I trust that you know that God's Church is near and dear to my heart, not an institution for me as much as a living and breathing organism to which I have answered His call to serve. This is the source of my passion for this topic, because I know how relevant and revealing the Church can be to a man in his relationship with his Lord. However, for men especially, I'm afraid the Church

Prayer without sincerity is futile.

often emasculates and castrates the power and passion we feel in exchange for compliance and domestic tranquility. So many men tell me that they tried going to church, tried participating and getting involved, but were bored and frustrated.

I'll never forget one gentleman in particular who came to me at a ManPower conference and told me that he appreciated my passion for God but that he simply couldn't access the same level of enthusiasm at his home church. When I pressed him for an explanation, he briefly told me about his troubled childhood and troubled adolescence as a gang member. When he encountered the personal God whom he now served, he turned his life around and got involved in a local church. "But I've never really fit in there, Bishop Jakes," he explained. "I feel like the little boy who's too rambunctious during the solemn service and all the little old ladies are looking down their noses at me." He made me laugh at his description, but I knew exactly what he was saying.

Men who are in touch with the heart of God run the risk of being just as dangerous as God Himself. They're willing to follow their dreams, question tradition, and think outside of conventional boxes. They are willing to risk conflict and speak their minds and reveal what God has laid on their hearts. They are willing to act irrationally and listen intuitively to the calling God sets before them. All of these endeavors can be incredibly threatening to others who are looking for a more stable, staid, and secure environment in the Church. And, truth be told, our Church today has largely fallen into a place where so often men hide behind the women who hold the real power and run the operations of the church without ever receiving credit. So perhaps now when some men are willing to stand up and take initiative, the church mothers feel threatened and view it as simply an immature phase of spiritual adolescence.

Furthermore, I find that men who have only found the Church after a life full of struggles often need a church that understands them and is prepared to confront and develop them as men. Often these men do not understand Christian colloquialisms. They are confused by some of the do's and don'ts that are customary in most of our churches. These young men, like many others, are truly interested in serving God but tend to be less "churchy" than most of its members. They try hard but often feel uncomfortable in conversations that do not always "keep it real."

Men need a more transparent, less complicated environment in which to grow. These men find our religious rhetoric intimidating and sometimes irrelevant. A man from an unchurched background wants to discuss openly his battles with lust, his struggles with boredom on Friday nights, his struggles with past angers and worries about worldly matters. He needs encouragement in fighting the poor decisions of his past as he often feels like he's behind the rest of the class. He finds himself often needing to break through the social barriers that are often invisible walls that alienate men from feeling at home in the Church.

Other men who grew up in the Church or feel comfortable in the culture must not confuse their relationship with God with their interaction and involvement in the Church. For all our criticism and concern, the Church can offer a man many wonderful arenas of support, service, instruction and fellowship. However, it cannot replace the personal connection he needs with the Living God who formed him in his mother's womb and knew him before he was a glimmer in his father's eye. So many men in their struggles along the journey long to be known and seen and appreciated for who they are. They feel like they are forced to conform and stretch themselves into being someone different for all the different players in their lives—a loving husband to their wives, a devoted father to their children, a dutiful son to their parents, a loyal friend to their network, a tireless worker to their company, and on and on it goes. And then we feel missed for who we really are without any place where all of these roles can be stripped and our true center revealed.

Our relationship with God provides us with this safe place in which to maintain our sanity and security. Through knowing and relating to His Son Jesus, we are invited to be transformed in this life and to become more than we could ever become if left to our own devices. He is the One who calls and coaches us to take risks that seem beyond our reach. He is the loving shepherd who comes after us when we go astray, leaving the ninety-nine so that when we fail to stay on the path He can rescue and redirect us. He is the fierce and passionate defender of our souls, thwarting the enemy who prowls and scowls and seeks to devour us. Jesus is the tender friend Who listens and understands even when we ourselves don't know what we mean or who we are. He is the compassionate Healer Who offers us peace and comfort and solace in the shadow of His wings.

PRIDE AND PREJUDICE

If He is all of these and more, then why do so many men view a relationship with God as a crutch, a sign of weakness? Why are those who have committed to Him willing only to set Him aside like a mistress who once offered a scintillating affair that has now grown cold and tiresome? There are myriad reasons and I won't attempt to explain or encapsulate them here, but please allow me to share my observations about the primary reasons that we men often give up on God or seek to relegate Him to a small portion of our lives.

So much of it comes down to pride and prejudice. No, I'm not talking about the Jane Austen book you read in high school or the film your wife may have dragged you to see a couple of years ago. I'm talking about the pride of self-sufficiency, which is, after all, the American male's credo, and the prejudice that develops when God doesn't come through for us the way we would like Him to. Please allow me to explain.

As we've discussed and examined, many factors in our culture condition men to stand alone and take care of themselves, stuffing their own needs down beneath a stoic mask of strength, certainty, and control. As little boys we're told not to cry, as young men we're told to control our hormonal desires, and as adults we're told to be responsible and productive. While these are all necessary and worthy endeavors in the right context, too many of us feel like there's no room to breathe, no space to be ourselves. So we work hard to be tough and appear to have ourselves and our lives together. And as we taste measures of success with such a strategy, we become more and more inclined to play this game of prideful management. "I'm a self-made man" has become the mantra of several generations of men. With our grandfathers' and fathers' generations, the phrase captured the essence of the hard-working, pulled-up-by-his-bootstraps kind of man who discovered an entrepreneurial niche and filled it to better his station and leave a legacy for his family. With my generation and that of my sons, the phrase often gets the emphasis placed on "self"-made man, meaning that we can invent and reinvent ourselves, being and becoming whoever we'd like to be, based on whatever makes us happy. If our first marriage doesn't work out, then there are plenty of other women out there for us to try. If this job doesn't pay enough, then we keep searching until one appeals to us.

On and on the merry-go-round spins as we try to catch a different brass ring each time our horse passes by, never realizing that we're stuck in place, spinning without advancing.

Pride is the one sin that has such potential for separating us from God and our need of Him because it blinds us and dulls our sense of perspective. Consider the way David insulated himself from the ravaging consequences of his sin with Bathsheba. After the king has taken another man's wife to his bed, had conceived a child with her, and had then ordered the execution of her husband to cover up their affair, David becomes blinded by his own power and arrogance. He is the king after all, chosen and anointed by God Himself. However, no matter who we are or how powerful we become, within the ministry or in any other realm, we are still human and must rely on God to satisfy us foremost. In the boredom of his midlife years, David finds the beauty of a woman, the lust of the flesh, a fitting diversion. But as his sin snowballs into an avalanche of desperation and deception, he allows his pride to callus his heart to the full effect of his wrongdoing. After Uriah dies and David takes Bathsheba as his wife—the least he can do, right?—it almost seems as if he's off the hook now. However, there's a short little understatement: "But the thing that David had done displeased the Lord" (2 Samuel 11:27).

> *God has grace for the challenge you face, so don't be afraid to cry out for His help.*

So in order to pierce through David's shell of pride around his heart, God sends Nathan to tell the king a story, a parable that is about David's own life.

Then the LORD sent Nathan to David. And he came to him, and said to him: "There were two men in one city, one rich and the other poor. The rich man had exceedingly many flocks and herds. But the poor man had nothing, except one little ewe lamb which he had bought and nourished; and it grew up together with him and with his children. It ate of his own food and drank from his own cup and lay in his bosom; and it was like a daughter to him. And a traveler came to the rich man, who refused to take from his own flock and from his own herd to prepare one for the wayfaring man who had come to him; but he took the poor man's lamb and prepared it for the man who had come to him."

So David's anger was greatly aroused against the man, and he said to Nathan, "As the LORD lives, the man who has done this shall surely die! And he shall restore fourfold for the lamb, because he did this thing and because he had no pity."

Then Nathan said to David, "You are the man! Thus says the LORD God of Israel: 'I anointed you king over Israel, and I delivered you from the hand of Saul.' "

(2 SAMUEL 12:1–7)

It's a brilliant strategy in many ways and once again illustrates both the power of story to reach us with truth but also the ways we try to justify and make our hearts impenetrable against serving and obeying God. If Nathan had simply walked into the palace and confronted David with a direct assault on the king's sin, the prophet would have been killed and the consequences of the royal cover-up would have grown that much deeper. David had developed a prejudice against God that prevented him from feeling repentence for his sin. "If God would only provide what I need, then I wouldn't have to take care of myself. But since He hasn't come through, I better get it while I can." David likely didn't articulate such a prejudice in these words nor do we, but when we pursue selfish pleasures and addictive idols to fill us instead of our relationship with God, then we have taken matters into our own hands and usually feel a measure of entitlement.

However, God knew that David was still a compassionate man at heart, a man who had a tender spot that could be reached with the right angle. God becomes a masterful fisherman using just the right bait to hook his agile fish. And David can't resist the bait, for he spots the injustice when the story is told in terms removed from his own circumstance. He's outraged that such an arrogant, selfish man should go unpunished while his poor, humble counterpart suffers such an injustice.

What does it take for you to become aware of your own transgressions? Where are you acting like the rich man and stealing the poor man's sheep, then hiding behind justification and entitlement? Most of us have our areas and build high fences around them. It may be the secret website that you go to on your laptop when you're traveling and alone in your hotel room. "It doesn't hurt anybody, right? It's better than going out and finding someone to get into trouble with in person," you think. It's not an addiction; it's just part of being a man and needing sexual relief.

Or perhaps it's the emotional affair with your best friend's wife, the one who seems to understand you better than your own wife. She always laughs at your jokes and nods sympathetically when you describe your workload and the hard day you're having. She gives you the attention you crave, and her touch on your shoulder seems to linger longer than it should. You have her cell number on speed dial, and you know you should quit confiding in her before something else happens, but you've come to rely on her compassionate glances and personal attention to get you through your day.

Maybe it's the way you justify your chronic workaholism and reliance on money to give you a sense of security and affluence. You're never home before eight at night and you frequently don't see your children for days on end, but you tell yourself that you're making a better life for them by your hard work and sacrifices. If it weren't for your hard work, there would be no half-million-dollar home with a pool, no deluxe SUV, no trips to Disneyland, and other luxuries. Yet somewhere in your heart you know the truth is that your family would rather have time with you instead of another Gameboy or DVD player. The truth is that you're avoiding the risk of emotional intimacy with your wife by telling yourself that as long as you keep money in her account and buy her a new bling bling at Christmas and on her birthday that your relationship is okay.

Or perhaps you've spiritualized your addiction and found a ministry outlet that consumes you and provides you with the soul gratification you can't get anywhere else. Having others need and depend on you, having them view you as godly and wise and spiritually mature can be a powerful aphrodisiac for your love of self. You feel doubly good about yourself because you're doing something for God and because you get so much positive feedback from His people.

On and on we could describe the ways that we let our pride blind us to the reality of our lifestyles and love affairs with things that pull us away from God and away from our true calling. But God loves us too much to leave us lost in our own delusions. He sends His Word to pierce through our defenses, and I believe He continues to send Nathans into our lives if we'll only listen, wise men who have been where we are and try to give us a reality check back to our true power source.

For we see in David's confession and repentance an acknowledgment that his real sin is against God and God alone. "Against You, You only, have I sinned, and done this evil in Your sight" writes David in Psalm 51. He finally quits playing games and gets to the bottom line. All that he's doing is worthless if he doesn't have relational intimacy with his God, the One who sought him and anointed him king, the One who believed in him and saw him through so many battles, so many close calls with a variety of enemies.

Recently, I was ministering to a young man who was an admitted adulterer and a long-time backslider. He was obviously under conviction. Yet I noticed that he harbored real bitterness for some of the Church persons he had met years ago. He confided to me that when he was in church over twenty years ago, one of the other young men had made a sexual advance toward him. Now this brother is far from being someone who has this type of struggle—to the contrary, he was leaning to the extreme in the other direction. Nonetheless, he said that this other young man had made an inappropriate and immoral advance toward him. Over the years, this other young man had gone on to marry and become a pastor while my acquaintance, the one who had backslidden, went on to succeed in business. Now, as I ministered to him, he was clearly hungry to come home.

He spoke about this brother, who was now a preacher, with disgust and anger. However, I asked him, "How many times have you failed yourself, your God, and your family over twenty years?" He said, "Many, many times." Then I asked him, "Why then are you holding this brother hostage to his mistake while you seek forgiveness for your own?" I pointed out that in twenty years anyone could change anything.

Many men sit in barbershops for hours, criticizing people who are trying to serve God while they themselves haven't the courage to fight their own weaknesses. These Monday-morning quarterbacks have great advice for what others ought to do, but in reality they have not had a personal, humbling encounter with God, which automatically should bring us to a place of introspection and humility.

The blame game often becomes a loophole that enables men whom God is calling to deeper consecration to escape the call and destroy a chance at a real relationship with Him. A failure in a church member is not an excuse to walk away from God. There are doctors who make mistakes, but we do not close down the hospital or stop dispensing medical aid to those in need. There are restaurants that don't meet the health code, but even they are given a chance to clean up their act before they are closed to business.

Men, you must remember that no one died for you but Jesus. He is the One we ought to seek for approval. It is against God that we sin. We cannot blame others and their weaknesses while we harbor areas in our own heart that need repair. I am not excusing the pastor who, as a young man, had allowed his behavior to mar his testimony. But I want to point out that many men confuse Church with God and forget to forgive others who are flawed like us. Apparently, this man and the events of twenty years ago did not stop him from seeking God, getting forgiveness, and moving on.

> *Don't be afraid to admit your sins.*
> *Our Father won't abandon you.*

Two men struggled with controlling expressions of their sexual lust. One man is married and happy, seeking God and being used by Him to move forward. But the other is groping for excuses to justify his unwillingness to surrender to God, and he'd rather use a twenty-year-old incident than come clean before God and admit that he needs forgiveness himself. Brothers, please don't let the past stop you from finding a vibrant life with God now.

REALITY PROGRAMS

One way I believe we can keep our heart plugged into our Supreme Power Source and maintain that vibrant life He offers is by keeping it honest before Him day in and day out. I recall my first impressions when the so-called reality television programs began airing. "What's the big deal? It's even kind of boring," I thought to myself. But when I expressed my feelings to my teenaged daughter, she pointed out that a lot of the entertainment was in the spontaneity of the contestants' emotions. She explained to me that it's not so much who gets voted off the island or offered a long-stemmed rose at the end of the episode as much as it's about how those players respond. Will they shrug it off? Did they expect to leave? Will they cry or plot to get even?

While I still harbor my doubts about the quality of entertainment these programs offer, I do believe that we must learn a lesson from this format and display our true selves to God. Even though we know that we can't hide from Him, we still resist going to Him with our problems and expressing our honest emotions. But another facet of David's life-long relationship with God emerges in the poems he wrote and collected as the Psalms. You may not think of yourself as a poet, but you can express the same kinds of feelings and thoughts that we see David composing. And in case you haven't read them in a while or don't know them at all, I invite you to take inventory of the full variety of emotions they express. These poems are not just warm, fuzzy praise songs repeated in endless variation over and over again. No, a perusal through the Psalms reveals fear, jealousy, anger, doubt, depression, regret, deceit, and a host of other dark emotions that most of us are uncomfortable expressing to anyone, but especially to God. However, this man after God's own heart has no problem sharing them with his Lord. I have pastored black men, white men, Hispanic men, Native-American men, as well as wealthy men, and even homeless men. You know what? When it comes to our need for mercy and grace, all men must meet at the cross and confess our need of God to survive manhood. You must be strong to be a man. You must be balanced to be a man. You must pray to be a truly great man.

May I share with you the truth of the matter? I have seen the shattering blows that come from poverty, and I have carried the stressful bruises that come from the demands of accomplishments. Neither of them is bearable without God. I strongly encourage you to go to church where you can be fed and strengthened. But far deeper than that, you must have your own personal relationship with God. Do not allow anyone or anything, past, present, or future, to dissuade you from seeking His face. Your weakness should not drive you from God but to Him. He is able to assist you as you grow and evolve, experience disappointment, and all that's entailed in the process of life and living. I know that I would have fainted, forfeited my destiny, and driven off into the sunset, much like my friend said he often wanted to do back at the beginning of this chapter. But when I would have driven away, God took the wheel. I am so thankful that He did. Why don't you allow God to take the wheel of your life and strengthen you and fortify you when life seems unpredictable and you feel empty from the constant demands of those who say they love you or need you?

God can handle us no matter where we meet Him on our journey. One of my favorite of David's psalms expresses not only his fear and uncertainty but also his trust and hope in God's goodness. Psalm 27 opens with "The LORD is my light and my salvation; Whom shall I fear? The LORD is the strength of my life; Of whom shall I be afraid?" and David continues on in this bold vein of proclaiming God's faithfulness and protection through various trials and adversity. However, by the middle of the poem, the tone shifts and the Psalmist cries out, "Do not hide Your face from me; Do not turn Your servant away in anger; You have been my help; Do not leave me nor forsake me, O God of my salvation." By the end of the psalm, he admits that he would have fainted had he not believed that he would see the goodness of the Lord in the land of the living. If David almost fainted, had it not been for his faith, then what about you and me?

Some biblical scholars have even wondered if this psalm was once actually two poems that were eventually combined into one. However, I don't think so. I believe these honest heart expressions convey the shifting moods and volatile emotions that we all experience. One minute we can be praising God and the next minute cursing Him. Our hearts are often fickle and our moods can change faster than the weather. The amazing thing about God is His ability to know the worst in us and lovingly bring out the best in us.

So as you reflect on your own relationship with God, even as you're reading this page, I encourage you to be as honest as possible about where you are and what you feel toward Him. You must trust that He can han-

---

How would you describe your present relationship with God? What do you wish you could change?

What keeps you from being totally honest before God? What keeps you from believing how much He loves you?

How often do you pray, read Scripture, and worship? What would it take to increase your commitment to these goals?

How can the important people in your life—your spouse, children, close friends—encourage you in your dependence on God?

What vision has God given you for your future? What do you need to do now in order to make it happen?

How can you encourage your man to be honest before his God?

How would you describe your own relationship with God? What affect do you have on the way he seeks God in his life?

How often do the two of you pray or worship together? What can you do to encourage this more without nagging or pressuring him into it?

---

dle it. If you need further evidence beyond what David writes in the Psalms, then I encourage you to check out Ecclesiastes, by David's son Solomon, or the book of Lamentations or Jeremiah or Job. God can handle the full brunt of all the pain we've experienced, all the trials we've suffered, all the tears we've shed. He wants to be intimately involved in each day of our lives, guiding and nurturing, shepherding and challenging, if we will only let Him.

My brothers, I pray that your prayer, like David's conclusion at the end of Psalm 27, would be one of hope and perseverance, regardless of your present circumstances and the weather of your soul. Keep your heart soft at its center, your pride under control, and your prejudice against God's goodness sovereign to His Word and the testimony you have seen from Him throughout your life.

> I would have lost heart, unless I had believed
> That I would see the goodness of the LORD
> In the land of the living.
> Wait on the LORD;
> Be of good courage,
> And He shall strengthen your heart;
> Wait, I say, on the LORD!
> (PSALM 27:13–14)

EPILOGUE

—⟨⟩—

EMBRACE THE RACE

Nothing in the world can take the place of persistence. Talent will not; nothing is more common than unsuccessful men with talent. Genius will not; unrewarded genius is almost a proverb. Education will not; the world is full of educated derelicts. Persistence and determination alone are omnipotent. The slogan "Press on" has solved and will always solve the problems of the human race.

—Calvin Coolidge

If you have built castles in the air, your work need not be lost. That is where they should be. Now put the foundations under them.

—Henry David Thoreau

All around me, as far as the eye can see, cerulean blue waters swirl and dance along the horizon like a woman's dark curls of long, luxurious hair caught in the breeze. The scent of salt water permeates the air almost as sharply as the sunlight illuminates it and reflects off the water. The large charter boat upon which I stand lurches and rocks as if the deck beneath my feet might suddenly buck me overboard like a wild horse throwing its rider. I am not seasick, having grown accustomed to the rhythmic rocking, although I can understand why others near me cling to the rail with expressions of nausea and distress.

I'm on vacation with my family in a tropical locale, enjoying the sublime beauty and intoxicating pace of time on the beach. This day I've ventured onto a fishing boat with my sons and a few other brave men who want to go deep-sea fishing off of the island's coast where we are staying. As images of the shore recede behind us, I notice dolphins arcing through the air up ahead. I'm aware that I'm entering another world out here.

As we were instructed on how to use the giant rod and reel mounted before us on the deck, I realize that I've come a long way from the banks of the creek where I fished as a boy in West Virginia. And even though I am supposed to be fishing alongside the others, I am soon too absorbed in watching the water and the drama that is about to unfold to seriously maintain my line.

To my left near the back of the boat stands an older gentleman who clearly knows what he is doing. He has already caught my attention with his native, non-tourist apparel and pleasant demeanor, someone who either lives on the island where we are merely vacationing or else a man who has been here many times before. Soon after our boat drops anchor and we cast our lines, this gentleman seems to display more care and deliberation with his bait, his cast, and his exertion of patience.

So I'm not entirely surprised that he is the first among our party to get a bite. But, oh, what a bite it is! The line suddenly grows taut and there is such a pull that the boat rocks in his direction. For a moment I imagine us on a ship to Nineveh with a mighty whale about to capsize our boat and swallow us all. And, I confess, I also have images from *Jaws* flash before my eyes—what if this is a shark?

But the creature on the other end of my new friend's line is neither whale nor shark but a magnificent swordfish. As it begins to struggle and thrash in and out of the waters, its body glistens as it catches rays of sun. I would panic and break the fishing line in such a tug of war or lose my grip on the reel altogether, but the mature gentleman remains calm and focused, smiling and obviously delighted at his potential catch.

That fish is not about to come in easy, to be reeled in gently and patiently like a small trout from the rivers where I grew up. No, we are in for quite a show as the swordfish jumps and jives his way up and down, back and forth, in an attempt to prolong not only his life but his freedom. He has to be at least ten feet long with considerable weight, several hundred pounds. In streaks of blue and silver, the fish pulls and yanks, darts and dances, while his master on the other end of the line firmly commands the line and slowly brings the fish closer and closer to us.

By the time the fish is alongside our boat and ready to be hoisted out of the water, it is clear that the fisherman is going to need some help. Three other men come over, lower a net from the side, and help maneuver the fish into it so that it can then be raised by a large crane-type device onto the deck. Just as we are all breathing a sigh of relief and marveling at such an incredible sight, the impossible happens. Or, if you know anything about fish stories, the most likely outcome happens. For this is a story of the one that got away. You see, that swordfish who finally seems to have relaxed as the net closes in around him, waits until the right moment and, just as the net is being drawn and raised, bucks and jumps like one of those trained porpoises at SeaWorld and arcs back into the water. All we can do is stand there in disbelief at such a sight, stunned. And then the old gentleman who has almost caught himself an incredible trophy begins laughing a low deep belly laugh. It is contagious, and soon we are all laughing and marveling at the splendor of this fish that got away.

"He was a fighter," the older man says. "I *like* that fish."

Later as I shared this anecdote with my wife and reflected on its message, I recalled the story that Jim Bakker had shared at the Back to the Bible conference. You remember, don't you? The story recounted in the Introduction of this book, about the man who kept an aquarium of exotic fish and accidentally caused them to boil while he was away for an extended time. The man then grieved and wondered if the fish had screamed out, trapped inside the glass case as the temperature increased and scalded the creatures to their death. Bakker shared how he knew what it was like to be boiling and imprisoned and to scream out in silence. I know what that is like as well, as do you.

However, the swordfish that had been snared and was fighting for his life suddenly seemed to represent the opposite of Bakker's fish tale. Instead of being trapped inside a glass prison, this fish knew the boundless ocean as his home and the incredible freedom, and danger, of living in such a tempestuous environment. This fish had apparently endured the tropical storms, hurricanes, and tidal waves that had plagued this island during past years. He had likely swam with the sharks and not been eaten. And he had evaded at least one determined fisherman, if not more. In the midst of certain capture and death, this fish had not given up but had suffered and endured until the time was right and he could seize his final opportunity to maintain his freedom. I know it sounds ridiculous to personify a swordfish this way, but I could just imagine him laughing at those ridiculous men on the boat who thought they were going to stuff him and mount him on a wall—either that or eat him.

I realized then as I compared the two stories that there are at least two kinds of fish. There are the small fish in the exotic aquarium who are fed and nurtured by someone else and left largely to the mercy of others. When the water gets hot in the tank, they are trapped and boil amidst the echoes of their silent screams for help, victims of limitation and isolation. And there are the big fish, contained only by their imagination and the distant shoreline beyond the horizon. These fish feed themselves, protect themselves, and develop a survival instinct that knows how to put up a good fight. That swordfish I observed wasn't merely emitting a silent scream; he was going to go down fighting, not giving up hope that there was a way to maintain his freedom by exercising insight and timing. Like David slaying Goliath, this fish seemed to face an insurmountable obstacle that he nonetheless managed to overcome.

I also thought about the two men's responses in these two stories. The aquarium owner and lover of exotic fish grieved and cried over his loss. He accepted his responsibility and felt remorse over his carelessness. Nonetheless, he couldn't bring back what he had lost. The older fisherman alongside me on the boat also lost his fish, but he had no regrets, for he had also put up an incredible fight and done all he could do to reel in his catch. When he lost his fish, he seemed to appreciate and identify the magnificence of a worthy opponent who had managed to best him that day. But I had a feeling this gentleman would be back and that someday in the near future a gorgeous ten-foot swordfish would be mounted above his fireplace!

GO THE DISTANCE

My friend, what kind of a fisherman do you want to be? Better yet, what kind of fish are you? I believe that inside each man is a swordfish who revels in his own beauty, strength, and passion. In innumerable ways for countless reasons, we lose sight of our own magnificence, of the masterpiece in progress that God is completing in us over the course of our lifetime. David possessed a sense of this wonder and appreciation, expressed so poetically in a psalm:

> When I consider Your heavens, the work of Your fingers,
> The moon and the stars, which You have ordained,
> What is man that You are mindful of him,
> And the son of man that You visit him?
> For You have made him a little lower than the angels,
> And You have crowned him with glory and honor.
> (PSALM 8:3–5)

As we conclude our he-motions journey together, I want to leave you with a few final words of encouragement. It's easy for us to be separated by the distance between us on the page. And even though we may never meet face to face, I hope that you feel like you know me better and can relate to my personal he-motions journey through the experiences and areas of my heart I've shared in these pages. And although I may never sit across from you and share a meal or a heart-to-heart conversation, I believe that I know your struggles, your weaknesses, and your strengths because they are part of what it means for me to be a man.

Since I'm not your father, your brother, your best friend, or your son, it's easy to dismiss me as a preacher with some thoughts collected in a book to sell. But I trust that you can feel me and know that the burden I carry for men struggling and striving on their journeys is legitimate and heartfelt. I can't be your counselor or personal coach, your therapist or pastor. But through these pages and our time together, I hope that I can be a small part of your journey, an encourager who helps you see the finish line and keep putting one foot in front of the other.

I want to be the mysterious giant my friend encountered while running a marathon last year. My friend Bill has taken up running as part of his midlife crisis–coping regime. A big, heavyset, linebacker-looking man over six feet tall, Bill has surprised himself and all of his friends, myself included, through his training and completion of many 10K races. Having lost weight and tasted the rewards of his new passion, Bill set his sights on a larger goal—a marathon in a nearby city.

On race day, the late spring weather promised a sunny, gorgeous day. Bill took off at a good pace and enjoyed the first half (thirteen miles!) of the race. But then the morning sun turned brutal and Bill began to dehydrate and struggled to down the Gatorade and water at the various aid stations along the way. Bill slowed and adjusted his pace, but by the time he hit mile twenty-five, he wasn't sure he could make it. With only a little over one mile left, Bill felt tears brimming in his eyes, and he experienced the fear that he had come so far and yet might not finish. By this time, his eight-minute-per-mile pace began to look more like a slow-motion jog, a parody of those runners striding along the beach in *Chariots of Fire.*

But just as he was about to give up, Bill heard someone behind him. "I just love seeing a big man hit his stride," said a low voice, chuckling. Bill looked up and saw a huge man, at least five inches taller and fifty pounds heavier, running alongside him with a big smile on his face. The man said, "Those little skinny wimps ahead of us think they're something for being fast, but they could never be an offensive lineman like me and you! The finish line is just ahead—see? Come on, brother!" And with that, the stranger took off, pacing himself about ten yards ahead of Bill.

Bill had to laugh at the man's words and found a renewed hope— no, a firm knowledge—that he could and would finish the race. He paced himself behind the giant for the last half-mile, smiling all the way. His newfound colleague reminded him of his purpose, of his accomplishment for having made it that far, and of the finish line now in sight. When Bill crossed the finish line, blinded by tears of joy, he searched and searched for his mysterious friend but couldn't find him. Nonetheless, the stranger had made an indelible impression that took Bill to new heights.

That is what I wish for you, my friend. I pray that my words here might touch you in some way and spark a greater awareness of your destiny, of that fire burning beneath the surface of your skin, of that dream held but not believed in and actively pursued. Take the next step, my brother, and pick up the pace. Look behind you at how far you've come—take in the view for just a moment. There have been hard things—of course, there have—but you've survived, you've been sustained, and you've made it this far. Now it's time to thrive, to flourish, and to pursue your dream more passionately than ever.

> Therefore we also, since we are surrounded by so great a cloud of witnesses, let us lay aside every weight, and the sin which so easily ensnares us, and let us run with endurance the race that is set before us.
> (HEBREWS 12:1)

And look ahead, my friend—the finish line is just around the corner. I have survived some tough places, failures too deep to ignore, frustrations difficult to explain. I have lost jobs, had cars repossessed, seen one of my companies collapse, withstood disappointments, and kept on going. To be sure, I know what it is to weep secretly while smiling publicly. After my mother died and the reality of both my parents' deaths sunk into my bones and reminded me of my own mortality, I moved beyond fear and morbid self-pity regarding my own death someday. Instead, I began to feel a sense of time running out before I can complete all the endeavors that I dream of accomplishing, running all of the races that God has called me to embrace. "Well done, thou good and faithful servant!" Those are the words that I long to hear, that beckon me forward in service to my king.

> Looking unto Jesus, the author and finisher of our faith, who for the joy that was set before Him endured the cross, despising the shame, and has sat down at the right hand of the throne of God.
> (HEBREWS 12:2)

Get your second wind, my brother. Take heart and steady your stride so that you can finish the race. And not merely finish, limping to a standstill, but cross the finish line with pride, knowing that you've run your best race, moved and maneuvered with fluidity and grace, with speed and precision, with passion and determination.

Running the race and going the distance may sound like clichés. But I promise you they contain the essence of truth needed to remain a man in motion, a man committed to finishing and reaching a destination that he could never have chosen for himself. My brother, take action this day to further your dreams. Learn to take better care of yourself so that you have more energy to engage with your woman, your children, and your calling. Face the giants in your life, slay them, and move on. Do not be daunted by the mistakes and failures in your life. Like David seeing God redeem his affair with Bathsheba, you should leave room for God to redeem your weakness and produce His glory. Leave a legacy that you will be proud to pass on to your children and their children. Feel the motion of your masculine soul and embrace all the dimensions of who you are as a man. Swim with this tide, my brother, and carry my blessing with you!